D0906321

YOUTH-LED COMMUNITY ORGANIZING

Youth-Led Community Organizing

Theory and Action

MELVIN DELGADO

LEE STAPLES

UNIVERSITY PRESS

2008

OXFORD
UNIVERSITY PRESS

Oxford University Press, Inc., publishes works that further
Oxford University's objective of excellence
in research, scholarship, and education.

Oxford   New York
Auckland   Cape Town   Dar es Salaam   Hong Kong   Karachi
Kuala Lumpur   Madrid   Melbourne   Mexico City   Nairobi
New Delhi   Shanghai   Taipei   Toronto

With offices in
Argentina   Austria   Brazil   Chile   Czech Republic   France   Greece
Guatemala   Hungary   Italy   Japan   Poland   Portugal   Singapore
South Korea   Switzerland   Thailand   Turkey   Ukraine   Vietnam

Published by Oxford University Press, Inc.
198 Madison Avenue, New York, New York 10016

www.oup.com

Oxford is a registered trademark of Oxford University Press

Library of Congress Cataloging-in-Publication Data
Delgado, Melvin.
Youth-led community organizing : theory and
action / Melvin Delgado and Lee Staples.
p. cm.
Includes bibliographical references and index.
ISBN: 978-0-19-518276-7
1. Youth movement.   2. Youth in development.   3. Youth development.
4. Community organization.   5. Young volunteers in community development.
6. Social action.   I. Staples, Lee.   II. Title.
HN19.D35 2008
361.20835—dc22   2006100993

Epigraph extracted from Andrew Malekoff's *want to make waves*
Reprinted with permission from *Families in Society* (www.familiesinsociety.org),
published by the Alliance for Children and Families.

1 3 5 7 9 8 6 4 2

Printed in the United States of America
on acid-free paper

This book is dedicated to
Denise, Laura, and Barbara (*Melvin Delgado*)
Louise, Josh, and Becca (*Lee Staples*)

want to make waves
     want to make waves
want to jump in
     want to make some waves
want to make waves
     want to make waves
 want to get wet
     want to make some waves

want to make waves.

Acknowledgments

The authors would like to thank Sara Perks, Patricia Soung, Alison Conway, Rebekah Gowler, Suzanne Hogan, Yi-Chin Chen and Youth 1st in Jackson Square, Boston (with particular thanks to Gian Gonzalez and Leo Peguero), and the following external reviewers of the initial book draft: Barry Checkoway (University of Michigan), Ben Kirshner (University of Colorado), Laurie Ross (Clark University), and Carmen Sirianni (Brandeis University).

Contents

Part I

Setting the Context

Today's youth are coming of age in a complex world impacted by global forces. However, they generally feel disenfranchised from socio-political processes.... Youths may turn to social action to speak out and effect change in relation to issues touching their lives.
—Lombardo, Zakus, and Skinner,
  Youth Social Action (2002)

1

Overview of Youth-Led Community Organizing

Youth organizing gives young people the potential to exercise power to affect key policy
decisions and create proactive new realities.
—YouthAction, *Why Youth Organizing?*
(1998)

There is no nation on earth that can afford to neglect its youth and still hope
to play a viable role in a global economy and meet the social and educational needs of its citizens. However, there also is no nation that will publicly acknowledge that it systematically and purposefully marginalizes its
youth. Rhetoric must be separated from reality and actions, as in the case of
the United States. A review of any standard statistic on child/youth well-
being would find the United States far from being a world leader in its
treatment of this population group (Males 2004). A nation that systematically neglects its youth must be prepared to invest considerable sums of
money in remedial services and correctional supervision, both now and in
the future. These resources, in turn, can better be spent as social capital
investment, helping to prepare youth to assume contributing roles in society
(Tienda and Wilson 2002a, b).

The price that a nation pays for not constructively engaging and supporting its youth is ultimately far greater than what any natural disaster or
armed conflict can possibly extract from its coffers (Jenkins 2001; Rizzini,
Barker, and Cassaniga 2002). But the true cost cannot be measured simply
in monetary standards, as some governments are prone to do. The social
and political consequences far exceed any financial costs (Mangum and
Waldeck 1997). Such nations must be prepared to have youth rebel under

dire circumstances or organize to change existing conditions (Anderson, Bernaldo, and David 2004; Welton and Wolf 2001). Both outcomes have tremendous implications for current and future generations. Further, disinvestments in young people effectively serve to divide a nation along age groups, which can compound other social relations based upon ethnicity, race, sexual orientation, class, and religion.

To say that the world around us is changing dramatically would be a serious understatement. There are few, if any, countries in the world where this statement does not apply, including our own. The United States has experienced significant demographic, technological, economic, and political changes in the past decade that have tied it more closely to the rest of the world. For example, a remarkable increase in the number of newcomers has fundamentally altered the composition of the nation's population (Levitt 2001). These new Americans have had a propensity to settle in cities, particularly on both coasts, essentially reshaping these geographic areas by making them much more diverse in character (Delgado, Jones, and Rohani 2005). This dramatic increase in newcomers, particularly those who are undocumented, has become a major political issue that threatens to further divide a nation that is already fractured along a variety of focal social, economic, and political lines.

The United States has also witnessed significant structural changes in its economy, reflecting growth in the service sector, increased prominence of communication and information technology, and the decline of manufacturing. Employment in the industrial sector, or in "skilled trades" that historically enabled members of immigrant groups and low-income youth of color lacking college degrees to achieve relatively swift economic success, is increasingly much more limited. The remaining service-sector jobs that are available usually offer few opportunities for career advancement, often trapping newcomers and other members of groups of color in low-paid, "dead-end" positions (Bartik 2001; Moss and Tilly 2001; Newman 1999). Consequently, youth sharing a particular socio-demographic profile are increasingly marginalized in this society.

At the same time as these demographic shifts have been occurring, the number of youth in American society, particularly adolescents, has grown at a rapid pace. This phenomenon also has played a prominent role in helping to shape day-to-day life as well as social policies (Damon and Gregory 2003; Delgado 2000, 2002; Tienda and Wilson 2002a). The number of youth aged 10 to 19 years increased dramatically between 1995 (37 million) and 2000 (almost 40 million). According to the U.S. Census Bureau (2000), it is projected that youth under the age of 18 will increase an additional 7 million to 77.6 million by the year 2020. The population under the age of 18 has increased from 62.9 percent in 1978 to 72.4 percent in 2000 (Lopez 2002).

Overall, there is nearly an even split along gender lines, with males accounting for 51 percent and females for 49 percent of that age cohort (U.S.

Department of Health and Services, 2002). However, when gender is broken down into ethnic categories, the discrepancy between males and females is greater and has a history of greater fluctuation. African-American/blacks' gender breakdown is approximately 54 percent female and 46 percent male, with the Latino youth population being approximately 47 percent female and 53 percent male; nonwhite Latinos, in turn, are nearly evenly split at 50 percent for each gender (Lopez 2002).

Diversity among youth becomes a factor to consider alongside numerical increases, particularly in urban areas. In 2000, it was estimated that 1.3 million immigrants entered the United States (Immigration Update 2002). Over the past ten years, 43 percent of the nation's population growth was attributed to immigration (Bayer and Bonilla 2001). Currently, the breakdown of youth under the age of 18 by race is 64 percent white, 16 percent Latino, 15 percent African-American/black, 4 percent Asian/Pacific Islander, and 1 percent Native American (ChildStats.gov 2001).

The amount of all children under the age of 18 living in poverty is 16 percent with great variation by race and ethnicity: 9 percent of white children, 33 percent of African-American/black children, and 30 percent of Latino children were living below the poverty level in 1999 (ChildStats.gov 2001). According to O'Hare and Mather (2003), the number of children living in severely distressed urban neighborhoods increased by 18 percent between 1990 and 2000:

> Of the 5.6 million children growing up in severely distressed neighborhoods, 55 percent are black, and 29 percent are Hispanic. Over a quarter (28 percent) of all black children live in severely distressed neighborhoods, and more than one in 10 Hispanic children (13 percent) live in severely distressed neighborhoods, compared with 1 percent non-Hispanic children. (5)

The changing socio-demographic profile of this nation's youth has had a major impact on how youth-led community organizing is conceptualized and implemented across the country and has effectively brought a new face and language to social justice work. Thus, this social and economic justice context shapes youth perceptions of issues of oppression related to socioeconomic class, ethnicity and race, gender, and legal status (Kim et al. 2002). Examples of youth-led community organizing reflecting these themes will be found throughout this book.

Despite the declining social conditions in which many youth live, recent studies show positive increases in certain behaviors. For example, the Urban Institute, in their study *Teen Risk-Taking: A Statistical Portrait*, found that 92 percent of youth were engaged in at least one positive behavior, such as earning good grades (54 percent), participating in school sports or other activities (53 percent), being involved with a religious institution (60 percent), or spending time with parents (76 percent; Lindberg, et al. 2000). Unfortunately, relatively few studies have focused on developing an understanding of positive youth behavior, values, and attitudes, particularly when compared to the large body of research highlighting deficits or the potential of young people as a market for consumer goods!

The field of youth services has experienced tremendous growth and change in the latter part of the twentieth and early years of the twenty-first centuries. A youth-development or youth-led paradigm has emerged, effectively transforming young people from their traditional roles as consumers, victims, perpetrators, and needy clients to positive assets who are quite capable of being major contributors within their respective communities (Eccles and Gootman 2002; Why Youth Development 2001; Kirshner, O'Donoghue, and McLaughlin 2003; Lerner, Taylor, and von Eye 2002; Villarruel et al. 2003a).

While this new paradigm has been widely embraced by professionals, society in general typically has been unwilling to view youth from such a positive perspective (Flay 2002). Aitken (2001) argues that our culture must be willing to reexamine the notion of what it means to be a youth before there is a significant shift in social perspectives on this age group. The so-called politics of growing up has changed, and this perspective takes on even greater meaning when marginalized youth of color, particularly those residing in the nation's cities, are the focus of attention (Garbarino et al. 1992; Kim et al. 2002; McNamara 1999; Roberts 2002). This focus invariably emphasizes a view of these youth as "dangerous" and "predators" (Breggin and Breggin 1998; May and Pitts 2000).

The scholarly literature helping to shape potential social policy has begun to address questions about which community actions most effectively promote positive development in young people (Booth and Crouter 2001; Camino 2000; Lerner 2003). The belief that youth must play an active and meaningful role (decision making) in shaping their own destiny has been very influential in grounding these policy interventions in a set of values that are participatory and empowering in nature (Barich 1998; Earls and Carlson 2002; Checkoway, Figueroa, and Richards-Schuster 2003; Villarruel et al. 2003a).

Checkoway (1998, 783) advocates for *youth action*, another term for youth organizing, as a means of helping youth politically mobilize their constituency to act on their own behalf:

> Youth action is based on a belief that organizing is central for people seeking to participate in the community. In pluralist political theory, it is assumed that each interest is free to organize a group and influence decisions. In practice, however, some interests mobilize more political resources, and thus have more influence, than others do. As an example, adults mobilize more political resources, both on their own behalf and that of youth, than do youth themselves. In the absence of special circumstances, adults thus produce the most powerful political inputs and, hence, dominate community decisions. It is only when youth organize that they can hope to have much influence, in this view.

Checkoway's (1998) views on youth action are predicated on the fundamental belief that youth ultimately are their own best advocates and are in the most favorable position to assess their issues and needs. Consequently, they are their own group's most effective spokespersons. Adults can be supportive or even allies in a youth-led social and economic change agenda; however, youth must play central and decision-making roles in shaping these initiatives and social-change campaigns, and they are in the best position to share their interpretations of why these actions have been undertaken (Zeldin et al. 2001).

The extensive number of books, as well as government and foundation reports, attesting to the importance of this paradigmatic shift speaks well to the popularity and future of youth development and youth-led movements. Youth participation or youth-led interventions can occur in a variety of ways, including but not limited to youth-led research (Checkoway and Richards-Schuster 2002, 2004; Delgado 2006; Sabo 2003; Suleiman, Soleimanpour, and London 2006), social enterprises (Delgado 2004), health education campaigns (McCall and Shannon 1999), philanthropy (Bjorhovde 2002), planning and program development (Delgado 2002; Mullahey, Susskind, and Checkoway 1999), and school reform (Scheie 2003; Sonenshein 1998).

There is no arena where young people cannot assume a participatory and leadership role in helping to shape their own destinies (Jarrett, Sullivan, and Watkins 2004). For example, the California Fund for Youth Organizing (2004) advocates youth-led organizing as a means of mobilizing a new generation of marginalized youth to challenge social and economic justice issues in institutions and communities: "This burgeoning youth movement draws upon the successes and lessons learned from community organizing and youth development, and weaves together the best of both theories. The resulting strategy is explicitly committed to individual development through civic engagement, as well as community change through political and collective action" (2). Age, according to the California Fund for Youth Organizing, is not a hindering factor in the development of social change campaigns.

YouthAction (1998, 13) defines *youth organizing* as involving "young people in a membership that does direct action against defined targets on issues that are important to young people and to the community at large. Youth organizing seeks to alter power relations, creates meaningful institutional change, and develops leaders." This YouthAction definition places an emphasis on social change and the development of leaders. Although short, it still conveys the immense potential of youth-led organizers to impact their environment while simultaneously achieving a transformative personal experience. Altering power relations cannot help but be a profound experience for any age group. However, it takes on added significance in the case of young people because of their almost total subjugation to adults and the opportunity that stands before them to practice the new lessons learned.

An article by LISTEN, Inc. expanded on YouthAction's conception of youth organizing, linking it to youth development and social justice as a strategy to reshape unequal power relationships with adults:

> Youth organizing itself escapes comfortable universal definitions. The definition offered above, derived from a standard description of community organizing practice in the United States, captures the approach of many of the organizers interviewed for this project, who focus on policy and institutional change. Others conceptualize youth organizing more broadly, prioritizing the forging of new political identities and challenging the wider forces of social and cultural exclusion faced by many young people. Others heavily emphasize the provision of direct services to youth as an entry point to engaging in individual advocacy or collective action. Many integrate an array of youth development functions with their organizing work. (2003, 9)

LISTEN's (2003) delineation of the various ways that youth can alter power relationships and bring about social change typifies the flexibility associated with youth-centered projects and activities. This creativity in constructing youth-led organizing campaigns takes on great significance for this age group. It allows young people to craft their organizing efforts to take into account local circumstances, which invariably are neighborhood based. Further, there is an acknowledgment that the personal needs of youth must be recognized and addressed in the course of community organizing. As noted in chapters 2 and 4, and other parts of this book, youth-led organizing takes a multifaceted approach, with young people often playing different roles as organizers, leaders, and consumers of services. Age limits the opportunities available for youth, separating them from adult organizers, who have more options for meeting their own needs.

In the course of reading this book, the reader will be exposed to countless numbers of frameworks, guides, and taxonomies pertaining to youth participation. This information is presented with the explicit goal of providing the reader with a wide range of perspectives on the subject matter, although it can certainly lead to confusion. These perspectives differ along a variety of dimensions; however, central to their differences is how they view youth in their relationship to adult allies. Hart (1992), for example, typifies the perspective of youth eventually working their way up a ladder of participation and sharing power with adults as the ultimate goal. Checkoway (1998), in turn, typifies the position taken in this book that youth can lead social interventions with adults as allies.

We, like countless others in the field and academia, are not arguing that "successful" youth organizing is predicated on the degree of "absence" of adults. Rather, adults can be present and active in aiding youth organizers (Young Wisdom Project 2004). However, their role and function are dictated by youth rather than the other way around. Terms such as *collaborators*, *mentors*, and *apprenticeship*, to list but three, often appear in the literature as an attempt to define youth roles when viewed from an adult-organizer perspective.

Young people are quite capable of achieving much more than they are usually given credit for by adults. Conversely, it would be irresponsible for us to ignore that youth may have less experience, knowledge, or expertise in community organizing when compared to adults. Our position is that youth are well aware of this situation, and that adult veteran organizers have much to offer them and the field. Nevertheless, this transfer of knowledge has the capacity of disempowering youth. Thus, in order to increase the empower-ment of young people, youth must eventually assume positions of leadership in their own social action campaigns. This, however, does not mean that youth-adult relationships are not complex or that they do not bring inherent conceptual and political tensions to the field of youth-led community or-ganizing.

Some practitioners may advocate for a more fluid relationship between young people and adult organizers. We recognize the advantages of this stance. Nevertheless, we hold that the field of youth-led community orga-nizing is legitimate and advocate a goal that adult community organizing organizations should embrace and plan for whenever youth are involved in social action campaigns. It is important to note that youth-led community organizing has emerged for very good reason—namely, that young people's voices have not found quality air time in the adult world and that their issues, although overlapping with adult-determined issues, bring a distinct youth flavor to the field.

There is general agreement, however, regardless of the perspective on the degree and importance of adult participation, that young peoples' signifi-cant participation in designing social change interventions has the potential of addressing and enriching a wide range of aspects in the lives of youth (Community Unity Matters 2000, 3):

> Current research shows that if young people are to become competent, caring and responsible contributors to their communities, they need meaningful opportunities to participate, to lead, to contribute, both side-by-side with adults and on their own. Why? Because such "stakeholder" opportunities satisfy their very deep-seated developmental needs for belonging, recognition and power, and help them develop the skills and values they need to succeed in school, work, and life.

Prevailing stereotypes of disengaged, apathetic young people do not reflect research results that show youth playing active roles in community life (Gauthier 2003; Weiss 2003; YouthAction 1998). And the benefits of the youth-led movement are both immediate and future oriented, stretching the imagination and its potential for personal and community transformation. This movement's goals are ambitious and of great consequence—and rightly so, focusing on changing power dynamics between those with a voice in shaping this nation's policies and those who lack a say.

Adults often must play catch-up to understand and appreciate this movement. They no longer can speak for or represent youth within this new paradigm; young people need to play a central role, with adults assisting them as needed. This shift in power brings with it an increased recognition that youth have ability, rights, and corresponding responsibilities. Young people as community assets become the organizing core of youth-led activities, placing youth in positions of leadership within their own communities with a mutual set of expectations that they can effect positive change (Delgado 2006). However, adults do not "disappear" from the lives of the young during these activities. Instead, they assume supportive/consultative roles based upon how *youth* view their own needs and the role that those *youth* wish adults to play.

Since successful youth work does not mean that young people are not actively involved in meaningful interactions with adults (Camino 2000), several frameworks have been developed to describe and prescribe youth-adult relationships for interventions. Advocates of youth-led movements have argued that these efforts are primarily about collaboration between youth and adults and not exclusively youth-led. The ability to foster these relationships helps to ensure the success of joint projects, but also equips both youth and adults with experiences and tools to draw upon in future undertakings. Adult–youth relationships based upon mutual trust and respect can be quite powerful and transformative in changing institutions, communities, and eventually society (Harper and Carver 1999).

The field of community organizing has not escaped this renewed attention to youth as key actors on their own behalf. Themes related to social and economic justice have resonated in countless initiatives that seek to bring about positive social change within schools and in the broader community. Community organizing by and for youth can be found in numerous fields, such as transportation, school reform, health promotion, safety, media, research, courts, disabilities, gender and racial equality, to list but several of the more prominent arenas (Delgado 2006). The goals for each of these fields may vary, but the central roles assumed by youth do not change, thereby casting them into positions of leadership, decision making, and shapers of interventions rather than as mere participants.

National and local efforts to further democratize this society have only further accentuated the need for youth to organize and exert greater influence over the institutions that regulate and impact their lives (Lombardo, Zakus, and Skinner 2002; Mokwena 2000). Most of these institutions have failed to carry out their missions in a manner that is both respectful of and empowering for youth. Youth-led community organizing has been advocated as an effective means for bringing disengaged or disconnected young people into the youth development field (Besharov 1999; Roth et al. 1999).

Not surprisingly, effective youth organizing must draw upon an extensive list of knowledge sources and competencies, which places youth organizing at the nexus of youth development (Ginwright 2003; Taylor 2000). A partial list includes reflection, recruitment, research, assessment, group facilitation, goal setting, development of public policy packets and position papers, strategic analysis, planning, public relations, direct action tactics, public speaking, negotiation skills, conflict resolution, video production, photography, writing, and editing. These competencies are often at center stage in any youth development program. However, in the case of youth organizing, the emphasis is on the achievement of positive social change, although individual gains undoubtedly will be part of the process.

Ginwright (2003) goes on to note that youth organizing brings two developmental "layers" to the youth-led movement: a sociopolitical capacity that effectively connects community problems and issues with the broader social and political arena, and the development of competencies naturally leading to community capacity enhancement (Benson 2003; Lorion and Sokoloff 2003). The former serves to ground or contextualize organizing in issues of significance to youth, their families, and community. The later results in youth acquiring key skills associated with building consensus, researching and advancing issues, and creating a social purpose that unites them with the broader community. These skills transcend the field of organizing and have applicability to other realms in the lives of youth.

Currently there is no book specifically examining the phenomenon of youth organizing that describes and analyzes the key advances in this area over the past decade. Such a book not only fills an important void in the scholarly/practice arena but also serves as a vehicle for delineating the youth-led/youth-development paradigm through which this movement can be understood best. Needless to say, this book will appeal to a wide range of audiences, both academic and practice centered, including such professional disciplines as recreation, education, sociology, psychology, social work, and media. Consequently, this book focuses on youth-led organizing from a multidisciplinary perspective, drawing implications and generalizations for a wide range of professions.

Book Goals

This book addresses five interrelated goals: (1) to provide an updated review on how the youth-led movement has evolved over the past five years, with special attention paid to its potential for further evolution in the future; (2) to present a conceptual and practice foundation from which youth-led community organizing can be understood, analyzed, and undertaken, with youth development as a theoretical backdrop and guiding force; (3) to introduce the key principles of youth-led organizing through the use of case illustrations and vignettes that will serve as templates for readers to better adapt their own practice; (4) to identify key facilitating and hindering factors for organizations wishing to embrace youth-led community organizing; and (5) to articulate a series of recommendations and reflections that will help move this field forward in a positive and progressive manner in the early part of the twenty-first century. Each of these goals is worthy unto itself; however, when taken together, they serve a synergistic purpose, illustrating the dynamic and fluid nature of the field of youth-led community organizing.

Book Outline

This book consists of eleven chapters and is divided into three parts: (I) Setting the Context; (II) Conceptual Foundation for Youth-Led Community Organizing; and (III) A View and Lessons from the Field. The first two parts of this book effectively ground the reader in the subject matter from an historical, theoretical, and philosophical perspective. The final part draws heavily from the field of practice, although practice issues and examples can be found throughout the first parts of the book.

Who Should Read this Book?

We envision this book as appealing to an audience of both academics and practitioners. However, we realize that embracing this vision brings with it a set of challenges inherent in reaching out to such a broad audience. Nevertheless, the importance of the subject makes this goal a necessity, even though the realms of academia and practice historically have been worlds apart, each with a distinctive orbit and only minimally crossing paths. Drawing these two domains together has enormous potential for advancing the field of youth-led community organizing by providing a meeting ground for theoretical ideas and practice methods that do not intersect as often as they should.

Each of these two arenas is dependent upon the other. Practice alone will continue to flourish only up to a certain point without serious scholarly scrutiny. Funders and policymakers invariably will request more and more evidence of the effectiveness of youth-led organizing to accomplish personal and community transformation, necessitating the involvement of academics in helping to document and explain this phenomenon. This is not to say that youth and other practitioners may not fear the arrival of the academics. Concern about academics usurping the voices of consumers and practitioners unfortunately is not unfounded (Weisbrod 1997), and the establishment of trust and dialogue is essential.

Academics, in turn, must be able to join practitioners to increase their relevance in helping to shape practice and social policy in support of any field of practice. In fact, academics are in key positions to influence future generations of practitioners through teaching and scholarship. For example, Strand and colleagues (2003) view sponsorship of community-based research involving collaboration among academics, students, and communities as a model with tremendous potential for impacting the future of research. All participants in this collaboration benefit from a working relationship that historically has been one-sided—namely, benefiting academics. Ansari (2005) warns about the challenges of research partnerships involving "disadvantaged communities," however.

The energy in the youth field is self-evident in the amount of activity and the number of publications over the past few years. Clearly, youth-led community organizing has moved forward without academics—or in spite of academics. Unfortunately, from an academic perspective, this is not unusual; nevertheless, effective collaboration between practice and academia serves to strengthen any field while making academia more relevant. The authors have approached this book with this goal in mind.

While we both are social workers, we firmly believe that this field is too important to be confined to one professional discipline, although we sincerely believe that social work can make significant contributions (Burghardt and Fabricant 2004; Fisher et al. 2001; Mary 2001; Rubin and Rubin 2004). Youth-led community organizing is a very specific method geared to a particular population group, and we hope that this book can find a home easily in social work, community psychology, sociology, youth development, and educational and recreational disciplines. Still, the task before us was demanding and we undertook it fully aware of the challenges that lay ahead.

We wanted to appeal to both the practice field and academia. In the latter, we sought to appeal to a wide range of disciplines. Undoubtedly, the reader will find moments of indiscretion when we have reverted to our social work roots. We believe that the social work profession has a distinct contribution to make to the youth-led community organizing field because of its historical embrace of social activism; however, we have striven to keep such lapses to a minimum and humbly ask that the reader be accepting of them. Last, we hope that youth organizers can read this book or take sections of it for use in training, writing proposals for funding, and as a field manual for supporting other youth organizers. Young people are the ultimate beneficiaries of this book, and they will be the ultimate judges of its worthiness.

Methodology

This book has used a variety of methods to bring forth the field of youth-led community organizing with the perspectives and voices of some of the youth and adults who are shaping this field as it continues to evolve. First, and foremost, the personal experiences of the authors have played an instrumental role in shaping the contents of this book; however, we also have relied heavily on a review of the professional and scholarly literature in a variety of fields that intersect to create youth-led community organizing. Foundation and governmental reports also have been used. We obtained some materials that normally would not be read by people outside of the organizations under study. Finally, qualitative interviews were conducted with young people and adults actively engaged along the entire spectrum of youth-led community organizing. All of these sources have found their way into this book.

This book represents a synthesis of the literature, the authors' experiences, and the interviews conducted with a wide variety of sources, youth as well as adult. No specific empirical-based study was undertaken to guide the conceptualization of the book, nor was research funding sought or obtained for the actual writing. However, we do not apologize for not undertaking this form of research. The empirical (qualitative and quantitative) findings from seventy sources have been integrated into this book. We cast a wide net in gathering materials and information, some more difficult to obtain than others, and we believe the current format makes that information reader friendly. To facilitate this process, we have reported research data, with some exceptions, in either summarized form or by highlighting particular findings. In cases where quantitative data were reported in a study, we have reported only key findings. This is a judgment call on our part; however, we believe that it facilitates the reading of this book without sacrificing empirical grounding. Chapters 5 and 9 contain systematically integrated key research findings from studies, reports, and books in a manner that we believe facilitates readability without sacrificing the presentation of research findings from the field.

Authors' Qualifications and Interests

The reader has every right to question the expertise and legitimacy of the authors to write on this subject matter. We bring extensive histories of both practice and scholarship in the area of macro-practice (planning, program development, and community organizing), as well as work within the youth development/youth-led field. We also share a commitment to marginalized communities and a fundamental belief in the dignity and assets of every human being. Professor Melvin Delgado has either single-authored or co-authored five books on youth development or the youth-led movement (Delgado 2000, 2002, 2004, in press; Delgado, Jones, and Rohani 2005). Professor Lee Staples has authored the first and second editions of a widely used text on community organizing (1984, 2004a) and has published numerous articles on empowerment and collective action for social change. We believe that the expertise each of us brings to the task of writing this book helps to capture the essence of youth-led community organizing.

In addition, we have relied heavily on the voices of youth, represented in a variety of formats, to help shape the central messages of this book. Youth voices articulating their experiences, both positive and negative, are critical to making this publication relevant for the field of practice. Essentially, this book is about youth and their efforts to bring about positive social change. It also considers the role of the adults who work as allies with youth, and it examines how they can best ensure that the rights of youth are not overlooked in this society.

Neither of us has previously published in this specific area, although we certainly have touched on the subject in some of our writings. The field of youth-led community organizing connects with many different arenas, professions, scholarly theories, and constructs. As already noted, it is receiving increasing national and international attention. Nevertheless, in spite of the field's breath, there is no book that focuses specifically on it.

Our experiences in writing for scholarly publications typify what commonly is found in such journals and books. Professor Delgado has published extensively in the field of youth-development/youth-led practice, but his prior books do not address community organizing. While Professor Staples has focused his scholarship on empowerment and community organization, his work to date has not concentrated on youth organizing.

Other Work in this Field

A number of excellent books on community organizing have been published during the past several years, reflecting an increased interest in this subject. But these works, although making important contributions to the field, essentially have viewed community organizing from an adult perspective, thus the need for this book. Murphy and Cunningham's *Organizing for Community Controlled Development: Renewing Civil Society* (Sage Publications, 2003) addresses the role of civic involvement within a community and societal context, but youth participation is touched upon only cursorily. Hardina provides an extensive review of strategies and tactics for community organization in *Analytical Skills for Community Organization Practice* (Columbia University Press, 2002); however, youth are not featured in her book. Homan also addresses change from the perspective of adults in *Promoting Community Change: Making it Happen in the Real World* (Brooks/Cole, 2004).

Terms

This is a good juncture to address the use of terms that play a critical role in shaping the content of this book. Four terms (*youth, youth-led, community organizing* and *marginalized/undervalued*) will be examined below. A lack of consensus about how these concepts are defined, their scope, and what constitutes optimum activities related to them should in no way discourage interested individuals and organizations from fostering youth-led activities. On the contrary, the proliferation of terms serves as an indicator that this is a field that is continuing to evolve. This is exciting as well as challenging.

Youth

There are tremendous challenges in developing a succinct definition of what constitutes "youth" in this society. Like any social term, there are multiple perspectives on how best to define it. The concept of youth has been viewed historically in a number of ways, including as a state of mind, a legal age, a developmental stage, or a cultural phenomenon. Gillis (1981, 3) notes: "Evidence of youth as a separate stage of life with its own history and traditions comes to us from a variety of sources, some literary and iconographic, others economic and demographic."

For example, a market-value orientation would derive a very different definition of what constitutes a child/youth (Nasaw 1985; Zelizer 1985) from one operating from a rights or developmental perspective (Earls and Carlson 2002; Hine 2000; Scales and Leffert 1999; Swart-Kruger and Chawla 2002; Zelizer 1985). Social perspectives bring with them a specific set of adult beliefs, expectations, and behaviors toward youth (Mortimer and Larson 2002). Thus, a definition of youth is influenced not only by professional discipline but also by the philosophical set of values that guide the definition (Young Wisdom Project 2004).

Not surprisingly, the Applied Research Center's (Weiss 2003) research on youth-led community organizing concluded that there is no consensus on what constitutes youth. There is little disagreement that individuals under the age of 18 years would fall into the youth category; however, there is some disagreement about the age range of 18 to 22 years, where the "young adult" label is meant to capture this age bracket, reflecting a trend toward expanding how society defines youth. An example of this expansion is the definition of youth that embraces the point at which an individual can be self-supporting economically. This has resulted in broadening the age category of youth to that of 25 years, or to the point when a young person has finished her or his college education and been gainfully employed for several years.

For the purposes of this book, youth are people under the age of 26 years, although some of the literature reviewed may extend it only to 25 years.

However, we focus on the ages 12 to 19. This age group bears the brunt of society's fears, as well as the vicissitudes of social policies and programs (Austin and Willard 1989; Furstenberg et al. 1999; Kipke 1999; Leadbeater and Way 1996; Mortimer and Larson, 2002).

Youth-Led

Any serious review of the field of youth-led programs raises many more questions than it actually answers, and this is to be expected in a field that is only growing in importance. The history of viewing youth from an asset, rather than a prevailing deficit, perspective can be traced back to the late 1970s and the pioneering work of Werner and Smith (1977, 1992). However, it was not until the early 1990s that this movement representing a paradigm shift started to take hold. In the early 1990s, Pittman (1991) identified six terms that were often interchangeable with youth civic engagement: *governance, organizing, advocacy, service, leadership,* and *engagement.* The time period since has only added to this list and further accentuated the overlaps and differences among these terms.

A review of the literature in the early twenty-first century uncovers terms such as *youth civic activism, community service, civic engagement, decision making, participation, empowerment, involvement, community-driven, development, positive development, community development, leadership,* and *led.* The terms emphasizing various aspects of youth intervention share much in common, although at a glance they seem to emphasize different elements. These terms express a fundamental belief in the rights and capacities (assets) of youth, their potential for positive contributions, and the importance of preparing them for adult roles in a democratic society (Halfon 2003). The term *youth-led* places emphasis on youth rights and the power of young people to define their circumstances and the direction of intervention, as well as the degree to which adults are actively involved as allies (Youth-Action 1998). This book focuses on youth-led community organizing as the vehicle, although as the reader will soon discover, there are numerous types of youth-led models and organizations that sponsor this form of intervention. Chapter 3 provides the reader with four models for viewing youth involvement in social change, and one of those models has youth in positions of power, with adults participating as allies.

Community Organizing

Simply put, *community organizing* is a process through which people sharing similar concerns can unite to achieve positive change, community betterment, and political empowerment (Rubin and Rubin 2004; W.G. Brueggemann 2002). Community organizations are structures, or vehicles, through which participants can exercise power collectively. Typically, they "engage in specific campaigns to change institutional policies and practices in particular arenas, ranging from education to income to the environment" (R. Sen 2003, xliv). Community organizing draws on models of union organizing, as well as political activism (J. Brueggemann 2002).

Staples (2004a, 1–2) has defined *grassroots community organizing* as "collective action by community members drawing on the strength of numbers, participatory processes, and indigenous leadership to decrease power disparities and achieve shared goals for social change." Three elements are central to this definition, which is used in this book. First, goals are established and decisions are made by the people most affected by a particular situation; the operative assumption is that community members should, must, and can organize effectively to set their own goals and to act on their own behalf. Second, grassroots organizing is based on the premise that social change is possible when constituency members undertake collective action that derives its efficacy from "people power;" large numbers of participants acting in concert are able to accomplish far more than atomized individuals. Finally, the leadership for a grassroots organizing effort comes from within the affected community, which has "the requisite strengths, assets, and resources to fulfill this function" (Staples 2004a, 2).

Youth organizing, like community capacity enhancement, seeks to achieve social change at the local level. It helps to transform both youth and their communities through an emphasis on knowledge and awareness, community and collective identity, and a creation of a shared vision (Gaventa and Cornwall 2001; Morsillo and Prilleltensky 2005; Transformative Leadership 2004). Youth-led community organizing is best understood and appreciated through a broad-angle lens (Turning the Leadership 2003, 3): "More than a training ground for decision-making and leadership assumption, youth organizing enables young people to participate in, shape and lead democratic processes, decision-making and innovation that impact their schools, homes and communities."

An authoritative definition of *youth community organizing* does not exist. However, the Innovation Center for Community and Youth Development (2003, 3) defines it in a manner that intersects both organizing and youth development: "Youth organizing is the union of grassroots community organizing and positive youth development, with an explicit commitment to social change and political action. Youth organizing is based on the premise that young people are capable of taking leadership to transform their communities." The operationalization of this definition, however, can take on a variety of forms and stress a range of youth-development core elements. For example, identity support seeks to provide youth organizers with the space and opportunity to develop a sense of identity affirmation and does so within a social and economic justice context (Gambone et al. 2004). Exploration of oppression is tied closely to young people's own experiences, with subordination based on what they have learned about their identities in this society. Critical consciousness is developed and linked to collective action in the pursuit of justice (Morsillo and Prilleltensky 2005; Prilleltensky 2003; Watts, Williams, and Jagers 2003).

Unfortunately, but predictably, this form of social intervention does not enjoy the same level of professional respect as do other more mainstream and less adversarial modalities, such as planning and program development. However, youth-led organizing clearly has emerged as a viable and significant method for involving disenfranchised communities. Youth organizing taps into this nation's long history of social activism, making this form of intervention relevant to young people. This, in turn, channels their enthusiasm and ideals in a direction that increases the collective power of their age group and the power of the community in which they reside. Further, it provides a viable avenue for youth dissatisfied with conventional electoral politics (Turning the Leadership 2003).

There certainly are critics of organizing youth as an identity group (Young Wisdom Project 2004, 11):

> Critics have argued that "youth" is a transitional identity—not a real community. On top of that, "identity politics" has major limits. Youth organizing, they said, risked having a narrow analysis, splitting youth from their communities and broader social justice goals. What these critics failed to see is how the youth movement actually used its understanding of adultism as a starting point for understanding and addressing other forms of oppression.

Thus, although youth is a transitional state, it can be fertile ground for enlisting a cadre of future organizers and public servants, making the benefits of youth-led organizing far greater than "just" the immediate.

McGillicuddy and James (2001, 2) bring a different response to critics of identity group organizing:

> The youth movement, in its boldest and most prominent expressions, is defined not primarily by age but by values. It is a movement for fairness: the right of all people for self-representation and self-determination. These values are often talked about in our culture but rarely realized in our institutions and daily lives. That hypocrisy—the discrepancy between the rhetoric of America and the brutal reality—is what young people, like the generations before them, are standing up to confront.

Marginalized/Undervalued

The concepts of being *marginalized* and *undervalued* seek to capture both a social condition and a state of mind that effectively render youth to be perceived by society as a surplus population group, along dimensions of class, race, abilities, and gender. Adults control the process of relegating these youth to low-status positions. Viewing youth as in need, reckless, preoccupied with immediate gratification, consumers, and a threat serves to substantiate this perception and the actions that follow.

Youth who are marginalized by virtue of their identity find themselves disconnected from key institutions and social systems. Conventional youth-oriented programs can fail them because of the depoliticized nature of the services and activities rendered, as well as an inability or unwillingness to confront the forces of oppression in the lives of these youth (Roach, Sullivan, and Wheeler 1999). This reluctance may stem from an interplay of several factors, such as fears about funding termination, a lack of clarity and understanding of how oppression operates, concerns about alienating constituencies, and confusion about how best to relieve the oppression in the lives of young people and their communities. Regardless of the reasons, not addressing the larger structural issues that serve to marginalize youth in this society represents a missed opportunity, as well as a serious breach of ethics from our standpoint.

Addressing these forces through consciousness raising and social action is critical in engaging and sustaining marginalized youth. All action must be cast in a broader context that systematically examines the underlying roots of social inequality in the lives of these youth and the communities where they live (Martineau 2005). Furthermore, young people must play an active role in developing such a critical analysis and drawing the conclusions that lead to collective action attendant to it. It would not be sufficient to have an adult come in and give a lecture or to provide written materials to read at home (homework). The journey that youth take is as important as their destination; a participatory process of consciousness raising carries equal weight with the conclusions drawn about their state of affairs in this society (Tolman and Pittman 2001).

Although commenting specifically on youth civic engagement, Gibson's (2001, 11) observations also are applicable in other arenas addressed in this book:

> The lack of consensus on what constitutes civic engagement and whether and to what extent young people are engaged has led to disagreement about which strategies are effective in helping young people become active and long-term participants in our democracy. Exacerbating this fragmentation is the tendency for those interested in this issue to adhere to and promote particular views about it, rather than to come together and engage in a thoughtful dialogue about how to enrich youth civic engagement.

Gibson's challenge never has been more appropriate than it is today as youth-centered activities proliferate (Balsano 2005). The search for common ground starts with clearly defining the meaning of key concepts and terms. It is important to remember that these ideas have origins in a wide variety of settings and disciplines, and therefore it is quite natural to have many different ways of describing the same phenomenon, as well as differential usages of identical terms. Clarifying and sorting out definitional confusion never has been easy in any field, and the area of youth-led organizing is no exception. However, the authors do their best to accomplish this goal.

Conclusion

The importance of youth to this country has historically been overlooked and undervalued, and at times systematically undermined. This societal neglect of the contributions and potential of young people effectively has marginalized this population. The United States and other industrialized countries can ill afford to cast aside a significant portion of their populations and later expect them to become contributing members of society as adults. Human life never can be conceptualized as a faucet that can be turned on and off at will. Although this and other societies always are quick to note that youth are the "future of the nation," those words ring hollow when we examine the treatment of this asset. Indeed, the phrase "Actions speak louder than words" certainly does hold true in this instance.

The phenomenon of youth seeking social and economic justice for themselves, their families, and communities in this country certainly cannot be confined to the twenty-first century; the following two chapters contextualize this perspective. Young people have played very important roles in helping to shape this nation. Unfortunately, their contributions either have gone unnoticed or simply have been minimized by adults. This chapter has attempted to highlight this injustice and the next two chapters help present present-day youth-led community organizing within the context of a rich historical past.

Youth-led community organizing is a field that is dynamic, growing, complex, and connected with many other areas of practice. Its origins can be found within a number of social paradigms, depending on the backgrounds and perspectives of those using this method of practice; youth development prominently is mentioned in many circles. While it can claim roots in numerous professional disciplines, youth-led community organizing has no home that it can call its own. Furthermore, many terms usually associated with this form of intervention are used imprecisely (or abused) by practitioners from other areas of the youth field, adding to a lack of conceptual clarity. One activity in youth-led organizing may be called by a different name in another field, making connections between fields that much more difficult to achieve and research, and increasing the likelihood of tension between young people and adults.

Youth-led community organizing has all of these limitations but still manages to enjoy tremendous popularity within this country and internationally. Social change as a central goal is very appealing to youth, particularly those struggling to overcome social and economic injustices. The following chapters systematically examine youth-led community organizing and provide the requisite historical background, exposure to various key theoretical concepts, and case illustrations and vignettes, thus contributing to a better understanding and appreciation of the virtues of this method of practice. This book attests to the importance of this field and its rightful place within the constellation we refer to as youth services.

2

Social and Economic
Justice Foundation

Social justice is the virtue which guides us in
creating those organized human interactions
we call institutions. In turn, social institutions,
when justly organized, provide us with access
to what is good for the person, both individually and in our associations with others. Social justice also imposes on each of us a personal responsibility to work with others to
design and continually perfect our institutions as tools for personal and social development.
—Center for Social and Economic Justice,
   Defining Economic Justice and Social Justice
   (2005)

Some would argue that the key element determining the authenticity of a
democratic society is how well it professes and carries out the values of
social and economic justice vis-à-vis all of its members. The following statement by Gibson (2001, 1) illuminates the lofty goals for a democratic society:
"The heart of a healthy democracy is a citizenry actively engaged in civic
life—taking responsibility for building communities, solving community
problems, and participating in the electoral and political process." This statement's simplicity masks the tremendous challenge, pain, and struggle that
a society faces if the true meaning of democracy is to extend to all age
groups and not be limited to adults. Citizenry, as the reader will discover in
this chapter, is a concept that is elusive for all age groups in our society
(Golombek 2006). Making the changes necessary to include young people

may prove quite troubling, if not threatening, for adults in positions of authority and power (Carlson 2006). It is against this backdrop that youth-led community organizing can best be understood (Suleiman, Solei-manpour, and London 2006).

A number of fields embrace values reflecting social and economic justice. For instance, social work and many of the other helping professions have espoused the goal of achieving social and economic justice as a guide to the development of social-based interventions (Gil 1998). The Social Worker's Code of Ethics explicitly singles out the goals of overcoming oppression and realizing social and economic injustice as central tenets of practice. The Council on Social Work Education, the accrediting body for schools of social work, also explicitly supports principles of social and economic justice. Other professions also make some reference to social and economic justice as part of their missions (Kiselica and Robinson 2001).

As additional forms of oppression have been recognized and many more marginalized groups have been acknowledged during the past several de-cades, the focus on social and economic justice has evolved and its scope has been expanded. However, only recently have children and youth been viewed as a disempowered group. Traditionally, this age group has been overlooked while social and economic justice has been viewed historically from an adult perspective. Adults have determined what is in the best interest of children and youth, ultimately defining what constitutes an in-justice and under what circumstances and forms it takes place. Scholarly publications, written by adults—as is this book—provide the theoretical foundations upon which to structure dialogue, debates, and research. Poli-cies and programs ensue, again developed by adults, to address the new-found oppression.

A perspective of social and economic justice facilitates the identification and inclusion of groups that historically have not enjoyed the status of being enfranchised within a society. The pursuit of justice provides an excellent framework for bringing together groups that have not collaborated in the past. The term *justice*, not surprisingly, generally consists of a set of uni-versal principles. Justice, according to the Center for Economic and Social Justice (2005), is one of four "cardinal virtues" in what commonly is con-sidered "classical moral philosophy." Courage, temperance (self-control), and produce (efficiency) are the other three virtues, which contrast with the more familiar religious virtues of faith, hope, and charity. Together these four ideal ethical qualities encourage members of a society to moderate self-interests in favor of the greater good.

Weil (2004) provides a simple but quite useful definition of *social justice* that is both broad and inclusive of an equitable perspective, and it is her con-ception that guides us in this book. According to Weil (2004, 8), social justice

essentially means fairness. As social refers to our human relations and interconnectedness in society, social justice implies commitment to fair-

ness in our dealings with each other in the major aspects of our lives—
the political, economic, social and civic realms. In society, social justice
should foster equal human rights, distributive justice, and a structure of
opportunity and be grounded in representative and participatory democracy.

As a consequence, social justice is a concept that serves a unifying
function within a society and lends itself to being part of a foundation for
youth-led community organization.

Embracing a social justice agenda such as that articulated by Weil (2004)
brings with it a responsibility to ensure that all sectors of society have rights
and that corrections are available to rectify any injustice. Purposefully over-
looking disenfranchised groups in a society because it is not politically
"safe" to consider their needs effectively undermines the establishment and
maintenance of a social and economic justice agenda for change. Such a
circumstance dramatically limits the potential of the affected group to maximize its inherent resources, including both its social and financial capital.

This chapter has the important goal of providing a four-part definitional
and philosophical foundation upon which to build a contextualization of
youth rights and their social-political status within this society. It includes
definitions of: (1) social justice; (2) adultism; (3) youth rights; and (4) a social
and economic justice agenda. Moral philosophy and sociology influence
these four perspectives on justice. Each is addressed as an entity unto itself,
an artificial but necessary separation. In reality, however, these four concepts are intertwined, and discussion of one necessarily involves discussion
of the others. Furthermore, a commitment to these four concepts is essential
if adults are to play meaningful roles in working respectfully and effectively
with young people in youth-led community organizing. We do not expect
the reader to accept our definitions or visions of these four conceptual un-
derpinnings, although it is always wonderful to achieve consensus. Rather,
the reader must be prepared to identify the elements that he or she embraces
and those with which he or she disagrees. This outcome will play a determining role in how the reader views youth-led community organizing as a
distinctive field of practice, and how he or she conceptualizes the role of
adults within this field (Ranjani 2001; Youniss, McLellan, and Yates 1997).

Social Justice

Language and concepts play such a critical role in any form of social intervention, and nowhere is this more the case than in community organizing. As a result, youth must use language and concepts that help them better
understand their social context and enable them to communicate successfully with those outside their own group. The saliency of the concept of
social justice and its roots in political philosophy represent an excellent

starting point for engaging youth in a discourse about their lives and the conditions of their communities, even though such an examination initially may result in a tremendous amount of pain and anger.

Social justice is a term that has almost universal meaning throughout the world. This concept encompasses *economic* justice in most fields of practice and in much of the related literature, especially in the social sciences (Center for Economic and Social Justice 2005). Social justice has a rich historical meaning in this country dating back to the Revolutionary War, when it provided a philosophical rationale for breaking away from England (Kurland 2004). Its meaning since that time has broadened and evolved to include a multitude of social perspectives that stress the importance of inclusion rather than exclusion, going beyond a limited number of social factors such as race, class, and gender.

Age has become the latest factor to enter the dialogue about social and economic justice in democratic societies, including the United States. *Child Welfare Across Borders* (2003) notes that viewing youth from an autonomy perspective implies that young people have the same rights to participation and decision making as adults, while using a social justice framework to assess the status of youth leads to the creation of social interventions to rectify injustices. David Miller (1999) advances the position that social justice has been the animating ideal of democratic governments in the twentieth century.

Separating rhetoric from reality, however, is essential for any group wishing to further a social and economic justice agenda in this society. Furthermore, the appeal of such an agenda can transcend groups and has equal applicability for examining the social conditions of both youth and adults, helping campaigns for social action cross this age divide. There are numerous ways in which such a social justice construct may be constituted, with the particular perspective taken influencing debate and corresponding actions.

However, social justice usually consists of three essential principles (Center for Economic and Social Justice 2005): (1) the principle of participation; (2) the principle of distribution; and (3) the principle of harmony. We believe that all three principles must be a part of any operational definition and agenda embracing social justice, whether it is youth-led or adult-led. Therefore, every effort must be made to bring these principles to life, rather than to hold them as abstract philosophical ideals. The greater the specificity with which they are operationalized, the more their attractiveness and utility for youth-led community organizing.

While a distributive paradigm is the prevailing manner in which social justice usually is conceived, discussed, and operationalized, the concept has been both elusive and the source of much contention over the past two and a half centuries (Garrett 2005; Kant 1797; Mill 1849/1973; Marx 1975; Rawls 1999; Nozick 1974; Dworkin 1977; MacIntyre 1981; Sandel 1982; Walzer 1983). Consequently, the tension usually associated with any meaningful dialogue on this concept is not new; and not surprisingly, it also is manifested in the youth-led community organizing arena. However, this difference of opinion must be recognized, since it will enrich debate and be relevant for those engaged in social action-oriented interventions.

Many scholars are quick to point out the difficulty in defining the concept of justice across national boundaries; yet the word still evokes an important emotional and sociopolitical response, regardless of country. O'Kane (2002, 698) captures this sentiment when he observes:

> Changing times and differing needs have affected its description. However, around the world, children of different cultures appear to share an acute sense of justice. The expression "it is not fair" is frequently uttered by girls and boys when exposed to situations of inequality, whether small or great. . . . How just and fair a society is depends on who has the power and how it is exercised. Good governance will ensure equity and social justice for all. It is said that the litmus test of justice or injustice in any society is how it treats its poor and powerless.

Additionally, social justice has tremendous meaning for both newcomers and longtime residents of the United States (Stepick and Stepick 2002). For example, unequal access to and distribution of resources have played an influential role in encouraging migration from Latin American countries to the United States. Long histories of dictatorships and political oppression have spurred revolutions in these countries. As a result, countless millions of Latinos have been uprooted and then have migrated to the United States, making the subject of social and economic justice very real for them, while creating a construct that can be used to help unite immigrant youth and their communities (Delgado 2007).

As noted earlier, a society's distribution of advantages and disadvantages to its members is an organizing perspective from which to determine who is valued and who is undervalued within that cultural context. Understanding why this is the case offers an opportunity for politicization that has great potential for youth-led community organizing. David Miller (1999, 17) notes, "Relations of domination and oppression are drawn into this picture because the systematic presence of such relations is clear evidence that the basic structure is unjust." Unequal distribution of resources and access to opportunities become the basis upon which to determine reasons for societal disparities, as well as the source of interventions designed and undertaken to rectify this imbalance.

Rawls (1999), in his widely acclaimed book *A Theory of Justice*, raises the concept of the social contract as a means of resolving the debate about political obligation by introducing the theory of "justice as fairness." Rawls goes on to articulate two principles of justice: (1) "First, each person is to have an equal right to the most extensive basic liberty comparable with a similar liberty for others" (60); and (2) "Social and economic inequalities are to be arranged so that they are both: (a) to the greatest benefit of the least advantaged, and (b) attached to offices and positions open to all under conditions of fair equality of opportunity" (303). Introducing fairness into discussions involving youth strikes a familiar chord and allows the concept of social justice to be translated in a manner and language that are understandable and attractive to young people (Kurland 2004). The concept of fairness is one that often is found in family and school discussions, and thus is not foreign to youth.

Any serious examination of how the odds are stacked against the young in this society cannot help but uncover how the power and domination of adults over youth are at the heart of many of the struggles fought and challenges faced by young people (McNamara 1999). Therefore, youth need to be able to understand how social and economic injustices relate to a host of social factors, including age. When economic variables such as changes in the labor market are added to the analysis, it becomes apparent that youth must cross barriers that previous generations did not face. And often they are expected to surmount these obstacles with minimal assistance from adults (Noack and Kracke 1997). Recognition of how these forces impinge on their lives often represents the first critical consciousness-raising step that young people take as they begin organizing to achieve a greater measure of social justice.

These barriers are most apparent regarding young people who are newcomers to this country, as well as immigrant parents who attempt to shape their children's cultural values (Delgado, Jones, and Rohani 2005). While the experiences of immigrant parents are different from those of their sons and daughters, there nevertheless needs to be a shift in power that promotes partnership between the generations rather than continued adult domination over the young.

David Miller's (1999) conclusions, although not focused on adult-youth relationships and the distribution of power and control, easily apply to age discrimination on the part of adults toward young people. Regardless of its particular form, such unfairness limits opportunities for the group being discriminated against to reach their potential. The emergence of a field like youth-led community organizing, we believe, is a direct response to adult discrimination and disempowerment of young people. The process of discrimination also takes a toll on those who discriminate, because of the time, energy, and resources that have to be expended to carry out such unjust, and often counterproductive, practices and policies.

Adultism

As noted earlier in this chapter, the importance of language in any social intervention cannot be underestimated. This is particularly the case for youth-led community organizing and youth rights, an area that only recently has begun to receive the national attention it so richly deserves (One and Four 2005, 1): "Language is important for new movements such as youth rights. We are given the very difficult task of presenting new ideas to a skeptical public, and as with anything else, very new concepts require new terms to describe them."

The power imbalance between adults and young people, and the negative consequences that result, necessitates the use of new language that quickly conveys its meaning to the professional, as well as the general public. However, creating such terminology never is easy and is not a task that can be taken lightly. One activist's statement about the oppression of youth helps illustrate how a single word can convey the meaning of a new concept (Felix 2003, 5): "Is it possible that America—a country that prides itself on working to end racism, sexism, and other -isms—could be guilty of committing countless acts of adultism?"

Not surprisingly, the professional literature has added a number of expressions to describe the power imbalance between young people and adults. The phrase *adult supremacist* recently emerged as an alternative to *adultism*, and this concept reflects the fundamental belief that adults have the moral authority to control youth. *Youthism* also is finding currency, although it is not as popular a term as *adultism* or *ageism*. The term *reverse ageism* also has been used to identify discrimination against the young. *Adultism* and *ageism* have been referred to as the Coke and Pepsi of the youth-rights movement (One and Four 2005).

We favor *adultism*, although the reader should not be surprised if he or she has never before heard this word. *Adultism* has been used only for the last decade or so, as the concept slowly has found its way into the professional literature on youth, particularly in writings embracing a rights perspective (Tate and Copos 2003). The term seldom has surfaced in discussions related to social oppression in this country; nevertheless, in order for youth-led community organizing to fulfill its mission, adults must be prepared to confront their biases, as difficult as that may be. Therefore, *adultism* captures the single greatest factor that threatens the ultimate success of adult–youth collaborations on social interventions such as community organizing.

Although Bell (1995) is widely credited with popularizing the concept of adultism, Flasher (1978) made what is probably the earliest mention of this term in the professional literature. In fact, there are various definitions of adultism in the field. Checkoway (1996, 13) defines it as "all of the behaviors and attitudes that flow from the assumption that adults are better than young people and are entitled to act upon young people in many ways without their agreements." Bell (1995, 1), in turn, defines adultism as the "assumption[s] that adults are better than young people, and entitled to act upon young people without their agreement." Consequently, a social and economic justice perspective on youth necessitates that issues related to oppression be integrated into interventions. This process of disempowerment can manifest itself in attitudes, behaviors, and language (Bergsma 2004;

Evans, Ulasevich, and Blahut 2004; Morrell 2004; Prilleltensky, Nelson, and Peirson 2001).

Some readers may prefer the term *ageism* to describe this power differential based on age. However, ageism is a term usually reserved for discrimination focused on elders, even though it is not restricted to this group (Macnicol 2006). Ageism still continues to be a major social issue in this and other countries. One study of ageism in Britain found that this form of oppression eclipsed racism, sexism, and discrimination based on disability (Age Bias 2005). As of 2003, only Alaska, Florida, Maine, Maryland, and Mississippi had employment antidiscrimination laws that specified no age limits, unlike federal law that specifies age 40 and over for legal protection (Armour 2003).

However, *adultism* has been used specifically to focus on youth, thereby giving this age group a unique term that helps capture a wide range of attitudes and behaviors by adults. The extent that adultism is central to youth-led community organizing remains an open question; however, as one young activist noted (Weiss 2003, 100): "While young activists often encounter and take on ageism, it is seldom the focal point of their struggle." Therefore, the reader may ask why this book pays so much attention to the *adultism/ageism* matter if this phenomenon is not the central feature of youth-led community organizing. The answer is quite simple: because the presence of this oppressive force permeates all contacts that youth have with adults and people in authority. This reality effectively serves to undermine any serious campaigns for social change, and it is ignored by youth-rights advocates only at great peril to their success. This form of social oppression serves as a catalyst, or rationale, for the important social-change efforts being led by young people, with or without the aid of adults.

Bonnichsen (2002, 5) identifies adultism as an ideology founded on family and governmental control of youth:

> The government echoes the structure of the family: adults, and only adults, get to make the rules. The breadth of rule-making power that adult government grants itself is almost unlimited. It elevates traditional parental authority to law, giving youth a status much like property. Yet, when the state does take an interest, parents' rights of private ownership are superseded, with the justification that youth are property ("resources") collectively owned by *all* adult citizens.

Adultism is the inherent belief that adults are the ultimate experts on young people—their issues, dreams, anxieties, and abilities. It places adults in the position of decision makers and arbiters of all policies, programs, and services regarding the young. What makes adults such experts on youth? Since adults have all been through the key developmental stages associated with this age group, their experiences, both positive and negative, have provided them with a perspective usually associated with being on the outside and looking in. Adults conduct research, write scholarly articles and books, gather and report the news, and generally are in positions of authority regarding all aspects affecting the lives of young people. Thus, why shouldn't they also be in a leadership position for achieving social changes that involve social conditions particularly applicable to young people?

However, Felix (2003) asserts that adult problems and responsibilities burden today's youth, unlike their own parents' generation. For example, high-stakes testing, illnesses such as HIV/AIDS, labor-market shifts resulting in minimal upward mobility, lack of health insurance, low minimum wages, and new and very powerful illicit drugs combine to create an environment that best can be described as challenging, if not toxic, for young people. Felix notes that the previous generation did not grow and develop within this much more difficult context. The failure of many, if not most, adults to be aware of and sensitive to such profound differences in contexts exacerbates adultist attitudes and actions.

Thus, it is irresponsible to discuss youth and cultural competence without addressing the deleterious role of adultism in the lives of young people (W.T. Grant Commission 1988). For example, HoSang (2004, 5) notes some of the other ways that adultism is manifested in subtle and not so subtle forms:

> Psychologists and other social scientists often refer to adolescence as a rehearsal of sorts, a "not quite" transitory period between the unqualified dependency of childhood and the full charge of adulthood. A natural temptation exists to assess youth organizing efforts from this same vantage point—a "not quite" dry run in anticipation of a more bona fide effort to build "real" power as adults.

As a result, one of the most significant challenges facing youth organizers is obtaining the respect of adults and ensuring that their contributions to the community and the larger society are acknowledged. The reader may argue that respect always must be earned; however, when this fundamental social need is absent from the very outset based solely on age, the deck is stacked against young people, who must earn that respect by proving their worth to the very adults who doubt their capacity to think and act independently and efficaciously. This is a quintessential catch-22 situation. Adults are in the powerful position of defining and determining the types of decisions and actions that are "worthy" of respect, yet the youth whom they are judging frequently are not given sufficient responsibility to "prove themselves." Meanwhile, there is no relationship of reciprocity whereby those same young people have the power to make such judgments about the commitment, competence, and comportment of their elders.

Bell (1995, 1) makes a similar observation as that of HoSang (2005) when stating: "To be successful in our work with young people, we must understand a particular condition of youth: that young people are often mistreated and disrespected simply because they are young." The process of adults' "discovering" and effectively addressing the consequences of adultism in the field of youth services represents the cornerstone of any effective social interventions involving adults as consultants or co-collaborators with youth (Delgado 2006). Adults in youth-led initiatives must be able to step back and trust that youth can be responsible, yet not tune out because they are in a position to provide support (Wheeler 2003). There is an underlying tension between usurping authority and stepping aside! Nevertheless, youth-led community organizing, like other dimensions of the youth-led movement, requires adults to assume roles that are secondary to young people; further, these roles in collaboration with young people are determined by young people themselves, and not the other way around.

It is necessary, however, to point out that the concept of adultism is not universally accepted in this society. Some of the most common arguments against its use are: (1) youth is a biological state that has permanent and immutable characteristics; (2) youth is a temporary legal status; (3) age is a continuum that differs by race, ethnicity, and subgroups; (4) youth is a universal state; (5) young people are part of families and thus are in partnership with adults, rather than outsiders; and (6) the young eventually become adults and will assume positions of authority, unlike some groups based on race/ethnicity, gender, and disabilities (Notepad 2003).

Our position is that discrimination of any kind, regardless of its transitory or temporary state, never should be tolerated in a democratic society that embraces values and principles of social and economic justice. The pain, as well as the social and economic consequences resulting from these experiences, will shape the long-term worldview of those being discriminated against and also the outlooks and attitudes of the perpetrators of such oppression. This behavior is not justified simply because a society has the "right" or power to exercise control over some group because of a time-limited characteristic (Nagle et al. 2003). A humanitarian perspective on youth must not differ from that on sexual orientation, race, and gender, regardless of the fact that this condition is not a permanent state. Thus, the common reasons about why adultism is not a true form of oppression simply have no legitimacy.

Adultism can manifest itself in overt and covert ways when adults discuss youth. Statements such as "You are so smart for your age," "You are not old enough to understand," "We know what is best for you," "Act your age," and "What do you know about life?" all represent the undermining forces of adultism at work, to one degree or another. Blaming youth for the challenges that they must overcome, without regard to the circumstances (barriers) that adults have created for them, is irresponsible, yet it is a common example of adultism in action.

Dysfunctional rescuing is another attitude that either has adults believing that youth cannot help themselves or that serves as a self-fulfilling prophecy, providing assistance to young people that limits their abilities to act independently and efficaciously (Community Youth Development Program 2005). Embracing a "rescue fantasy" effectively disempowers youth, further questioning their competencies. As a result, human service professionals and educators must guard against "the need to rescue youth from themselves." When adultism intersects with other oppressive forces such as racism, classism, sexism, ableism, mentalism, and homophobia, the social situation is compounded. This can result in young people's experiencing further loss of self-esteem, hope for the future, and disengagement from the community, to list but three consequences for self, family, community, and society.

One youth organizer made this poignant point to show how adults tend to take over (LISTEN, Inc. 2004, 15):

> [A]dults are just so quick to speak for young people. They're quicker to speak for us than we're able to speak for ourselves. So we can't speak for ourselves. Everybody wants to represent youth. Everybody wants to be young. These are hard times for young people. We're too busy trying to be adults and adults are too busy trying to be young. That's a problem.

This statement articulates the ambivalence adults feel about youth. We envy them, yet we do not trust them! But the argument based on experiential and theoretical expertise neglects to take into account the fact that adults were young during another time period, when circumstances and challenges were vastly different.

Adultism can manifest itself in countless injustices and social dynamics; however, the term does not explain why this phenomenon exists. The National Youth Rights Association (2003) identified three key manifestations of adultism: (1) youth inequality, or the failure of adults to share humanity with young people, resulting in stereotypes and discrimination; (2) lack of youth power, tied to a long history of viewing the young as human property, with adults holding the right to command obedience; and (3) repression of youth culture by adults who view it as a threat to stability in society. The consequences of adultism for youth and the larger society are far-reaching. Young people lose self-confidence, develop feelings of powerlessness, and ultimately may give up their dreams for a better tomorrow, effectively limiting the potential contributions they can make to their families, community, and society. They also are more inclined to treat others with the same disrespect. Disillusioned young people enter adulthood without the desire and repertoire of competencies necessary to play active roles in their communities and in society in general.

Kim McGillicuddy (2003, 1), a young community organizer, summed up the importance of youth participation quite well:

> I think that for many people our commitment to youth organizing is because of both the personal and community transformation it brings. For example, the skills youth (and adults) get from organizing are endless.... Youth organizing teaches young people not only a large set of very important skills together, in a way that's immediately relevant to people's lives, and that gives it special strength.

As a result, young people are thrust into positions of helping and teaching not only one another but also adults, which can be quite empowering.

Essentially, competencies cannot be separated from values and commitment, since each addresses current needs while also serving as a foundation for future actions within a democratic society. Nevertheless, for youth, the value of immediate gains far outweighs potential benefits that may accrue at a later time, when they become adults. This focus on the present may appear minor; however, as will be discussed later, this stress on immediacy is critical to understanding how youth-led community organizing operates, and often dictates, the manner in which campaigns unfold and individual youth organizers function.

It is quite fitting to end this section with a quote from Eleanor Roosevelt (1940), who poignantly raised youth/adult power relations for scrutiny: "I wish we could look at this whole question of the activities or youth-led organizations from the point of view of the wisest way for old people to help youth. . . . We must go and deal with them as equals, and we must have both courage and integrity if we expect respect and cooperation on the part of youth."

Youth Rights

A rights perspective invariably is associated with a legal definition and the role of the courts in determining who has rights and if, and when, they are violated. Nevertheless, when applied to youth, a legal perspective usually has served to disenfranchise this age group, not grant them the same rights and privileges given to adults. *Youth rights* usually refers to a philosophical stance that focuses on the civil rights of the young (Golombek 2006). This is counter to the more traditional perspective held by child rights' advocates that emphasizes youth entitlements, a viewpoint that usually rests on a paternalistic foundation (Wikipedia 2006). In fact, youth rights organizers seek equal rights with adults by having young people play central roles in crafting their own strategies and campaigns to change their status. The National Youth Rights Association calls the youth rights movement the "last civil rights movement."

It always is so much easier for adults to view youth as victims—needy, reckless, and out of control—and also as markets for goods and services. Considering youth as resources, social capital, citizens, and partners with adults represents a radical departure from the existing norm. In effect, this latter position requires a shift in paradigms. Any paradigmatic change away from the prevailing view is bound to cause a severe reaction from those in positions of authority (adults), who have a vested interest in maintaining the status quo. Viewing youth as a constituency with inherent rights and privileges represents a significant challenge to the negative forces associated with adultism. A youth rights movement, otherwise called *youth liberation*, places the status of youth within a social context and proponents can expect to encounter numerous speed bumps on the road to equality for all, regardless of age (Watts and Serrano Garcia 2003).

Edelman (1977), like many other scholars, argues that children have much in common with African-American/black people and women—namely, each has historically been regarded as chattel in society and rarely has shared the rights and privileges enjoyed by the dominant group. O'Kane (2002, 701) identified three social domains for a child/youth rights perspective that have direct implications for youth-led community organizing:

> The principles of child rights programming are based on the principles of human rights, child rights and childhood development, namely: *indivisibility/holistic*: consider all the children's development needs; *accountability*: children are rights holders and adults are responsible for child rights; *equity*: ensure non-discrimination and inclusion of all children (age, gender, ability, ethnicity, religion, origin, etc); *participation*: promote children's rights to participate and to have their views considered; and *best interests*: always consider children's best interests and be accountable.

A rights perspective on social and economic justice serves to broaden this concept to include a wide variety of undervalued groups (Youth Liberation Program 1977a). For example, civil rights, women's rights, gay rights, disability rights, senior rights—all have currency in most fields of practice. However, youth rights has *not* been widely accepted, as argued by Holt (1974, 1977), Farson (1974), and Parson (1977) over thirty years ago.

The 1989 United Nations Convention on the Rights of the Child often is credited with popularizing youth rights across the world. Besides Somalia, the United States is the only nation out of 193 countries that has not ratified the outcomes of this conference (Males 2004). More recently, the United Nations Ad Hoc Working Group for Youth and the Millennium Development Goals (United Nations 2005) has cast further global attention on the importance of tapping the human capital represented by 1.2 billion (ages 15 to 24) young people and on developing mechanisms to increase their participation in decision making.

Youth rights as a guiding tenet for social justice has been underappreciated and ignored in a fashion similar to the failure to acknowledge the important role of young people in helping shape U.S. history. Embracing a youth-rights perspective helps politicize the existence of young people and the issues that they confront. This shift in perspective easily finds a home within a social and economic justice framework. Affirmation of youth rights is an excellent mechanism for bringing attention to the status of youth within this society, raising consciousness within their own group, and setting forth an agenda for social change to rectify their disenfranchisement.

A Declaration of the Rights of American Youth, promulgated on July 4, 1936, at the American Youth Congress, still holds significant meaning more than seventy years later and provides an excellent example of how social and economic justice can guide a youth-led agenda (American Youth Congress 1936, 1–2):

> Today our lives are threatened by war, our liberties threatened by reactionary legislation, and our right to happiness remains illusory in a world of insecurity. Therefore, on this Fourth Day of July, 1936, we, the Young People of America, in Congress assembled, announce our own declaration— A Declaration of the Rights of American Youth. We declare that our generation is rightfully entitled to a useful, creative, and happy life, the guarantees of which are: full educational opportunities, steady employment at adequate wages, security in time of need, civil rights, religious freedom, and peace. We have a right to life. . . . We have a right to liberty. . . . We have a right to happiness. . . . Therefore, we the young people of America, reaffirm our right to life, liberty, and the pursuit of happiness. With confidence we look forward to a better life, a larger liberty and freedom. To those ends we dedicate our lives, our intelligence and our unified strength.

This declaration of youth rights is quite powerful in conveying the belief and principles of an agenda of social and economic justice that is just as relevant today as it was in the 1930s. Edelman (1977, 206), although speaking almost thirty years ago, raised the specter of a youth rights movement: "It will probably never be a 'movement' in the mass-action sense that the civil rights, the women's, and the peace movements have been. Even so, the growing effort is showing enough potential strength and effectiveness that it may soon be worthy of the term." A rights point of view conveys respect and a set of societal expectations that cast youth as citizens with privileges, including the right to organize for social change.

Roche (1999) introduced the language of citizenship as a means of raising the status of youth by examining how a sector of society effectively is disenfranchised of its rights. *Youth citizenship* generally refers to young people having access to and exercising the rights and obligations for civil rights, political rights, and social rights. This multifaceted perspective broadens youth participation within all aspects of society and provides a framework for assessing their status. As a result, the denial of youth citizenship is an excellent handle for young people organizing campaigns, particularly ones that they lead.

Ginwright and Cammarota (2002), in turn, commend youth organizing by taking the position that a social justice-driven model makes at least three direct contributions to the field of youth development: (1) shifting from an individual and psychological modality to a community/society focus provides an ecological perspective on better understanding and addressing youth issues; (2) young people are empowered to address environmental concerns through opportunities to achieve positive social change; and (3) critical consciousness and collective action results in a social justice agenda by recognizing societal inequality and encouraging change efforts to alter conditions and power relationships. We, however, believe that Gainwright and Cammaroa's stance brings youth-led community organizing more into the youth-led field and away from youth development.

The youth-led movement, it must be acknowledged, has raised the political consciousness of youth who occupy marginalized positions in society. Increasing numbers of young people understand that their situation and identity are very much based on inequalities in social and economic justice. As a result, many youth are drawing on their politicized identities to organize collective action to achieve social and economic justice for themselves and their communities (Ginwright 2003). One youth organizer's vision for organizing operationalizes a social and economic justice agenda quite well (Transformative Leadership 2004, 3–4):

> Driving youth organizing is a vision for economic and racial justice. Youth organizers and their adult allies believe that regardless of race, gender and socioeconomic status, people should be treated with respect and have equal access to a decent quality of life. For low-income, of color, and other disadvantaged populations, inequality and discrimination are persistent barriers to achieving this vision.

Thus, it is not surprising that the goal of achieving social and economic justice has become a central part of the youth development, and particularly the youth-led, field. For example, Brown and colleagues (2000, 33) argue that community youth development (CYD) is a method for creating positive social change that harnesses the power of youth: "No community can be considered 'developed' if relations between individuals or groups are based upon social injustice or an imbalance in power relations. As such, social justice [must be] the bedrock of all forms of community development. Community Youth Development is no exception."

The Social and Economic Justice Agenda

The youth-led community organizing field has its marching orders, so to speak. Concepts such as social justice, adultism, and youth rights set the stage for this form of social intervention. Commitment to a social and economic justice agenda, without question, is alive and well with this country's youth, particularly those who are systematically marginalized. Weiss (2003, 6) summed up this point quite well:

> [O]ver the last two decades, youth have joined the ranks of "favorite scapegoat" for politicians and news pundits. . . . This crackdown on young

people is based on a change—both real and imagined—in *who youth are,* grounded in two interrelated factors: (1) demographic shifts among young people; and (2) stereotypes of youth among elected officials, the media, and society as a whole.

The interplay of demographics and stereotypes identified by Weiss (2003) has helped shape a youth social and economic justice agenda for action and change, and has set the stage for a movement that will apply well into the early part of this century. A total of sixteen key issues for the youth rights movement have been identified in the literature (Wikipedia 2006):

Drinking age	Unschooling
Voting age	Corporal punishment
Age of candidacy	Zero tolerance
Curfews	Student rights
Emancipation	Ageism
Age of majority	Driving age
Age of consent	Child labor laws/right-to-work
Gulag schools (schools for youth with behavioral issues)	Adultism

The above youth-rights issues are the foundation for a social and economic justice agenda in youth-led community organizing. However, the average adult undoubtedly would have great difficulty acknowledging *any* of these issues for youth; and this epitomizes the struggles youth have in achieving their civil rights in this society. Thus, this points to the need for a youth-led community organizing model that places youth in charge of a social-change agenda based on their worldview and voices.

The set of beliefs, values, and principles associated with the concept of equity, an important element of youth rights, no doubt will continue to benefit from the input of young people, as noted by one youth organizer (LISTEN, Inc. 2004, 2):

> The whole [youth] generation is going to change what the whole social justice movement does.... I think that there is a new spirit of sort of militancy and rebellion to a certain extent that's coming up everywhere, across the country. That's going to rejuvenate and revitalize the social justice movement in this country, and some of the tactics—the lack of fear, the use of hip hop and culture—is incredible and beautiful.

Youth must define "equity" in their lives, and we as adults must be prepared to accept this definition, regardless of how narrow or broad that definition is. Adults must determine what role they are willing to accept in helping this youth-led, social justice–influenced agenda progress in this country. Youth, it is important to emphasize once again, will determine if, when, and how adults are a part of youth-led organizing!

Youth-led community organizing must be a social intervention that is inclusive, rather than exclusive. A philosophical commitment to diversity must play a central role in any youth-led social and economic justice agenda (Velazquez and Garin-Jones 2003). The reader will see these and other social and economic justice values prominently represented in the guiding principles for youth-led community organizing and the analytical framework presented in chapter 4.

The acceptance and celebration of diversity must be backed by a similar commitment to action, often forming the foundation for initiatives embracing social and economic justice. For example, gender diversity necessitates that youth organizing efforts must reach out to women, creating an organizational climate that confronts patriarchy, provides opportunities for leadership and high visibility, and addresses social and economic issues of great relevance to women (Weiss 2003). Anything short of these goals will ultimately compromise any legitimacy that young people gain in their social-change efforts.

The sexual orientation of youth also takes on an influential role in dictating organizing initiatives (Hagen 2005). Youth who are gay can organize on the same general issues as straight youth, such as with regard to education, but they will do so with a special focus on their population group. This issue specificity highlights broad educational matters of inequality, but it also seeks redress of particular concerns of interest to that group (Weiss 2003). Commitments to other underrepresented groups require similar sets of values and actions. As a consequence, youth who are organizing on specific issues, must endeavor to identify how their interests and concerns intersect with other issues and organizing groups. There must be a strategic determination about when they can unite and when they must go their separate ways (Sears 2005).

Conclusion

The philosophical foundation upon which youth-led community organizing rests will help young people frame their perspective on social and economic injustices, provide them with a language to use, and be the base for their plans and social action campaigns. Not surprisingly, it is difficult to identify and arrive at consensus definitions for the key principles and belief systems for social and economic justice that underpin this organizing effort. Such challenges are not restricted to youth; they are a common problem when anyone attempts to delineate the philosophical and theoretical roots of any social intervention. Nevertheless, it is essential to explore the basic premises and operating principles that animate youth-led community organizing.

This chapter has provided a perspective on how young people can best be assisted in identifying key issues in their lives and the means by which they can communicate their visions and goals for change to other youth, as well as to adults. A social and economic justice lens provides optimum perspective for bringing together disparate groups in search of a common understanding of their situation, helping them to create an agenda for action that is inclusive. Further, it highlights the complexities in achieving social justice in a society that has a long history of discrimination and that has essentially selected adults to decide which social issues are legitimate.

However, there is little question that we adults must be willing and able to confront and change the roles we play in disempowering youth. Unfortunately, this journey of self-discovery is painful and unsettling. Nevertheless, as addressed in this chapter, there is no denying that youth are oppressed in this society, and that even the most understanding professionals harbor attitudes and have behaviors that stem from adultism, even as we embrace the youth-led movement. Achievement of social and economic justice for youth will necessitate the involvement of adults as collaborators and facilitators, as dictated by youth. Our failure to act in such an empowering and facilitative manner will bear bitter fruit in our society. In effect, adults will become (or continue to be) part of the problem facing youth, even if our intentions are honorable!

3

Overview of Community Organizing, Youth-Led Field, and Youth-Led Organizing

> The United States is the most anti-youth society on earth. This is not because American youth suffer absolute deprivations worse than youth of other nations, though we fall far short of the standards of health care, housing, economic support, and opportunity afforded youth in similarly affluent Western countries. What characterizes America's singular hostility is that youth here are worse off *relative to adults* than those of any other country for which we have reliable information.
> —Males, *Youth and Social Justice* (2004)

Contextualizing youth-led community organizing is possible only when we learn about its origins. The emergence of an intervention such as youth-led community organizing is rarely an overnight occurrence. In fact, this approach has deep historical roots and can be appreciated best only when we examine adult community organizing over the course of the twentieth century, as well as the development of the "youth-led" field dating back to the 1980s. A context of social and economic justice, we believe, helps us better understand and appreciate the emergence of youth-led community organizing, as noted in the previous chapter.

Having laid this groundwork, we now chronicle the growth of youth-led organizing since the mid-1990s. Without knowing this history, our understanding of the current status of youth-led community organizing is severely limited. And while projecting into the future is, at best, a noble endeavor with no guarantees of accuracy, understanding the historical context increases the likelihood of our successfully identifying new trends, prospects, opportunities, and challenges.

Historical Overview of Community Organization

It is important to note that the roots of community organizing for achieving social and economic justice reach deep into the social work profession, and the effort dates back to the settlement movement, although organizing certainly cannot be considered the exclusive domain of this profession (Weil 1996; Garvin and Cox 2001; Betten and Austin 1990; Fisher 1984; Ross 1955; Lane 1939; Steiner 1930). However, the debate about social reform versus individual treatment is well over 100 years old and parallels the history of the social work profession, persisting to this day in various arenas (Haynes 1998; Specht and Courtney 1995).

The 1960s witnessed the emergence of community organizing as a distinct practice, with a set of theoretical concepts, principles, scholarship, and graduate-level courses of study in schools of social work across the United States (Lurie 1959, 1965). Probably more than any other profession, social work has adopted this practice alongside planning, program development, and human services management within the macro-practice arena (Weil 1996; Rothman 1995), and community organizing continues to be studied and learned in social work and other human service programs.

Nevertheless, community organizing is by no means restricted to practitioners who are formally educated or belong to any particular age group. Unlike planning, program development, and management, this practice has a long history of being democratic and within the reach of anyone and any organization wishing to bring about social change. Community organizing has been undertaken and embraced by numerous undervalued groups in this society, and excellent examples and scholarship can be found on how this method has addressed the concerns of women (Hyde, 1986, 1994, 1996, 2004; Weil 1986; Withorn 1984), women of color (Gutierrez and Lewis 1994), communities of color (Morales and Reyes 1998; Rivera and Erlich 1998), people with disabilities (Staples 1999; Checkoway and Norsman 1986), the elderly (Minkler 1997; McDermott 1989), and gays/lesbians (Wohlfeiler 1997; Tully, Craig, and Nugent 1994).

Indeed, most social work practice is not actively engaged in community organizing, and the majority of organizing efforts are not carried out by social work professionals. Organizing also is firmly planted in other arenas, including labor, agrarian reform, civil rights, welfare rights, neighborhood improvement, environmental justice, disability rights, the lesbian, gay, bisexual, and transgendered (LGBT) movement, immigrant rights, the women's movement, and social action efforts at the citywide, state, regional, national, and international levels. Quiroz-Martinez, Wu, and Zimmerman (2005), in their report *Regeneration: Young People Shaping Environmental Justice,* do a superb job of highlighting how the environmental justice movement has benefited from the infusion of young people. Thus, professional community organizing has a long and distinguished history within social work along with connections outside the profession, and all indications are that the influence of this means of social intervention will only grow in future years.

Over the course of the twentieth century, the degree and impact of various forms of organizing was episodic, with periods of popular insurgency and social activism followed by periods of relative quiescence. For instance, the Progressive era that immediately preceded World War I featured a wide variety of organizing initiatives involving social settlements, agrarian reform efforts, workers in the skilled trades, and the women's suffrage movement. The war dramatically changed the sociopolitical context, generally retarding most organizing efforts; and the political economy of the "return to normalcy" that followed, 1918–1929, also was inhospitable for popular collective action (Garvin and Cox 2001; Fisher 2005).

The Great Depression ushered in a new era of social unrest that was animated by the labor organizing of the new Congress of Industrial Organizations (CIO), by direct action through the Unemployed Councils of the Communist Party, and by Saul Alinsky's first community organization in the Back of the Yards neighborhood of Chicago (Piven and Cloward 1977; Fisher 2005). World War II effectively eliminated or minimized the significance of progressive organizing initiatives in the United States, and the cold war period that followed had a distinct chilling effect on most forms of social action.

Then in the mid-1950s, the civil rights movement launched an unparalleled period of activism and organizing that extended all the way through the 1960s (Piven and Cloward 1977). During this time, a broad array of constituency groups organized to assert their rights, including welfare recipients, farm workers, the elderly, women, gays and lesbians, people with disabilities, prisoners, tenants, environmental activists, blacks, Chicanos, and Native Americans (Garvin and Cox 2001; Fisher 2005). Turf-based community organizing also began to gather momentum, as Alinsky started new projects in a number northern and Midwestern cities (Finks 1984). And most relevant to this present study, there was an explosion of student activism, including the Student Nonviolent Coordinating Committee (SNCC) in the civil rights movement, Students for a Democratic Society (SDS) in the mid-1960s, and a host of groups mobilized against the Vietnam War (Gitlin 1989; Garvin and Cox 2001; Fisher 2005).

While fallout from the end of the war and the Watergate scandal dominated the national news in the early 1970s, federal funding for community organizing rapidly dried up, effectively ending many groups that were dependent on public dollars (Garvin and Cox 2001). A political backlash from large segments of the working and middle classes also led organizers to rethink their approaches and strategies that had focused exclusively on low-income people. George Wiley, director of the National Welfare Rights Organization, left to found the Movement for Economic Justice (MEJ), where he worked with colleagues to develop a "majority strategy" that was "aimed at uniting most Americans, black and white, poor and middle income, women and men, against the rich and powerful" (Boyte 1980, 53).

A number of ambitious new community organizing initiatives of unprecedented scale appeared. The Association of Community Organizations for Reform Now (ACORN) was founded in Little Rock, Arkansas, in 1970, to organize low- and moderate-income people around a mix of neighborhood and economic justice issues. Over the next three and a half decades, ACORN moved rapidly to build organizations at the statewide, regional, and national levels. As this book was being written, there were 175,000 family members in 850 chapters in seventy-five cities across the United States, plus cities in Canada, the Dominican Republic, and Peru. Other statewide efforts of note that attempted cross-class organizing included the Citizens Action League (CAL) in California; Massachusetts Fair Share; Connecticut Citizen Action Group (CCAG); Carolina Action; Illinois Public Action Council; Ohio Public Interest Campaign; and Oregon Fair Share.

Saul Alinsky died in 1972, but his Industrial Areas Foundation (IAF) continued his work during the 1970s, beginning a number of large-scale projects in cities across the United States, including Baltimoreans United in Leadership Development (BUILD), Communities Organized for Public Service (COPS) in San Antonio, Oakland Community Organization (OCO), and United Neighborhoods Organization (UNO) in Los Angeles. Other major organizing efforts spun off from the IAF, such as the Citizens Action Project (CAP) in Chicago, which in turn helped generate the Citizens Action organizing network; National People's Action (NPA), which by 2006 had organized 302 grassroots neighborhood groups based in thirty-eight states; and the Pacific Institute for Community Organization (PICO), currently working in 150 cities in seventeen states.

The election of Ronald Reagan in 1980 brought forth sharp cutbacks in welfare-state programs, as a taxpayers' revolt led to decreased government revenues at all levels. This decade also marked the start of a conservative era that lasted for twenty-five years and was "characterized by three central challenges: (a) the private marketplace and the practices of global corporations dominate and permeate almost all areas of life; (b) issues become increasingly private and individual rather than public and social; and (c) people are increasingly isolated and less able to build community and social solidarity" (Fisher 2005, 48). This context hardly was fertile ground for community organizing. Indeed, many of the large statewide organizations founded in the 1970s were out of business by the mid-1980s.

Nevertheless, the large organizing *networks*, such as ACORN, NPA, and PICO, have continued to grow while other associations and training and support centers have been created, including the Center for Third World Organizing (CTWO), the Direct Action and Research Training Center (DART), Gamaliel Foundation, Grassroots Leadership, Midwest Academy, National Housing Institute, National Organizers Alliance, ORGANIZE! Training Center (OTC), Organizing and Leadership Training Center (OLTC), Regional Council of Neighborhood Organizations (RCNO), Southern Empowerment Project (SEP), and Western States Center (Delgado 1997). During this time, the Industrial Areas Foundation also moved forward with such new organizing projects as Valley Interfaith in Texas, Greater Boston Interfaith Organization (GBIO), and ONE LA-IAF in Los Angeles. Hundreds of smaller, independent grassroots organizations not aligned with any of the major networks also sprouted up across the country, and many community development corporations now include an organizing component (Traynor 1993).

The past twenty-five years also have given rise to initiatives and innovations whereby community organizations have entered new arenas. For instance, ACORN now operates two radio stations, produces several publications (including *Social Policy*), runs a housing corporation, administers a voter registration network, and helped spin off the Working Families Party in New York State, which is expanding into several other states as this book went to press. Indeed, many community organizations have entered the arena of electoral politics within the constraints of their corporate status. There also have been many attempts to build cooperation between community organizations and organized labor, as evidenced by the work of ACORN with the Service Employees International Union (SEIU), a number of successful community-labor coalitions, and Living Wage campaigns across the country (Simmons 2004).

Finally, there have been literally thousands of organizing efforts to address specific issues or bring constituents together based on a shared identity. An illustrative, but not exhaustive, list of issue-based organizing projects includes affordable housing, environmental justice, lending policies, recreation, crime, utility rates, corporate responsibility, global capital, health care, public assistance, neighborhood improvement, tax reform, clean government, education, and employment (Staples 2004a, 5):

> Still other organizations are formed by constituency subgroups as *communities of identity* along dimensions such as race, ethnicity, gender, age, sexual orientation, immigrant status, religion, and physical or mental disability. Examples might include a senior citizens' group, a Vietnamese mutual assistance association, a lesbian/gay task force, or a social action organization of disabled people. While such groups will have a geographic location and may work on a range of issues, their primary focus and raison d'etre link to their members' shared characteristics of identity. Over the past several decades there has been explosive growth in identity

organizing. Much of this can be attributed to the failure of many turf and issue organizations to adequately address the interests and concerns of constituency subgroups within their membership. Since constituency group members often experience discrimination most directly and painfully along these very dimensions, they have frequently felt the need to organize separately to effectively challenge the oppression that so profoundly impacts their lives. Identity politics has fueled the civil rights, women's, LGBT, and disability rights (physical and mental) movements and continues to be a primary focus for grassroots organizing.

The youth-led organizing that this book examines most clearly falls under the category of *identity organizing*. Indeed, Williams (2003, 1) goes so far as to argue that youth organizing is no different from traditional forms of organizing, and he defines this approach simply as "a group of young people arranging themselves to change the status quo." However, youth have been involved in many of the large-scale organizing efforts of the twentieth century, especially the civil rights movement, and much of that long history has suffered the unwillingness of scholars to recognize youth's contributions to significant social change in this country. Nevertheless, with the exception of the student movement of the sixties (which was dominated by white, middle-class college students or recent graduates), young people seldom were in positions of leadership and responsibility in these organizing efforts. At best, these community organizations included youth, but almost never was the agenda *youth-driven* nor were the groups *youth-led*. This theme will be revisited in the third section of this chapter, but first we turn our attention to the evolution of the youth-led field.

Historical Overview of the Youth-Led Field

As addressed in chapter 1, the term *youth-led* often is interchangeable with numerous other phrases, such as *youth civic engagement, youth decision making, youth empowerment, youth leadership*, and most notably, *youth development*. A historical review of youth development is beyond the goals of this chapter; however, the reader is advised to read the book *Community Programs to Promote Youth Development* by Eccles and Gootman (2002) for an appreciation of the history and expansiveness of this paradigm. This evolutionary process has taken many years, if not decades, with no one timetable that applies to all processes.

Initially, a field may receive very little attention, and then, after an extended period of time, its origins may be uncovered, validated, and studied. We believe that youth-led community organizing follows this evolutionary pattern, and only now are we starting to appreciate its origins and manifestations. The authors believe that this historical context is of sufficient importance to warrant attention in this volume, although an entire book, or even a series of publications on this subject, is very much in order.

If we hope to comprehend the present form of the youth-led movement and seek to help shape its future, it is essential that we understand its origins and evolution. This is no easy task, particularly for adults:

> Some of the most significant and well-documented resources on youth action are less accessible than the ones you have on your book-shelves and bookmarked on your Web browser. [These inaccessible resources]. . . . tell an important story: our understanding of young people's engagement is both deeper and broader than we often assume. Yet, much of what we "know" is hidden from view, either because the literature documenting it went out of print decades ago, or because it was learned by grass roots organizations with little capacity to share their lessons. (Two Decades 2002b, 11)

This assessment of the paucity of historical knowledge and understanding about the youth-led movement, and particularly about youth activism is very much on target, from our perspective. It underscores the need for developing a fuller and more in-depth appreciation of the history of youth organizing.

The birth of this social intervention has been traced to the 1980s and the emergence of the "prevention" field of practice. Blum (1988), in one of the earliest articles on youth development, articulated the four C's of healthy youth: (1) competence in literacy and interpersonal skills; (2) connection to others by engaging in caring relationships; (3) character building by embracing individual responsibility and community service; and (4) confidence building through goal setting and achievement of goals. These points are manifest in virtually all definitions of youth development and have applicability to the youth-led movement.

There are few scholars who would disagree about the importance of youth development in influencing the youth-led field (Scheve, Perkins, and Mincemoyer 2006; Sherrod, Flanagan, and Youniss 2002). The youth-development paradigm also has evolved over the past decade or so (Delgado 2002; Rauner 2000). Initially, this model significantly shifted how society viewed youth. No longer were youth viewed and portrayed as victims, perpetrators, empty vessels, or a potential market for commercial goods. The shift from a deficit to an asset perspective redefined youth as positive contributors to society, both in the present and for the future.

Advocates for a more contextualized and politicized view of youth development articulated a "positive youth development" stance (Granger 2002; Lerner et al. 2002). This perspective further accentuated the assets that all youth have and the importance for adults to facilitate youth capacity enhancement, rather than focusing on development exclusively. *Development* signifies the need to "put into place what is missing," while *enhancement* is predicated on the belief that much is in place and it needs only to be

cultivated. Finally, those advocating a change agenda based on a foundation of social and economic justice introduced "community youth development" in order to emphasize these goals.

A conference on youth organizing embraced this important point (Youth
Organizing 1998, 4):

> Organizers generally agreed that the model they envision and seek to
> facilitate is, as one youth organizer described it, "youth development with
> a difference." For these youth organizers, the optimal model is one in
> which youth function holistically both in terms of self improvement and
> community improvement.... Young people are viewed as key agents—
> as the activists—in their communities around issues that impact them
> directly.

LISTEN, Inc. (2003) traces the emergence of youth organizing to three
important elements: (1) the legacy of traditional organizing methods emphasizing the work of Saul Alinsky; (2) the progressive social movements of
the 1960s and 1970s; and (3) the emergence of positive youth development.
These three elements represent the key ideological, conceptual, and practical foundation for what many consider much of youth organizing's theory
and practice.

The currency of community youth development has facilitated the rapid
growth of youth organizing because this paradigm couches youth development within the broader context of community (Booth and Crouter 2001;
Eccles and Gootman 2002; Gambone et al. 2006; Miao 2003; Villarruel et al.
2003a). Further, personal development often is a key component of youth-
led community organizing. Development in one area (individual) cannot be
maximized without development in the other area (community). In essence,
youth cannot flourish and grow without consideration for their environment or ecology (Massey 2001). Thus, it is best to view community youth development from a broad perspective that encompasses enhancing the power
of youth to achieve social change. In the process of attaining social change,
youth are able to enhance and develop competencies that facilitate their
transition to adulthood, with a tool kit that makes them valuable members
of a civic, democratic society (What Is the Impact 2002a).

As noted in chapter 1, the youth-led field also has evolved into a variety
of streams emphasizing different social causes. This expansion has not
weakened the field but, instead, has increased the attractiveness of this paradigm, allowing various fields to claim youth-led organizing as their own.
Social youth enterprises (Delgado 2004), health promotion (Delgado and
Zhou in press), and research (Delgado 2006) have been the latest arenas for
increased scholarship, and a number of new books on these subjects have
been published. However, this field also can encompass media, transportation, philanthropy, courts, recreation, and prevention. For example, Carroll, Herbert, and Roy (1999) report on the role and value of youth-led
violence prevention in the late 1990s. Thus, there are all kinds of indications

that the youth-led field will only continue to expand and mature in the coming decade; practitioners as well as scholars would do well to make note of this development.

We believe that the youth-led field can be conceptualized as evolving in parallel fashion with youth development. At times, these two fields are inextricably intertwined, as when attention is paid to individual youth acquisition or enhancement of knowledge and competencies. In other cases, the fields view youth from separate perspectives emphasizing significantly different values and principles. One field (youth development) highlights *positive community change*, while the other (youth-led, especially, community organizing) stresses *change in power distribution* based on social and economic justice themes (YouthAction 1998). Both fields, as will be discussed in greater detail below, retain a focus on the individual; however, the youth-led approach never loses sight of the community and the role of oppressive forces in shaping the daily lives of youth and their families. Thus, the youth-led field embraces a broader domain for practice that makes it very attractive for and consistent with community organizing (Irby, Ferber, and Pittman 2001).

The success of a youth-led social intervention such as community organizing has been achieved by its ability to "connect the dots between issues" (Young Wisdom Project 2004, 11):

> Young people understand better than anyone else that if their families are suffering, they will suffer. By exploring the intersections of age with race, gender, class, disability and sexuality, many organizations have developed a sophisticated analysis for how issues interact to impact their communities. As a result, many youth groups not only work to create power for youth in their communities, they also have the broader goal of community empowerment.

Checkoway (1998), a strong advocate of involving youth in community development, identified five distinctive forums for youth participation: (1) citizen action; (2) youth action; (3) youth development; (4) neighborhood development; and (5) neighborhood-based youth initiative. Citizen and youth action each feature youth initiating and organizing themselves for social change. Although both forums are based on empowerment principles, youth action places young people in a central decision-making role vis-à-vis issues specific to them. Citizen action, in contrast, can have youth involved, but not necessarily in key decision-making roles, and the issues addressed may have broad appeal to all ages rather than being youth-specific.

The Forum for Youth Investment (2006) also has developed a Youth Engagement Continuum with five stages: (1) youth services; (2) youth development; (3) youth leadership; (4) civic engagement; and (5) youth organizing. A youth services approach "defines young people as clients," and "provides services to address individual problems and pathologies" with programming designed around treatment and prevention (3). The youth development model also features services, but focuses on growth and development by tapping into assets and strengths as it "meets young people where they are," building on individual competencies, emphasizing "positive self identity," and supporting "youth/adult partnerships" (3). While youth leadership includes many components of youth development, it also "builds in authentic youth leadership opportunities within programming and organization." This approach entails young people's participating in community projects, as they "deepen historical and cultural understanding of their experiences and community issues" and develop skills and capacities for decision-making and problem solving (3). Civic engagement moves youth further into collective empowerment by adding "political education and awareness," skills for "power analysis and action around issues," the development of "collective identity of young people as social change agents," and involvement in advocacy and negotiation (3). Finally, youth organizing emphasizes the need to build a "membership base," which "engages in direct action and mobilizing" and also works through alliances and coalitions with other groups. The organizing model includes "youth as part of [the] core staff and governing body" of a grassroots community organization that seeks to alter relations of power and bring about systemic change (3).

Those who subscribe to the youth-led approach, particularly those embracing community organizing, have separated themselves from the youth development field, which they consider too apolitical (Innovation Center for Community and Youth Development 2003, 72): "The reluctance of youth organizing groups to emphasize the youth development aspects of their approach belies the amount of time and resources they committed purely towards supporting the individual development of their core youth organizers." Advocates of youth-led community organizing have referred to the relationship between this field and youth development as "two ships passing in the night" (Wheeler 2003). These two ships meet on occasions but essentially are using different navigational systems and have different destinations. At first glance, they look the same; however, upon closer scrutiny, they are different vessels that sail the same ocean (community).

The Aspen Institute Roundtable on Community Change (Lawrence et al. 2004) identified the critical nature of structural racism and the need for youth development programs to both acknowledge and address this form of oppression when targeting youth of color. Such a perspective relies heavily on a social and economic justice perspective to help youth better contextualize their experiences. Achieving this goal requires interventions that do not exclusively focus on individual behavior. An asset-driven paradigm, such as youth development centered on progress toward individual development and achievement outside of a broader community context cannot be expected to achieve lasting and significant change when youth of color and other marginalized young people are the focus of interventions.

A broader social context allows youth to better understand how this nation's core values, policies, institutions, and practices severely limit youth from achieving their potential, particularly low-income youth of color (Nygreen, Kwon, and Sanchez 2006). Further, a more comprehensive approach enables participating youth to develop an in-depth understanding of how these forces shape their personal destinies, their communities, and the roles they can play in larger arenas. Youniss and colleagues (2002, 13) note:

> Youth did not create the post-1989 global uncertainty nor the sprawling global economic structures that can easily breed a sense of impotence. Nonetheless, youth will be the critical participants in the processes that achieve stability, even out the widening gap between rich and poor, preserve the environment, forcibly quell ethnic enmities, and render a balance between globalization and cultural traditions.

The reader may well argue that an asset paradigm, even if focused on individual youth, still is promising. There certainly is an intrinsic value to this approach. However, when youth development programs target youth who confront a litany of social and economic injustices, without systematically addressing those forces, injustices are perpetrated under the guise of helping youth develop their potential! Under such circumstances, youth cannot develop a more sophisticated understanding of the conditions that shape their individual development. Any results achieved and solutions found will fall far short of ultimate success when these larger dimensions are ignored.

Natural values such as personal responsibility, individuality, meritocracy, and equal opportunity have different operative meanings, depending on the social profile of the youth being served (Ginwright 2006). Addressing power inequalities is a natural response when injustice is experienced (Cohen 2006; Lawrence et al. 2004). Thus, the embrace of a change agenda for social and economic justice as a central goal or theme separates youth-led community organizing from the more conventional forms of youth development that emphasize personal growth and positive change within the community (Sherman 2002).

Change can focus on improving services, expanding access, and enhancing other dimensions that affect the quality of life for youth and their families within existing power structures (Checkoway 2005; Knox et al. 2005). However, justice-based change goals also can seek to alter power relationships in a redistributive manner, even when this may not be the norm or be explicitly stated. Collective action for a safer environment, civic engagement, antiracism, gender equality, LGBT rights, peacemaking and conflict resolution, electoral politics, and education reform all can be constructed within a framework of youth-led economic and social justice.

Activism connected to themes of social and economic justice is without question one of the most vibrant areas of the youth-led movement, nationally and internationally (Brown et al. 2000; Terry and Woonteiler 2000). Social activism is undertaken within an extensive set of public arenas. Each of these arenas, in turn, easily can be subdivided depending upon the focus and goals of the campaigns. Mullahey, Susskind, and Checkoway (1999, 5) do a splendid job describing youth-led initiatives that have social change as a central focus:

> Youth-based initiatives for social change are those in which young people define the issues that they work on and control the organizations through which they work and the strategies they use. In this form, youth employ a variety of strategies, including advocacy, social action, popular education, mass mobilization, and community and program development, to achieve their goals for social change.

According to the Applied Research Center's survey of youth organizing (Weiss 2003), essentially there are four defined components of youth-led organizing: (1) political analyses and education; (2) arts and culture; (3) personal development; and (4) interpersonal and coalition work. The reader may well argue that these components also can be found in adult-led organizing; however, as will be discussed throughout this book, these components take on unique and quite prominent manifestations in youth-led community organizing because of historical and social forces.

Youth-led community organizing, unlike most definitions of youth development, seeks to accomplish a multitude of goals in addition to addressing its primary end of social and economic justice within a community-societal context (Lafferty, Mahoney, and Thombs, 2003). The youth-led movement has managed to combine a variety of youth-focused goals that incorporate academic, social, cultural pride, and service learning objectives (Cervone 2002). This approach effectively embraces a holistic perspective on youth assets and needs, in a fashion similar to how the youth development field has incorporated cognitive, emotional, moral, physical, spiritual, and social core elements.

HoSang (2004, 2) highlights the importance of a holistic perspective in youth-led community organizing:

> First, many youth organizing groups have developed an integrated approach to social change, often combining issue-based organizing with leadership development programs, service learning activities, cultural enrichment programs, and even academic and personal support components. In comparison to adult-based community organizing groups that typically focus on policy outcomes and the organizing skills of its constituents, youth groups have crafted a more holistic approach to social change that addresses the many issues young members face.

The use of a community-based service-learning perspective is one promising mechanism for helping youth organizers integrate individual goals with community-focused goals (Camino 2005; Cervone and Cushman 2002; Eyler and Giles 1999). Wheeler (2003) identifies the integration of youth leadership development as an influential step in tying individual youth development to community development in general, with a corresponding validation of the importance of this connection within philanthropic and academic circles.

This holistic perspective opens avenues for rewards, but also raises challenges in creating a "proper" mix of personal and community-focused goals. The ability of youth-led community organizers to achieve both social and individual change will be a key factor in the success of their efforts, in both the short and long term. HoSang (2004) goes on to note that this holistic perspective takes on greater meaning with youth organizers, because social-action campaigns can take a great deal of time before success is achieved. Deriving a series of instrumental and expressive benefits along the way helps ensure that youth reap concrete benefits that can help with immediate needs. Unlike their adult counterparts, youth-led organizing campaigns rarely are affiliated with national organizations or support networks. Consequently, they do not enjoy the benefits of training, consultation, and technical support from national organizations, necessitating that their efforts basically create everything from scratch.

Further, these organizing efforts have the advantage of crafting their campaigns with specific local issues in mind and do not have to exert energy and resources responding to national directives. However, lacking the advantages of an infrastructure supported by an external body, youth-led organizing groups invariably have to create local solutions that would benefit from the experiences of other youth-led groups across the nation (HoSang 2004). Youth-led organizing victories, not surprisingly, are restricted to small-scale reforms focused on single issues. Lack of collaboration across groups, adult as well as youth-led, has precluded focus on broader social issues with national policy implications.

Youth-led community organizing easily can incorporate the elements and goals of decision making, leadership development, skills building, relationship building, community service, and identity development, to list a few goals usually associated with youth development (YouthAction 1998). This flexibility, or as critics would say, "looseness," allows sponsoring organizations and youth organizers to select a wide range of projects and individual goals for youth organizers. Thus, youth-led community organizing and youth development conceptually can co-exist without severely compromising each other. Youth development is the overarching paradigm, with organizing being the preferred mode or method for achieving the lofty goals inherent in this approach. Nevertheless, as will be discussed later in this book, advocates of youth-led community organizing who embrace a social and economic justice change agenda take issue with this point of view.

Gainwright and James (2002) and other advocates highlight the centrality of political empowerment within a social–political–ecological approach, which effectively transforms youth and their communities. Burgess (2002) grounds youth leadership development within a social-change agenda that ties in youth development, community development, and youth organizing. The emphasis on creating "social consciousness" as an integral part of youth development leads to a natural tendency for youth to engage in activism as a means of achieving positive individual and community change (LISTEN, Inc., 2003). Mohamed and Wheeler (2001) stress the importance of leadership as a vehicle for youth to acquire a range of competencies that will result in their becoming "engaging" citizens. These competencies can entail critical thinking, public speaking, written communication skills, and group facilitation. As a result, outcomes must encompass both individual and community change to maximize the benefits of youth organizing and youth development for this form of social intervention.

Mokwena and colleagues (1999) advocate the position that youth development and social change must address two goals: (1) youth participation is a critical segment of positive development; and (2) youth participation ultimately must contribute to the development of community and society. The nexus of these two goals helps shape the evolution of youth-led organizing as a vital part of the youth development field. This phenomenon is destined to increase in importance as more youth organizing projects are funded and more scholarship on the subject emerges. Nevertheless, the emergence of an agenda driven by social and economic justice promises to cause considerable tension in the field of youth development by necessitating a balance between goals for individual growth and those for social change.

Historical Overview of Youth-Led Community Organizing

As noted above, it would be a serious mistake to ignore the contribution of youth to a number of important organizing efforts in U.S. history (Cohen 2006). In fact, youth activism is as old as this country, having played an influential role in gaining America's independence, ending slavery, and improving working conditions, as well as gaining civil rights for all (Hoose 1993). Unfortunately, most history books have totally ignored its role in these and other important national events. While the legacy of youth in community organizing can be traced back well over two hundred years, it remains largely unappreciated in both organizing and nonorganizing circles. Sadly, this invisibility of youth's contributions is not restricted to any one era or social campaign, and is due primarily to the inability or unwillingness of adults to recognize assets that youth possess. Furthermore, when history is written, adults invariably are the authors and they tend to view significant events and circumstances through a narrow, adult-centric lens, failing to recognize the important roles played by young people (HoSang 2005).

Nevertheless, writers such as Hoose (1993) and Gross and Gross (1977) have made an important contribution by highlighting historical examples in which youth took action to help shape their own and others' destinies. These authors do a wonderful job giving voice to this nation's youth and explaining their role in creating a better society for all, including its youngest members. They have made significant strides toward correcting a picture of history that essentially omitted the significant parts played by youth in creating positive social change.

It is instructive to examine the role and influence of youth in this nation's civil rights movement, as a case in point. The importance of the civil rights movement in this country is well understood, and social work, probably more than any other profession, owes much to this movement for popularizing the practice of community organizing. As already noted, historians have largely ignored the role of youth in this field, even though the birth of the civil rights movement is arguably a watershed in youth organizing (McElroy 2001). Large numbers of youth participated in lunch-counter sit-ins across the South, and college students played an active and influential role in helping to integrate many other segregated settings.

One demonstration had children, primarily elementary-age, march out of the Sixteenth Street Baptist Church onto the streets of Birmingham, Alabama, on May 2, 1963. So many African-American adults had been arrested that it was difficult for Dr. Martin Luther King, Jr., to replenish their numbers. Until that point, large numbers of children had not participated in the demonstrations. But children began joining the ranks with adults to help maintain the large size of the protests. Eventually, over six hundred children were arrested. In fact, scenes of children being arrested, being blasted by water from firehoses, and being chased by attack dogs played a crucial role in changing public opinion.

Hoose (1993) argues that young people's conscience, energy, and courage helped shaped American history. Davis (2004), when chronicling the early civil rights movement in Mississippi, notes the central role played by youth (junior and senior high school students) in moving forward a social justice agenda in that state. Civil rights organizer Ed King commented appreciatively in 1963 on the contributions of youth to this movement (Davis 2004, 1): "When nobody else is moving and the students are moving, they are the leadership for everybody."

The experience of one youth activist during Mississippi's civil rights actions also helps illustrate the point that childhood activism can have a lifelong impact (Open Society Institute 1997, 1–2):

> Leroy Johnson wasn't even in elementary school when his education as an organizer began. Growing up in rural Trouble Grove, Mississippi, his early memories include sitting on his father's lap at meetings of the Student Nonviolent Coordinating Committee—SNCC. "In 1963, I was five years old, and my dad decided that it was time, for me—as the oldest child—to be involved in what was going on in my community. I didn't understand everything, but the singing, the energy and the spirit in those meetings was the thing that I took with me." His childhood role as a "lap activist" was the beginning of a lifetime commitment to community organizing. Today, as the Executive Director of Southern Echo, Johnson

integrates young people in all the organizing efforts led by Echo's membership.

McElroy (2001, 1) makes similar observations and adds another important perspective:

> In history, black leadership positions often have been undertaken by the youngest of society. In these instances, the leadership positions are assumed by the children, by those who have not yet been conditioned to feel uncomfortable with second-class citizenship. The youth organizers of past generations have become the adults of this one. Now these leaders are 40 to 50 (years old) and are still forced to undertake the leadership responsibilities. The torch must be passed. . . . The key to developing strength in black leadership is to give young people a very strong sense of their own power. The surest path by which to achieve this goal is through education, both conventional and totally unconventional.

Clearly, the involvement of youth by adults in the civil rights movement had immediate and long-term consequences by creating a cadre of future social activists. In fact, the 1960s were an influential period for youth activism throughout the country. For many, this era represented a critical turning point for youth engagement in political issues across a wide age spectrum. It should come as no great surprise that some of the leading exponents of youth civil rights, as well as social and economic justice for this group, were heavily involved in social actions during this decade. Spann (2003) and Kreider (2002) describe the many contributions made by youth during this period and show how these acts of civil disobedience changed society.

Hefner (1998) identifies the significance of the 1960s U.S. Supreme Court rulings concerning due process (juvenile courts) and student rights to wear black armbands to protest the Vietnam War. HoSang (2003) also acknowledges the important role youth played in the civil rights movement, and he goes on to examine youth leadership in antiracist movements through such groups as the Student Non-Violent Coordinating Committee, the Black Panthers, the Young Lords, and the Brown Berets. The term *student power* emerged to signify the presence of youth as a viable constituency and age group for achieving social change (Kreider 2002). Unfortunately, the faces and voices of youth in these and other social movements have gone largely unnoticed by historians.

Thus, some would argue that youth as a political identity did not emerge until the 1980s and 1990s. Not coincidentally, this period witnessed tremendous advances in the use of the media and telecommunications, effectively enabling youth to access and create information of particular value and relevance to their lives. It is during this time that the youth-led paradigm clearly began to be incorporated into community organizing that heretofore had been restricted to *including* youth to varying degrees. Indeed, this new model put youth *in charge*. The mission, goals, priorities, agendas, recruitment methodology, leadership, organizational culture, decision-making processes, selection of strategies and tactics, and actions undertaken were all youth-driven and youth-defined. Most important, heavy emphasis was placed on leadership development, which drew on principles of both traditional community organizing and the youth development field. Youth leadership was now at the center of this organizing—which is of, by, for, and about youth, their culture, and their concerns. Figure 3.1 provides a visual representation of several prominent streams of influence on youth-led community organizing.

YouthAction, based in Albuquerque, New Mexico, is an organization that has a distinguished history of sponsoring youth-led community organizing. This group has identified seven concepts and initiatives that often are incorporated in youth organizing, but in fact cannot be substituted for youth-led community organizing: (1) leadership development; (2) community services; (3) youth entrepreneurism; (4) civic participation; (5) service to youth; (6) cultural work; and (7) spontaneous high-school walkouts. Each of these forms, although means of achieving worthy goals, lacks a political analysis of social and economic justice and therefore cannot bring about significant changes in power distribution and relationships in this society. Youth-led community organizing enables youth to view their circumstances beyond their local boundaries and helps them better understand and appreciate the magnitude of the social forces that create inequality in the larger society.

For example, issues related to classism, racism, and sexism are quite openly addressed in youth-led community organizing initiatives, because youth bring the consequences of these oppressive forces to their worldview, as well as to the organizations in which they participate (Ginwright 2006; Quiroz-Martinez, HoSang, and Villarosa 2004). Acknowledging and integrating these themes into a campaign help ensure that the group's actions are relevant to larger social conditions. Certainly, there is a natural and strong connection between youth-led community organizing and recognition of neighborhood issues, city and state electoral processes, and national politics (Building Nations 2001). The leap from community building to nation building is one of the positive consequences of youth engagement in community organizing and other forms of civic activism and participation. Data from one national youth initiative reinforced the use of community organizing as a method for engaging youth and achieving positive community change (Mohamed and Wheeler 2001).

Youniss and colleagues' (2002) assessment of youth participation in political and civic arenas led them to conclude that the "general picture" was one of apathy toward conventional politics but active interest in "nonmainstream" civic involvement that leads to mobilization, social action, and youth's synthesizing of social and economic justice material, individually and collectively. Gauthier (2003) concurs with Youniss and colleagues (2002), and suggests that the concept of political participation be expanded to include involvement in social action and social movements such as anti-globalization demonstrations.

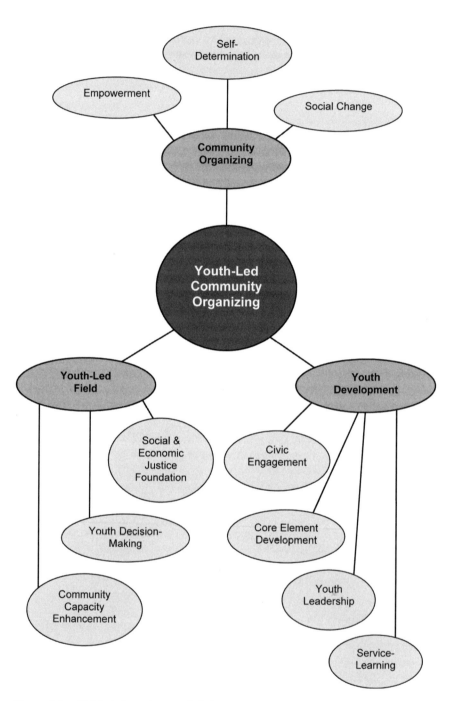

Figure 3.1. Fields influencing youth-led community organizing.

The call for civic action on the part of youth has not been viewed without skepticism and some resistance on the part of youth, for very good reason. This type of activity should not be confused with decision making and social action. Mendel (2004, 31), in quoting Jean Baldwin Grossman, notes:

> Grossman, a Princeton University youth scholar, warns that civic action programs are "harder to pull off than one might think, because often—and the kids smell it really quickly—it's a pretend. There's no real cause that's being served. 'We're gonna clean up this park. We're gonna help this organization by stuffing envelopes.' . . . The kids know they're being used. If it was to have a sit-down strike in the mayor's office, they'd be there with you in a minute. But there's sort of a backlash amongst a lot of kids against that kind of Mickey Mouse community service."

Grossman's assessment of the challenges that organizations face in recruiting youth highlights the difference when discussing youth as decision makers in community organizing campaigns. Youth-led community organizing, unlike more conventional programs where youth may share decision making with adults and the programming is more on community development, relies on themes of social and economic justice and strategies oriented toward social change as prime recruiting mechanisms. Youth-led community organizing has continued to broaden its appeal well into the new millennium, as evidenced by the increasing amount of funding and scholarly literature, as well as the increasing number of workshops and conferences highlighting this method (Fletcher 2004; Funders' Collaboration on Youth Organizing 2003; Pintado-Vertner 2004; Price and Diehl 2004). Youth organizing rightly has taken its place at the nexus of youth-related fields and emerged as a field in its own right. It has provided a viable alternative to youth development programs and activities that focus almost exclusively on individual growth without addressing social justice for all.

This area of practice will continue to inform the fields of youth development, youth-led, community development, civic engagement, and community organizing while engendering a new generation of youth workers known as *youth organizers* (Sullivan 2001). The specific designation of youth-led organizing as a field unto itself bodes well for its future. Such categorization helps attract the requisite attention (policymakers, academia, and local stakeholders) needed to move the field forward.

Hip-Hop Activism

The use of culture as a construct usually is reserved for discussions of race and ethnicity in this country. In many ways, this discourse has been shaped by historical events related to slavery and the racial and ethnic conflicts of the twentieth century. However, this perspective, although of great importance in influencing this country's view of itself and the world, is much too narrow in scope. It is necessary for both academics and practitioners to undertake a broader analysis of culture. Thus, hip-hop activism is understood best by using a social and economic justice lens and considering the historical backdrop.

Youth, too, have a culture that is greatly influenced by contextual factors and is worthy of extensive analysis and discourse in both academic and practice circles (Aitken 2001; Giroux 1996, 1998; Thornton 1996). Youth culture, like its racial and ethnic counterparts, shapes beliefs, values, behaviors, and worldview, effectively intersecting with other cultural dimensions such as gender, sexual identity, socioeconomic class, race, and ethnicity.

Weiss (2003, 95) underscores the importance of art and cultural events for the field of youth-led community organizing:

> One unique, and pervasive, characteristic of youth organizing is the significance of art and culture. Young organizers across the country organize hip hop concerts and spoken word workshops, sponsor poetry reading and fashion shows, host club nights and break dance competitions, and curate galleries. Like Generation Y, with its monthly "café Intifada," four out of five youth groups across the country use performing arts and cultural events to draw new members, sustain and nourish more experienced ones, breach ethnic and language barriers, and cultivate pride and positivity. . . . As organizer Marinieves Alba explains, "In the Puerto Rican community we have a saying that, in order to reach the masses, you have to speak to them in rice and beans. So hip hop is rice and beans for a lot of young people. . . . Fundamentally it's a tool. It's the bridge."

The emergence of the term *hip-hop activism* serves to ground youth culture within a social and economic justice orientation that seeks social change when young people attempt to alter environmental circumstances that are toxic and even lethal to their existence. Societal forces serve to target youth of particular backgrounds, rendering them marginal and undervalued from the mainstream perspective. (Ginwright 2006; Taylor 2004)

Hip-hop has undergone an extensive journey (Open Society Forum Institute 2002, 1):

> Hip-hop culture has transformed the popular landscape of modern youth identity and created a new forum of self-expression. In three decades hip-hop has expanded from a Bronx youth subculture into a global commodity, driving a multibillion-dollar industry that reaches into music, film, fashion, art, dance, and style. But that's not all. Hip-hop culture has also given voice to a new generation of activists, who have tapped its special, even prophetic, sensitivity to youth and urban issues in organizing their communities.

Chang (2003), in turn, places hip-hop activism within a broader social world that consists of youth organizers, thinkers, cultural workers, and activists. Furthermore, hip-hop activism can be considered a lens for understanding young people's reaction to social injustice and their desire to create social change.

Focusing on the role of social capital in urban black youth culture, Sullivan (1997) notes the richness of connections and informal social networks in this community. However, our larger society either has not bothered to examine this form of social capital or has misunderstood it and underestimated its significance. There has been a general disinvestment in the lives of these young people by all levels of government in the United States. Many of these young people of color feel a deep sense of alienation from mainstream society, including most black leaders. As a result, urban black youth have turned to each other and the hip-hop movement as a means of increasing connectedness, using this youth culture to provide a common identity, a collective voice, and a shared vision for a just society.

The influential role that youth culture plays in shaping youth-led community organizing is well acknowledged in the field. For example, art and other forms of youth culture help provide a meaningful context for the engagement of a large percentage of young activists (Delgado 2000; Ross and Rose 1994). This culture is brought to life through hip-hop, poetry readings, spoken-word workshops, breakdancing, curated galleries, murals, and graffiti (Kitwana 2002). These cultural forms of expression demonstrate the outrage felt by inner-city youth, who experience the pain of societal injustice and marginalization. This perspective is well over a decade old (Lipsitz 1998).

There are many different ways that young people can engage in self-discovery to find their place within the broader context of positive and negative societal values (Stokes and Gant 2002). Cerone (2002, 9) highlights important ways that art and culture can be used, quoting one youth organizer in the process:

"Hip hop attracts a lot of kids, especially those who feel on the outside," explains a 14-year old with Books Not Bars. "Kids go to it knowing it's political. They go to listen, but then it opens their eyes, and they get hooked on the issues." Kids First recently added two young artists to help with outreach. Film festivals like "Keeping it Reel," a youth-organized event held at the San Francisco Museum of Modern Art in May 2002, encourage young people to create or see films that highlight the importance of community institutions that, as the flyer announcing the festival says, are "youth-inclusive and supportive of youth representation."

Culture and the arts help youth develop an identity that draws upon racial and ethnic pride and anger; sustain that membership by providing a viable and culturally synoptic means of communication; and serve as a bridge across socio-demographic divides, such as race, ethnicity, and language that often are found in undervalued communities in this society. There is no aspect of youth organizing where these factors do not exert influence. For example, arts and culture serve multiple purposes, ranging from recruitment to helping youth develop a better sense of self. Exhibitions and performances provide young people with an opportunity both to be heard and to be praised. Art and culture also fulfill important roles in helping to nourish and sustain youth organizers (Weiss 2003).

Hip-hop often is seen as an effective vehicle for political and civic engagement of the young, particularly those who are urban, of color, and economically and socially marginalized in this country (Boyd 2003; Bynoe 2004; Ginwright 2006). This form of art is manifested in a variety of media, such as graffiti, dance, and music. Music, arguably the most sensational of hip-hop's manifestations, has offered the greatest potential for engaging urban youth because it is considered political and relies on language to push the envelope. It provokes people and makes them think critically about their circumstances (Boyd 2003). The accessibility of music makes this form of expression particularly attractive for youth.

Although hip-hop music is fraught with controversy, particularly its lyrics (violence, crime, sex, women as objects, anti-gay), certain aspects of this art form have tremendous implications for community organizing. This phenomenon was recognized well over a decade ago (Flores 1994; Rose 1994). Kitwana (2002, xiii) used the terms *hip-hop generation, hip-hop culture,* and *black youth culture* interchangeably to refer to a social–political perspective on life that is held by this primarily urban-based segment of the youth population. Tasker (1999) drew on hip-hop music to provide important insights into the life of a black female adolescent. Entrance into this world enabled the practitioner (social worker) to gain a profound understanding of and appreciation for how rap music gives voice to the dreams and struggles of marginalized youth.

Bynoe (2004), in turn, identified five central points:

1. *Content is not neutral*: Invariably there is a sociocultural context that highlights issues of inequality, as well as social and economic justice themes.
2. *Focus on history*: Looking closely at social conditions grounds these issues and problems in a historical context.
3. *Leadership development*: There is stress on the importance of indigenous leadership development and a viewpoint that the future of a community rests on itself.
4. *Fight image with image*: The importance of introducing positive role models is emphasized.
5. *Thinking beyond voter registration*: The importance of voter registration is cast within a broader structural analysis that stresses the need for dramatic collective action to alter existing social conditions outside and beyond conventional mechanisms such as voting.

As the reader will see in the chapters that follow, these themes all play central roles in shaping youth-led community organizing. Bynoe's (2004) themes highlight the politicized nature of hip-hop music as it attempts to inform and comment on issues of social oppression and the need to fight for social and economic justice. Marginalized youth rarely are seen on television or movies articulating these themes; rather, they usually are portrayed as perpetrators of crime and members of gangs (Giroux 1998). Thus, music is one of the few avenues by which these issues can be raised in an unfiltered manner. This venue will exist as long as it generates considerable profits for the music industry, along with money-making spin-offs such as clothing and other commercial products.

Organizational Settings and Youth Organizing

There is a wide variety of ways that youth-led organizing has been conceptualized and implemented. This diversity is stimulating and exciting, but it also poses difficulties, since various organizing efforts evolve differently as they take local circumstances into account. Such a lack of uniformity brings with it challenges for anyone wishing to understand and possibly shape local efforts. This section attempts to provide the groundwork for better appreciating the scope and range of the organizational settings in which youth-led organizing is carried out. As in the preceding two chapters, our discussion is not exhaustive; rather, we simply touch on some of the critical dimensions of this variable and the impact it has on youth-led community organizing. These factors will be examined in greater detail in the chapters that follow.

As noted earlier in this chapter, fields of practice and scholarship never emerge out of thin air, suddenly achieving acknowledgment and universal acceptance. Youth-led community organizing is no exception. Invariably there are circumstances or forces that converge to cause a phenomenon such as the youth-led field to appear, draw attention to itself, attract resources, and evolve into new forms. For example, there is general agreement in the field of youth-led organizing that intermediary organizations can play important roles by providing direct assistance to local groups. Such organizations also can act as conduits between practitioners and researchers or academics interested in youth organizing. Thus, intermediaries can help support the emergence of this field of practice and also help to sustain it. The W.K. Kellogg Foundation (2000, 19) concluded that intermediary organizations are vital to youth-led social interventions:

> Programs learn from and rely on intermediaries for the growth and development of their organizations. Leaders spoke about the role that intermediaries play in creating connections and building and maintaining networks. When intermediary services are fully funded by foundations, programs are able to take full advantage of them; when there are significant fees for services, programs cannot.

Tracing the exact origins of the youth-led approach in general, and youth-led community organizing in particular, is difficult. It is necessary to identify the major contributing, operative factors and forces when a theoretical model and set of new ideas and practices develop into a field of practice. Setting the context for youth-led community organizing first requires an examination of how the overarching youth-led field emerged and expanded. It is important to develop a better appreciation of the diverse approaches to youth organizing, including the youth-led model. This appreciation of the scope of youth-led community organizing also requires broad understanding of how this form of social action takes on regional qualities and circumstances (HoSang 2005). It must be placed in context (Youniss et al. 2002), but this "flexibility" makes it difficult to generalize key concepts and methods across geographical regions.

The organizational setting in which youth organizing is undertaken also is a key element for better understanding how social action by young people is conceptualized and carried out in the field. Therefore, we cannot underestimate the importance of viewing youth community organizing within an organizational context. Such a perspective helps both practitioners and academics to categorize, understand, and learn from youth-led community organizing efforts, whether locally, nationally, or internationally (Larson, Walker and Pearce 2004). The classification of these forms of organizing must take into account the degree of decision making, or power, that youth possess in shaping, initiating, and sustaining an organizing campaign. Furthermore, youth-led organizations must contend with a host of challenges that are shaped by the age of membership.

The social and economic issues that drive youth-led community organizing generally fall into five categories: (1) educational justice; (2) criminal and juvenile justice; (3) community development/capacity enhancement; (4) economic justice; and (5) immigrant rights (Weiss 2003). Youth-led community organizing, like youth development, can be carried out in a variety of social arenas. A quick review of these groupings will not reveal any surprises, particularly since educational, environmental, criminal, and juvenile justice issues often are mentioned frequently in the literature. The organizations that sponsor youth organizing play a critical role in shaping these efforts, so it is essential to understand both their commonalities and differences. Fortunately, there is an emerging body of literature specifically focused on analyzing youth organizing from a regional perspective; reports such as that by HoSang (2005) and Spatz (2005) typify the latest examples. Of course, there are differences *within* regions and by cities, with certain characteristics of the political as well as physical environments leading to particular adaptations.

Questions are frequently raised about the universal elements of these efforts. Consequently, this section examines the critical question, "What are the common characteristics of youth-led community organizations?" There is no simple answer, and the discussion that follows will likely result in further debate on this subject. We believe, however, that raising this question is healthy, and that it will lead to a keener appreciation of the complexities of the field, ultimately influencing how organizations and funders view youth-led community organizing (Gambone et al. 2004). To examine this question, we must separate organizations from organizers, although there certainly is a degree of overlap. Indeed, the question we raise highlights the interconnections among organizations, youth organizers, and communities.

There is no one single organizational model of youth organizing that would be successful regardless of local circumstances, and therefore it is difficult to specify an "ideal" blueprint for maximum effectiveness:

> When evaluating your organizing model and its impact, it is important to recognize that working for justice and creating social change is a long and complicated process that requires lots of creativity and a diversity of models and approaches. No one model is best for creating social change because there are many goals that must be accomplished for real systems change to occur. But for groups trying to accomplish similar goals, there is great benefit in sharing different methods for reaching the same goal. (Youth in Focus 2004, 1)

Although this book emphasizes a particular model of youth organizing, we recognize that the field is vibrant, not monolithic, and many different approaches to youth organizing have currency.

Local factors usually determine the ultimate success of social interventions such as youth-led community organizing. The decision-making structures of youth-led organizations may vary depending upon specific circumstances, such as the degree to which young activists have power in decision-making processes, the amount of autonomy they exercise within adult-led organizations, and what their funding base is (Young Wisdom Project 2004). There certainly is no single "type" of youth-led organization, and this situation presents advantages and disadvantages for carrying out a youth-led organizing mission.

If an organization wishes to sponsor a youth-led organizing project, it must believe that young people are capable of leading the effort for social change and reform. Both the field of practice and the scholarly literature have examined organizations that sponsor youth-led community organizing from a variety of perspectives, and have highlighted the influences of various social factors and how they have shaped organizational culture, structure, and mission in the process (Gambone et al. 2004). The introduction of a social-change agenda brings an added dimension to this organizational analysis, accentuating how a mission that indicates commitment to social justice influences organizational structure, staffing, and vision.

There is no denying the importance of school settings in youth-led campaigns, particularly in cases involving the low-income youth of color who typically grapple with problems of educational equity and justice on a daily basis (Scheie 2003); consequently, this section emphasizes schools. However, youth-led organizing can occur in a number of other organizational settings, such as community development corporations, youth serving organizations, and adult community-based organizations (Gambone et al. 2006). For example, Murphy and Cunningham (2003) note how community development corporations across the nation have shifted to comprehensive, place-based change efforts, including community organizing. Youth-led community organizing initiatives easily can be a part of these comprehensive efforts to achieve positive community capacity enhancement.

Much to the surprise of many, we are sure, youth-led community organizing is alive and well within schools. (Soundout.org, for example, provides countless examples of school-based youth organizing for school reform.) However, this statement certainly should not come as a surprise to anyone who has significant contact with young people (Fletcher 2004; What Kids Can Do 2001; Wilson-Ahlstrom, Tolman, and Jones 2004). Youth spend an incredible amount of time during their first eighteen years of life in school, which with rare exceptions, is when they are completely under the control of adults.

Zimmerman's (2004) classification lends itself well to better understanding youth-led community organizing because of its perspective on the roles of young people within an organization, and it provides a conceptual context from which to comprehend the various forms of youth activism, including those that are youth-led. Zimmerman's six-part typology for classifying organizations delineates the various levels of youth power within organizations, with the ultimate two forms being youth run (young people fill all staff and managerial positions) and youth led (young people fill all major leadership positions, such as executive director, and hold majority membership on the board of directors, with adult support as needed and requested). We have merged the categories of "youth-run" and "youth-led" for purposes of discussion in this book.

There is little question that new models of organizational development, structure, and governance will need to be developed to sustain youth-led initiatives, particularly youth-led community organizing, which very often entails use of a wide variety of strategies and tactics to bring about social change. For example, the model of Youth Liberation Organization recently has been conceptualized to capture those groups that are youth led and that embrace social activism by and for youth while challenging adult power as a central principle of their organizing (Generator 2005). Being youth led permits tremendous flexibility in crafting social-change agendas, as illustrated by Denver, Colorado's, One Nation Enlighten (ONE): " 'We're now a youth-driven organization, and having this independence allows us more control over the political message we develop, the campaigns we choose and how we build our movement' " (HoSang 2005, 22).

This book is a testament to the need for new models to better understand youth-led initiatives. We believe that such models should highlight the core factors that apply across the board to organizations that sponsor youth organizing, and also that are sensitive to unique local considerations, such as geography, history, and the socio-demographic composition of the young people who participate. One youth organizer responded as follows when asked to describe youth organizing:

> Although a wide range of youth organizing models exist, all approaches integrate several aspects into the process. First, all youth organizing models engage in leadership development and skill building among young leaders and members of the organization. . . . Second, all youth organizing involves young people in identifying, analyzing, researching community issues and power relationships. . . . Third, youth organizing groups develop, conduct, and evaluate campaigns to assess how their community and institutional change efforts influence institutional decision-makers around the issues they determine. (Turning the Leadership 2004, 5)

The Innovation Center for Community and Youth Development (2003) uses a definition of a civic activist organization that is sufficiently broad to allow projects such as increasing voter registration and education to occur alongside initiatives that take on a social-reform agenda such as boycotts, sit-ins, and other forms of direct action. Civic activist organizations are "place-based settings focused on supporting young people's healthy growth and development, engaging youth in leadership and decision-making roles, and in identifying and addressing barriers facing youth, families, and communities" (Innovation Center for Community and Youth Development 2003, 3).

Intergenerational organizing campaigns—another form of youth-involved organizing—bring with them both the potential for breaking down traditional barriers between adults and youth and the possibility of reinforcing these barriers. When young people work with adults to organize for various initiatives, this activity serves to build community and establish connections across age groups, pooling resources and experiences, and increasing the likelihood of sustained social changes. Nevertheless, young people in intergenerational efforts can confront limited leadership opportunities, restricted decision-making powers, and issues framed from an adult perspective—all of which can be to their detriment (Weiss 2003). Yet such opportunities, although fraught with potential limitations, also can prove fertile ground for youth to develop their competencies as organizers and their skills in working in partnership with adults. Important mentoring can take place, eventually allowing young people to break with adults and lead their own campaigns in which adults act as allies rather than mentors.

However, it is important not to romanticize youth-led organizations or to ignore the critical challenges they face in similar fashion to their adult counterparts. Zimmerman (2004) is careful to note that youth-led organizations invariably have problems involving staff development and management (creation of sustaining structures and guidelines), leadership transitions (opening up opportunities for changes in leadership as other youth leaders age out), capacity development (lack of experience and professional training), burnout (challenging situations can lead to disengagement), self-care and individual development (provision of support that may not be found in adult-led organizations), intergenerational relations (the unleashing of adultism), fund-raising (lack of experience and training in this specialized operational function), legal contracts (roadblocks in negotiating legal agreements), strategic planning and organizational development (terminology and process that may be foreign to youth), independence versus fiscal sponsorship (strings attached to funding that compromise an organizational mission), isolation and network development (developing organizational relationships can be labor-intensive and even hazardous to an organization), and documentation and evaluation (lack of resources, experience, expertise, and time to record and analyze initiatives).

The importance of these challenges should not be minimized; indeed, many of them are addressed in other sections of this book. While burnout is a phenomenon well understood by adults, it also can be experienced by young people. Finding effective vehicles to minimize this experience is significant because experiences and opportunities for young people are more limited than for adults (Young Wisdom Project 2004). But such hurdles are not insurmountable! Identifying these problems serves to normalize them, thereby taking them out of the local sphere (neighborhood) and placing them on the national stage. In essence, the uniqueness of these issues is rendered typical for youth. Dealing with the challenges helps prepare young leaders and organizers for the obstacles they most likely will encounter in their quest to bring about positive social change.

Models of Youth-Led Community Organizing

Earlier in this chapter we raised serious questions about the organizational sponsors of youth organizing; as the reader has no doubt surmised, it is a complex field of practice. The question is, "Is youth-led community organizing simply a junior version of adult community organizing?" Youth-led organizing does share many commonalties with adult organizing; however, it also has the distinctiveness of the age of the organizers and some of the issues that are targeted as particularly related to young people (Lawrence 2004).

YouthAction (1998) identified two organizational models for conceptualizing and planning youth-led community organizing: (1) youth are the primary and exclusive members and they define and carry out organizing campaigns based on issues affecting their membership; and (2) youth represent a strategic constituency among several others, taking action on issues specifically defined by a larger, intergenerational community organization. The first model places youth in central decision-making roles in all facets of a campaign; the second locates youth organizing within a broader community agenda for social change that involves adults as well as young people.

Contrary to what scholars would expect, or perhaps demand, not every youth-led community organizing campaign starts off with a distinct model. As noted by one young organizer:

> We didn't have a model! By the end of my time, we made some progress, but we still didn't exactly get there. I never had youth leaders that were conscious about turning out other youth leaders. That was the puzzle that I never had a chance to figure out. We had talented young people who were articulate and understood the organization. We had youth on the board, and I think they did a great job. But could they mobilize other young people to take on issues? No. (Beyond Base 2004, 5)

However, failure to use a "distinctive" model (and sometimes even avoiding doing so) severely complicates any serious efforts to evaluate processes and outcomes, as well as to refine the theory guiding organizing models. Of course, models never should be viewed as only serving the interests and needs of theoreticians seeking to develop a better understanding of a social phenomenon. Models also must help practitioners shape social-change interventions and campaigns. Thus, they can bridge the worlds of academia and practice, and this goal never should be minimized in any form of social intervention. Furthermore, models are not static in composition; they evolve and take into account new sources of information and experiences as they mature.

Youth and adult involvement in social-change efforts can be, and has been, conceptualized in myriad ways in the field, as already noted in chapter 1, but it is well worth revisiting. In turn, we classify these efforts into four distinct models along a continuum based on the degree of youth power and control over a community organizing initiative or campaign, as noted in figure 3.2.

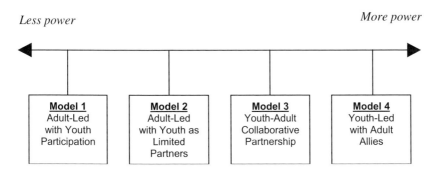

Figure 3.2. Continuum of youth power in community organizing.

These four models vary according to the degree of power exercised by youth in planning and implementing community social-change initiatives:

1. *Adult-Led with Youth Participation*: Youth are actively involved in change efforts as participants but do not share power, and there are no efforts to systematically bring them into power positions.
2. *Adult-Led with Youth as Limited Partners*: Youth decision-making powers are dictated by adults who are always the leaders.
3. *Youth-Adult Collaborative Partnership*: Youth and adults share power equally.
4. *Youth-Led with Adult Allies*: Youth are in charge and adults play supportive roles as needed and defined by youth.

The last is the model examined in this book. The youth-led community organizing model advanced here may not appeal across the spectrum of youth organizing; some practitioners and academics may advance a more "flexible" or "inclusive" definition or model whereby youth can learn the ropes, so to speak. We certainly can appreciate the appeal of such a long-term developmental perspective. However, a youth-led community organizing model such as the one presented in this book has a rightful place in the field. We believe that adult-led community organizers and organizations most actively sponsor this model.

Conclusion

The reader, we hope, has developed an appreciation of how geographical and historical context, as well as organizations and models, influence youth organizing and the way the issues they address are framed. Across the board, there is explicit acknowledgment of the importance of the work that youth organizers do in their communities and their role in advancing this field of practice, youth-led or otherwise. Seeking justice to address conditions of social and economic oppression no longer is the exclusive domain of adults. Youth rightfully can take their place alongside adults as allies, and also can become advocates for their own causes and social agendas.

This field of practice has deep historical roots that include the ideals of achieving social and economic justice. Failure to acknowledge and explore this background limits our understanding of the role that young people have played in promoting social and economic justice in this country. But familiarity with this context makes it possible to recognize and appreciate current trends in youth-led community organizing, such as hip-hop activism. (The tensions and issues inherent in this form of practice are addressed later in this book.)

Unfortunately, the role of youth in this country's history of community organizing generally has gone unnoticed or been mentioned only in passing by most mainstream accounts. This slight has perpetuated the propensity to view the nation's youth from a deficit perspective. However, the development of youth-led community organizing as a field will help rectify this oversight and lend a strengths and assets perspective on youth in this country. The stage has been set for in-depth case studies, scholarship, and historical recognition of the achievements of young people in the United States, as well as the contributions they will make in the future.

We think it appropriate to end this chapter with a quote that describes what youth-led community organizing is all about, one that is a wonderful prelude to the remainder of this book:

> Across the nation, youth organizing continues to be a strong, developing, yet under-resourced, approach to positive youth development and community change. Steering young people away from an inward, self-interested focus towards an outward concern for the community and world, youth organizing helps young people move from a place of anger, despondency and defeat to one of empathy, compassion and action. (Turning the Leadership 2004, 6)

We would like to add that youth-led organizing also can lead to self-discovery and a lifetime commitment to social causes.

Part II

Conceptual Foundation for Youth-Led Organizing

From coast to coast, a new wave of youth organizing is taking form, built on a historical foundation of youth activism, and shaped by the current cultural and political landscape. As in other countries, young people in the United States have played major roles in social justice movements. . . . Buoyed by a new crop of intermediaries and a handful of progressive foundations, the recent proliferation of youth-led and youth-focused organizations has even led to talk in organizing circles of a bona fide "youth movement."
—Weiss, *Youth Rising* (2003)

4

Guiding Principles
and Analytical Framework

Practice consists of methods and process. . . .
The terms go together because conceptions of
processes are necessary to design methods
to intervene in and to encourage, guide, stop,
or redirect processes.
—Brager, Specht, and Torczyner, *Community
Organizing* (1987)

The importance of principles and an analytical framework for youth-led community organizing cannot be over emphasized, and it is necessary to see their origins and relevance within a values foundation and historical context. Social and historical forces shape modern-day social interventions. Practice, as noted in the opening quote to this chapter, is shaped by methods and process. Practice is also shaped by principles and analytical frameworks.

Principles for youth-led community organizing provide both practitioners and academics with a navigational tool to keep the focus on the goals of social intervention, such as youth-led community organizing. An analytical framework, in turn, fulfills important theoretical and political functions, helping both practitioners and academics better conceptualize, plan, implement, and evaluate social-change efforts. Historically, the field of community organization has benefited from these tools. The best analytical framework serves to guide without being prescriptive; yet it is descriptive enough to allow practitioners to develop an in-depth sense of the key stages and elements that must be addressed in a social intervention, such as community organizing.

The subjects of guiding principles and analytical frameworks for community organizing have a long and distinguished history, replete with examples that show how community organizing must be conceptualized and implemented. Weil and Gamble (1995) present a historical overview of the models and frameworks commonly used in bringing about social change. Burghardt and Fabricant (2004) look at community organizing with a social work and labor movement perspective. Rubin and Rubin (2004), in turn, provide a framework for better understanding the skills required of a community organizer involved in social mobilization.

This chapter, as noted in figure 4.1 and figure 4.2, presents a set of guiding principles and an analytical framework that will navigate the reader through the rough terrain of community organizing—in this case, one that is conceptualized and led by youth. The principles and analytical framework bring together many key elements usually associated with social change, as well as integrate many key concepts and constructs that make up the field of

Figure 4.1. Analytical framework: The nine principles serve as the core around which the ten elements of the framework are built.

Elements

Principles	Participation	Leadership	Staffing	Structure	Goals and Objectives	Target Systems	Strategies and Tactics	Finances	Allies	Communications
Inclusive membership										
Social & economic justice values										
Support for change										
Training, mentoring, and leadership opportunities										
Adult involvement										
Long-term agenda										
Consciousness-raising										
Fun and learning										
Share common goals										

Figure 4.2. Analytical framework chart.

youth-led community organizing. Some of these concepts and constructs are not unique to youth; however, this chapter is written from a youth-led perspective and thereby will emphasize the latter whenever possible.

The reader, we believe, will note how language plays a significant role in both principles and analytical frameworks, and youth-led community organizing is certainly no exception. It is relatively easy to equate community development and change with certain phrases such as *community needs* and *community problems*. Youth-led community organizing emphasizes a view of the community that focuses on *issues, challenges, capacity, opportunities*, and *assets*. Embracing the following principles and using the analytical framework, in effect, requires using a new language—and for the uninitiated, you are warned!

Finally, two words of caution are in order before we proceed to outline our principles and analytical framework for youth-led community organizing. First, it is important to differentiate between a framework and a model. The latter is a conceptual construct, generally consisting of sequential stages or phases that embrace a particular theoretical perspective on a social intervention. An analytical framework, in contrast, is a series of factors, considerations, or what we call elements, that must be taken into account to bring a model to life, so to speak. A conceptual framework provides practitioners with a guide or a series of points that must be addressed to operationalize a theory. Second, principles help practitioners better operationalize the various facets of an analytical framework. Principles and framework can exist apart from one another; however, when they are brought together, their use in moving the field forward can be exceptional!

Figure 4.1 and figure 4.2 provide different ways of viewing the relationship between guiding principles and an analytical framework. Figure 4.1 lays out an analytical framework that ties together the different dimensions of youth-led community organizing. Figure 4.2 is a tool to use in determining how and when principles can inform elements. We expect that no youth-led community organizing initiative and sponsor will share all of the principles being operationalized in the same manner, throughout all of the elements. However, figure 4.2 helps practitioners and academics better understand and appreciate how principles and frameworks—in this case, one focused on youth-led community organizing—get carried out in a social change campaign.

Research Informing Principles and Framework

Writings about social interventions such as youth-led community organizing invariably bring to the foreground the tension between being descriptive and being prescriptive. The importance of local circumstances in shaping how youth-led community organizing gets conceptualized, implemented,

and evaluated will make either extreme of description or prescription un-
feasible. This book has emphasized the critical role local circumstances play
in youth-led community organizing, and we recognize that one size does
not fit all. Thus, this chapter travels between these two extreme approaches
to achieve a better understanding of practice. Such an attempt to moderate,
however, may have the unintended consequence of not appealing to either
side of the debate.

As noted in chapter 1, an extensive number of research studies from
youth development (including leadership development and civic engagement), the youth-led field, and more specifically youth-led community organizing have shaped the content of chapter 4. This book draws on more
than seventy research studies involving a variety of methodologies from
a multitude of fields that inform youth-led community organizing. Several
studies, however, have wielded extraordinary influence in our developing
this and other chapters of the book.

The ten scholarly publications listed here influenced the formulation of
the key principles that are discussed in the following sections.

- An extensive evaluation of the Innovation Center's *Youth Leadership
  for Development Initiative* (Innovation Center 2003) resulted in a
  wealth of data (qualitative and quantitative) about youth involved
  in social change efforts (principles 1–5, 7, and 9).
- The senior author's book on youth-led research *Designs and Methods
  for Youth-Led Social Research* (Delgado 2006) represents a meta-
  analysis of national and international research findings on youth-
  led research (principles 1–3, 5, and 7–9).
- Eccles and Gootman's (2002) seminal book *Community Programs to
  Promote Youth Development* represents the latest and most comprehensive national assessment of research on youth development
  (principles 2, 4, 5, and 7).
- The *Aspen Institute Roundtable on Community Change* (Lawrence et al.
  2004) synthesized numerous studies on youth and community
  change (principles 1, 2, and 9).
- Lerner and Benson's book (2003) *Developmental Assets and Asset-
  Building Communities* provides a wealth of data on youth and community development (principles 1, 3–5, and 7).
- The Philanthropic Initiative for Racial Equity's multi-level study
  titled *Changing the Rules of the Game: Youth Development and Structural Racism* (Quiroz-Martinez, HoSang, and Villarosa 2004) re-
  searched sixteen youth-development organizations and specifically
  focused on racial equity and the challenges and rewards youth face
  in addressing social justice issues in the field (principles 1–4, 6, 7,
  and 9).
- The Carnegie's Young People Initiative's (Cutler 2002) research report *Taking the Initiative—Promoting Young People's Involvement in*

Public Decision Making in the USA presents findings on over forty youth programs across the country (principles 1–5).

- The Movement Center has produced three reports that have direct applicability to youth-led community organizing. The first report (James 2005), *Bringing it Together: United Youth Organizing, Development and Services for Long-term Sustainability*, provides results from an analysis of six community organizing sponsoring organizations and provides a different perspective on youth organizing (intergenerational and youth-led; principles 1, 2, 5–7, and 9). The second report (Quiroz-Martinez, Wu, and Zimmerman 2005) is *ReGeneration: Young People Shaping Environmental Justice*; as the title implies, it analyzes a series of case studies specifically focused on environmental social justice and social change (principles 1–4, 7, and 9). The third and final report is *Making Space, Making Change: Profiles of Youth-Led and Youth-Driven Organizations* (Youth Wisdom Project, 2004); this report profiled research involving six organizations and provided key lessons and action steps for increasing youth leadership in organizations (principles 1–5, 7, and 9).

Principles of Youth-Led
Community Organizing

As noted earlier in the introduction to this chapter, principles fulfill a variety of important functions. Anchoring an intervention, however, stands out. The field of youth-led community organizing has borrowed widely from other fields such as youth development. As the youth-led field has evolved as a social intervention over the past decade, it has developed principles to help guide its operationalization on a daily basis. These principles and operating guidelines effectively serve as bridges between theory and practice, helping to unite academics across disciplines while at the same time linking practitioners who may share only geographic residence.

Pittman and Zeldin (1995, 2) tie practice principles to organizational approaches:

Defining practice principles is integral to the effectiveness of any organization but critical to effectiveness of these organizations approaching work with youth and families from a development rather than a problem perspective; and, linking principles to practice within an organization or to standards of practice across organizations is a challenging and sometimes controversial task.

Consequently, the importance of principles cannot be cast aside as simply an academic exercise, with little practical purpose and meaning. Instead, we envision principles as setting the requisite foundation for bringing academic disciplines, practitioners, and communities together in pursuit of a unified vision for youth-led community organizing.

Youth-led community organizing, as with its adult counterpart, brings with it organizing principles that are both unique to this age group and also shared with adult organizing. The National Conference for Community and Justice in Los Angeles raised four questions that effectively strike at the heart of youth-led community organizing and set the stage for identifying common principles for this method of practice (Anderson, Bernaldo, and David 2004, 3):

How to develop a positive identity in a world that is dominated by bias?
How to un-learn stereotyping, prejudice, and discrimination?
How to examine the root causes of systematic oppression and hate crimes while proposing real alternatives for positive community development?
How to create a safe environment for youth to dialogue with each other around difficult issues?

It is no mistake that these questions are deeply rooted in social and economic justice, since this perspective also informs youth-led community organizing, just as it informs its adult counterpart (Balsano 2005; Camino and Zeldin 2002).

The following nine core principles of youth-led community organizing are sufficiently flexible in nature to take into account the multitude of organizing campaigns that transpire in practice, yet they also capture some unique dimension of this form of intervention that does justice to its importance. Some of the following principles, the reader may argue, may not be restricted to youth and can easily also apply to adults; other principles, however, may have particular relevance for youth when compared to their adult counterparts. Nevertheless, each principle is clearly colored or "flavored" by a youth perspective:

Principle 1: Youth-led community organizing must seek to be inclusive rather than exclusive in nature with the exception of age-restrictions. Each youth organizing group ultimately must determine who qualifies as a youth participant based upon that person's age. Urban communities are never monolithic in composition regarding ethnicity, race, gender, sexual identity, abilities, or social class. Youth leaders must reflect the population that makes up the areas where they work in order to have legitimacy both within and outside of their communities. It is also important to give a voice to subgroups that historically have not enjoyed recognition within and outside of their own communities.

Principle 2: Youth-led community organizing must embrace principles and values associated with social and economic justice. Social-change campaigns must be guided by a common vision that can help unite young people and their communities. A social and economic justice perspective is powerful in helping view the experiences of marginalized youth in this society and that viewpoint can inspire youth to achieve positive social change for current and future generations.

Principle 3: Youth leaders must be supported in their quest for positive social change. Youth participation in community organizing can be supported in a multitude of ways by providing expressive, instrumental, and informational help. Young people bring tremendous assets to social action campaigns; however, they must have the requisite support, including financial help, to sustain them and their families while they pursue social and economic justice.

Principle 4: Opportunities must be built into the organizing experience that will enable youth to gain training, mentoring, and chances to exercise leadership roles. Personal growth must be an integral part of the experience of young people in youth-led campaigns (Huber et al. 2003). Such personal growth is multifaceted, and opportunities to exercise leadership always must be available for all youth participants.

Principle 5: Youth-led community organizing does not exclude possibilities of adult involvement when necessary. Adults are very much a part of the lives of young people and they should continue to be involved in the experiences of youth leaders and organizers. However, adult participation should be dictated by the needs and requests of youth, and not the other way around.

Principle 6: Youth-led campaigns must never be viewed as episodic but rather as part of a long-term change agenda. Positive social change is never easy, fast, or predicable. As in other aspects of life, both victories and setbacks can be expected. Youth participants must be prepared for some failures and need to have a vision of social change with long-term goals and objectives.

Principle 7: Youth-led campaigns must actively embrace a consciousness-raising agenda that addresses key issues of social oppression based on individual characteristics and beliefs. Youth-led community organizing provides young people with an opportunity to better understand how social forces bring about oppression in undervalued communities and how different groups are pitted against each other, rather than coalescing to achieve a common goal. The oppression of one group invariably means the oppression of many groups.

Principle 8: Youth-led community organizing is serious work, but it is essential to build fun and learning into the experience. Youth organizing still involves young people! They must be able to engage in serious work; however, opportunities to have fun and enjoy learning should be a central part of their experiences as well. The greater the integration of fun and learning, the higher the satisfaction and the more likelihood that youth activists will become lifetime organizers, either formally or informally.

Principle 9: Youth must share a common vision of what they mean by achieving social and economic justice goals. The construct of social and economic justice has many different definitions and dimensions. Youth participants must have an opportunity to explore these dimensions, arriving at consensus, if possible. This not only facilitates their work on organizing campaigns for social change but also opens up the possibility of sharing this vision within their community.

The above nine principles are by no means exhaustive; however, they represent what we consider to be the core elements of youth-led community organizing, separating this form of social intervention from that of its adult counterpart. The reader may well identify different or additional principles that contextualize youth-led community organizing in their particular circumstances—this is to be expected and encouraged. The manner in which these principles are brought to life in youth-led community organizing will vary according to various factors and forces. Nevertheless, any successful youth-led community organizing campaign will show these principles played out in a variety of ways, as will be shown in this book. When these principles are tied to an analytical framework, not only do they take on greater significance but so does the analytical framework. Bringing principles and framework together highlights the dynamic nature of the field of youth-led community organizing.

Analytical Framework

Grassroots community organizing takes place in four different arenas: turf, issue, identity, and workplace (Staples 2004a). Organizing by *turf* is concentrated in a particular physical area that might include a neighborhood, housing development, electoral jurisdiction, church parish, business area, government zone, trailer park, *colonista*, or school district. Anyone living within the turf area of focus generally is eligible for participation.

Community organizations also may be established to deal with particular *issues*, such as education, employment, housing, the environment, the criminal justice system, or recreation opportunities. Participants in an issue-based organization may be drawn from a wide array of geographic areas.

As discussed in chapter 2, constituency subgroups may organize as *communities of identity* based on shared race, ethnicity, gender, age, sexual orientation, immigrant status, religion, and physical or mental disability. A youth organization, disability rights group, lesbian student caucus, or Brazilian immigrant task force would be examples of identity-based organizations.

The *workplace* also is an important arena for organizing. Beyond labor unions, which really are distinct from community organizations, grassroots groups may be formed to deal with issues such as immigrant rights, safety, or working conditions where no union is present or likely to be established. Community groups also can provide support for workers who are attempting to unionize or join with unions to work on issues outside the immediate workplace (Fine 2001) that relate to a particular business, such as issues of noise, traffic, odor, waste management, water pollution, and other community health hazards.

These four arenas are not distinct and dichotomous. Many community organizations combine turf, issue, identity, and workplace orientations. Youth organizing clearly is tied to identity by age; however, usually there also are other elements. Certainly, most youth organizations have a specific geographic locus—the neighborhood or school, for example. These groups also may have a particular issue focus, such as after-school employment, creation of a new youth center, violence prevention, or relations with the police. And they may even be created around a particular workplace—for instance, a municipal summer youth employment program. Nevertheless, the primary criterion for membership is age, and youth identity always is of paramount importance.

Within these four arenas, there are two distinct approaches to community organizing: community development and social action. According to Staples (2004a, 7), "community development involves participants in constructive activities and processes to produce improvements, opportunities, structures, goods, and services that increase the quality of life, build individual and collective capacities, and enhance social solidarity." Cooperative strategies and processes to address problems and build communal infrastructure are central to this organizing method (Rothman 1968; Rubin and Rubin 2001; Fisher 1994; Shragge 1997; Pantoja and Perry 1998). Community development places much emphasis on self-help, integration, internal development, capacity building, social solidarity, and the exercise of power to find constructive solutions to community problems. There is no attempt to redistribute power or resources, and external decision makers are not confronted to redress the grievances of organized community groups.

On the other hand, according to Staples (2004a, 9), "social action brings people together to convince, pressure, or coerce external decision-makers to meet collective goals either to act in a specific manner or to modify or stop certain activities." Adversarial campaign and/or contest strategies (Warren 1975) are employed to overcome resistance from powerful actors in the private and public sectors who have conflicting interests with community members. Social action is undertaken in order to compel targeted individuals and institutions to do what they otherwise would not do. This approach stresses the need to build an organizational power base, features conflict, seeks to alter existing relations of power, is redistributive in nature, and enables the organized membership to wield power vis-à-vis other groups (Rothman 1968; Fisher and Shragge 2000; Staples 2004a).

Despite such fundamental differences, these two community organizing approaches share elements, including the resolution of mutual problems through collective action, a strong emphasis on broad-based involvement by community members acting on their own behalf, a commitment to indigenous leadership, and the formation of organizational structures as the vehicles through which joint action is undertaken. Community development and social action also are not mutually exclusive and may be combined in the same effort. For instance, a youth organization might pressure city officials to permit members to organize a clean-up day to resurrect a baseball field that has fallen into disrepair. Or, the same group might invite the media to observe when they begin painting an abandoned recreation center, hoping to embarrass the mayor into making a commitment to rehabilitate and staff this facility.

This book examines youth organizations that use both community development and social action methods. A range of models is presented, and a ten-dimensional framework is used to compare the approaches. That framework includes the following variables: participation, leadership, staffing, structure, goals, target systems, strategy and tactics, resources, allies, and communications.

It is only logical to ask a basic question whenever one analyzes a community organization, "*Who* wants *What* from *Whom*, and *How* will the group accomplish its goals?" (Staples 2004a). Clearly, there are four distinct questions in this overarching query, and the answer to each requires the investigator to address all ten of the above variables in turn. *Who* refers to the action group (community organization) that has been developed, and anyone wishing to understand the nature of this aggregation of people must focus on its membership, leadership, staffing, and structure. *What* relates to the goals and objectives that the community organization is pursuing. *Whom* is the target systems or institutions (e.g., municipal government), organizations (e.g., Girls and Boys Club), groups (e.g., a youth gang), and individuals (e.g., a landlord) the action group is engaging in an attempt to achieve its goals and objectives. And *how* involves the strategies and tactics, resources, allies, and communications systems (both internal and external) that the organization uses to carry out its action program.

1. Participation

The number and type of active participants in collective action are crucial variables when examining any community organization, and youth groups are no exception to this rule. Indeed, chapter 5 focuses on participatory democracy as a fundamental principle and theme in youth-led organizing. Elsewhere, we examine the reasons youth are attracted to organizing efforts, the recruitment methods that have been most effective in engaging them, some common barriers to youth participation, and the motivational elements and techniques that sustain active involvement. A variety of factors is analyzed, including the importance of pre-existing peer networks, the process of relationship building, organizational culture, and the collective actions taken for social change, individual development, and social activities.

We also consider both the *breadth* of participation in the organizations studied (how wide the pool they draw from) and the *depth* of activism by the groups' members. For instance, the total number of participants might be strong, yet whole segments of the youth community could be underrepresented in terms of race, ethnicity, language, gender, age range, social class, sexual orientation, religious affiliation, and physical or mental disability. And there certainly is a critical distinction between active participants and "paper members" who are involved only sporadically. Attendance at meetings, events, and actions (without focusing on too many large "one-shot turnouts") provides a direct means for assessing membership involvement.

2. Leadership

Indigenous leadership goes to the heart of community organizing principles. A group's leadership should be individuals who are representative of its general membership. Leaders may hold formal positions or may fulfill functional roles as needed. Leadership may be centralized (one or several youth) or may be shared. Second-line leaders are core activists who participate regularly in meetings, activities, events, and committees; they serve as links between the top leaders and rank-and-file members, helping maintain accountability and two-way communication. Frequently, but not always, new first-line leaders emerge from this group. Regardless, second-line leaders usually function as worker bees and provide the honey that holds the group together.

Leadership development is a central element of youth-led organizing, and chapter 6 examines this subject in detail. Throughout the book, we explore a range of topics related to youth leadership, including typical organizational roles and tasks, the process of gaining new skills, the development of critical consciousness, and the unique problems related to rapid turnover and transition as youth leaders age out after a relatively short period of time. Given the latter phenomenon, a steady flow of new blood from the second-line ranks is especially important to maintain the ongoing viability of youth-led groups that may have formed through the extraordinary efforts of a core of committed, talented, and charismatic initial leaders.

3. Staffing

There are two basic models for paid organizing staff who function as community organizers:

1. They may play a facilitative role, in which they do not act as leaders and seldom, if ever, speak publicly on behalf of the group; here, there is a strict separation of roles between leadership and organizing.
2. They may wear both hats, combining the roles of *leaders* who take charge, directing their followers, and *organizers,* who work to get others to take on key roles and responsibilities. When one person

acts as both a leader and an organizer, it is important to strike a balance between the two roles or else the organization may experience inadequate leadership on one hand or a lack of organizational development on the other.

The field of youth-led organizing has embraced a multifaceted definition of leadership that prepares youth to assume roles as community organizers that transcend traditional views of leadership, including recruiters, motivators, agitators, consolidators, facilitators, strategists, and tacticians. Thus, youth tend to function both as organizers and as leaders. Most, but not all, the youth organizations examined herein have paid staff, and frequently, former youth leaders move into these salaried positions. Three common experiences for first-generation paid organizers/leaders are: (1) the development of political consciousness in high school; (2) college activism; and (3) learning from veteran organizers (Pintado-Vertner 2004, 82). Where paid staff does not exist, youth leaders usually function as organizers by default. Chapter 7 examines the recruitment, screening, preparation, and support of youth-led community organizers.

4. Structure

Organizational structure enables one to see who is responsible for the various facets of a group's operations, including formally elected officer positions, permanent and temporary committees, and the general membership. Permanent or standing committees help maintain continuity; while temporary or ad hoc committees provide structural access points through which new members can become active. Other structural factors include operating procedures for choosing leaders, running meetings, making decisions, and forming committees. The old saying that form follows function is operative; there is no one best structure for all community organizations. Structures that enable an organization to accomplish its basic goals and objectives should be put in place.

Youth organizations often have more streamlined structures than those created by many organizations of adults. Most are *locally based* and are not affiliated with any national training or support networks (HoSang 2004). California, where there are some intermediary organizations, is an exception. In New York City, the Northwest Bronx Community and Clergy Coalition (NWBCCC) "reinvented its youth organizing, moving it out of the neighborhood level and creating a central youth organization—Sistas and Brothas United" (Sistas and Brothas United 2005). On the other hand, most rural areas and much of the South lack sufficient community organization infrastructure to develop separate, freestanding youth groups. Thus, there is wide variation in how youth-led organizing projects are structured across the United States, and structural factors will be considered throughout the chapters that follow.

5. Goals and Objectives

The analysis of this variable should include what the organization has accomplished in the past, what its present standing is, and what its goals are
for the future. The examination can begin with a look at the organization's
age and history, the rationale for creating it, key actors in its formation, the
original mission that moved it forward, and its accomplishments to date.
Goals include long-range visions about desirable circumstances in the dis-
tant future, as well as middle-range aspirations that are more concrete. Objectives operationalize these goals by specifying measurable outcomes within
a particular time period. Grassroots groups use community development or
social action methods to meet their goals and objectives, employing a variety of strategies and tactics to influence the relevant target systems.

Youth-led community organizing easily can incorporate elements and
goals associated with youth development, such as decision making, skills
training, relationship building, community service, identity formation, and
leadership development (YouthAction 1998). However, an organizing approach can combine youth development with social justice initiatives to focus on *youth power* for systemic change goals, such as environmental justice,
civic activism, antiracism, youth rights, gender and age equality, LGBT rights,
peacemaking/conflict resolution, exercising political power, freedom to express youth culture, and education reform (Russell 2002). These broad goals
of youth-led organizing are explored in chapters 4–6.

Examples of specific organizing campaigns identified in this study are
illustrative rather than exhaustive, but they include keeping an alternative
high school open; opposing racial profiling in schools; monitoring sexual
assaults in schools; seeking student fares on city buses; improving school
lunches; cleaning up a chemical waste dump; obtaining school repair; increasing police security; ensuring educational equity; and fighting the crim-
inalization and incarceration of young people. Case materials in chapter 9
also present more in-depth illustrations.

6. Target Systems

When community organizations attempt to achieve their objectives, they
focus on a target system whose members they engage, activate, or influence.
Depending on a group's organizing approach, target systems may be either
internal or *external*. Both community development and social action require
a high degree of participation and constituency involvement. Therefore,
community members are internal targets to become active in any grassroots-
organizing change effort. Success will depend on how much the community
buys into and invests in the effort. A community development approach
also may target external institutions to collaborate on or in partnerships

while, as previously discussed, social action *always* pressures external decision makers to do something differently.

This study examined a range of internal and external target systems impacted by various youth organizing models. Internal recruitment and engagement of youth in both community and school settings is examined in chapter 7. All of these organizing initiatives also have attempted to alter power relations between adults and young people. A community organizing approach enables youth to undertake collective action to hold adult institutional decision makers more accountable. Efforts by youth-led organizations to impact common target systems, such as schools, police departments, courts, business corporations, and municipal governments, are recounted throughout the remainder of this book.

7. Strategy and Tactics

According to Staples (2004a, 56):

> Strategies are methods designed to influence targets to act in a manner that enables an organization to achieve its goals and objectives. Tactics are specific procedures, techniques, and actions employed to implement strategic approaches. There can be *internal* strategies to engage and motivate community members to take collective action, as well as *external* ones to convince or coerce organizational targets to act as the group wishes. If a strategy is like a stairway to get from one floor to another, tactics are like the individual stairs.

There are three broad types of strategies: collaborative endeavors, persuasive campaigns, and adversarial contests (Warren 1975). On the other hand, there are an almost infinite number of tactics to pressure an internal or external target.

Effective strategies and tactics are critical variables for how youth organizing goals and objectives are realized. According to the Innovations Center for Community and Youth Development (2003), there are three essential strategies of successful organizations with social change initiatives: (1) organizational leadership is able to inspire action and partnership among all members of a community; (2) leaders are able to develop the capacity of their organization to plan, implement, and achieve its social change goal; and (3) the changes created can be effectively sustained and supported over an extended period of time.

HoSang (2004, 67) notes:

> Many youth organizing groups have developed an integrated approach to social change, often combining issue-based organizing with leadership development programs, service learning activities, cultural enrichment programs, and even academic and personal support components. In comparison to adult-based community organizing groups that typically focus on policy outcomes and the organizing skills of constituents, youth groups

have crafted a more holistic approach to social change that addresses the many issues young members face.

Political education that develops the critical consciousness of youth leaders is a second cross-cutting strategy employed by a high percentage of youth-led organizing initiatives; and "an unusually heavy reliance on the talents and commitment of a core group of staff members—many of whom are in their twenties or early thirties—who can successfully balance roles as mentors, political strategists, trainers, and fundraisers" is a third strategy (HoSang 2004, 68).

Strategies have been developed to meet the particular challenges of organizing a youth constituency. Thus, the absence of a well-developed youth service infrastructure throughout most of the United States has led youth organizers to take a broader, more comprehensive and holistic approach that includes the educational, personal support, and developmental aspects discussed above. Parham and Pinzino (2004) have combined the best of both community organizing and youth development in developing their model of youth organizing.

Also, because most youth organizing efforts are locally based, they often have considerable leverage on specific issues of immediate concern, but usually have difficulty achieving broader systemic change (Parham and Pinzino 2004). This localism, plus the shortage of national training and support networks for youth, often leads to "a lack of access to replicable campaign models" (HoSang 2004), which is a challenge frequently not faced by adult community and labor organizing projects that can draw on such larger affiliations. However, the youth-led organizing approach has drawn effectively on the lived day-to-day experiences of young people and has developed highly successful strategies for integrating culture as a central component of its organizing model.

The strategies and tactics specific to youth-led organizing are central to success in overcoming the challenges inherent in building power for this constituency. The approaches and methods briefly identified above will be revisited throughout this book along with other strategies and techniques that have proved effective.

8. Resources

The adequacy of capital resources, as well as the sources and means by which community organizations are funded, have a profound influence on almost every facet of how organizational operations are carried out. Adequacy of funding was identified by Sherwood and Dressner (2004), and countless others, as a major challenge—and more specifically, "too little and too uncertain" funding. Too little funding, for example, translates to limited physical space (inadequate office and meeting space) and restrictions on the number of youth who can participate. Further, inadequate funding limits organizations from undertaking important strategic planning functions. Uncertain funding, particularly sizable grants, necessitates that valuable time and energy be devoted to writing many small grants.

External funding may be public (federal, state, county, municipal) or private (foundations, churches, businesses, contracts, individual donors), and usually is most secure and insulated from a funder's whims and constraints when it is diversified. Groups that engage in social action should be especially wary about accepting money from potential institutional targets. *Internal* sources of capital may include membership dues, door-to-door canvassing for contributions, and a variety of grassroots fund-raising projects such as raffles, banquets, dances, carnivals, bake sales, ad books, car washes, or potluck suppers. But regardless of the source, there are organizational costs attached to almost all types of funding.

Raising sufficient funds to pay for staff is demanding for all community organizations, but is especially difficult for youth groups. We found that there are particular opportunities and challenges for funding youth-led organizing, which typically operates with limited capital resources. When adult organizations are the sponsoring bodies, money must be squeezed from existing budgets, and youth organizing staff usually are the first to be cut whenever a funding crisis occurs (Parham and Pinzino 2004). Miller (2004, 65) observes that "the growing foundation-related infrastructure... supports youth organizing in which projects, uniqueness, and separate identity are what is required to obtain funds," rather than "the development of a healthy youth and student movement" with a collective mentality. Skeptical funders also may doubt the capacity of youth-led efforts to function independently, without active adult involvement and supervision. The particular challenges for securing adequate financial resources to support youth-led organizing are explored in chapter 10.

9. Allies

Community organizing depends on people power to wield the requisite clout to bring about social change. Frequently, grassroots groups look beyond their own membership to determine how they can increase their power and capacity by working with allies who will support and assist their efforts. Both individuals and other organizations may function as allies for a community organization. At the organizational level, there may be an *alliance* in which two or more groups work together on a common goal while maintaining their own identities and autonomy. In other instances, a *coalition* may be formed, creating a new and separate structure—an organization of pre-existing organizations in which members give up their independence and agree to share decision-making power.

The relationship with adults (both individuals and organizations) often is complex for youth-led organizations (Youth Wisdom Project 2004, 20): "Even with all the challenges, youth-led organizations are powerful models for youth empowerment and organizational and community development. Young people involved with youth-led organizations develop skills and knowledge they cannot learn any other way." Within this movement, youth need to play a central role, with adults assisting them only as needed. Adults no longer speak for or represent youth, and this shift in power incorporates an increased recognition that youth have rights, abilities, and corresponding responsibilities. Youth-led organizations typically are wary of being dominated and controlled by adults. "Youth as community assets" becomes the organizing core of youth-led activities and places young people in positions of leadership within their communities with a corresponding set of expectations that they can effect positive change (Delgado 2007).

However, adults do not "disappear" from the lives of youth during these activities. Advocates for youth-led movements have argued that these efforts are primarily about collaboration between youth and adults, not exclusively youth-led (Evans, Ulasevich, and Blahut 2004). The ability to foster these relationships helps ensure the success of joint projects, but also equips both young people and adults with experiences and tools to draw upon in future undertakings. Adult–youth relationships based on mutual trust and respect can be quite powerful and transformative in changing institutions, communities, and eventually society. Both positive models of collaboration and common sources of tension within these relationships will be examined in this book.

10. Communications

Grassroots community organizations need to establish how they will communicate quickly and effectively *internally* with their members about a range of matters, including upcoming events, actions, decision-making processes, and other activities. It is important for lines of communication to flow democratically in a two-way fashion, not simply in a top-down manner from the leadership or staff. Open and inclusive communication processes help maintain member involvement and also make it easier to attract potential activists who have yet to join the organization. The group also must address the challenge of how it will reach out *externally* to these prospective recruits, as well as the larger community, through word of mouth, networking, mailings, telephone calls, small community meetings, larger public forums, newsletters, local media, brochures, e-mail listservs, and presentations in multiple settings.

Youth organizing frequently is on the cutting edge of technology, using it for both internal and external communications. Cellphones (instant contact), e-mail (informal and quick-to-spread messages), and computers (offering new marketable skills) hold great appeal for youth and often are combined with traditional patterns of youth communications through networking and word of mouth. Technology also facilitates youth transcending the geographical boundaries of their communities, exposing them to a world not normally within their reach. Exchanges with peers at a trans-community level can facilitate learning, consciousness raising, and activism.

This generation of youth grew up with these forms of technology around them, especially youth from privileged backgrounds. While youth from lower income families also are familiar with the technology, access is not a universal phenomenon, particularly when examined from a social-class perspective (Beamish 1999; Sanyal and Schon 1999). Much attention has been directed to the "digital divide," which marks the differential access to computers and the Internet (Kitlin 2004; Tardieu 1999). The divide is wearing down, but it still exists in many areas of the United States, especially the South. Electronic communication in youth organizing must take such technological disparities into account; however, we discuss the creative use of technology for recruitment, leadership development, information sharing, politicization, mobilization, networking, linkages outside the immediate community, and regular communication among group members at a number of points in the remainder of this book.

Beyond technology, youth culture as manifested through art and music plays a central role in virtually all models of youth-led organizing. Youth culture gets brought to life through a variety of media, including hip-hop and rap music, poetry and other forms of the spoken word, break-dancing, curated galleries, films and video, improvisational theater, and graffiti. These forms of individual and collective expression are essential elements in the process of engaging, motivating, politicizing, and holding the interest of youth activists. Leadership development cannot be separated from the infusion of youth culture into every aspect of youth-led organizing. Indeed, the importance and significance of youth culture is an ongoing theme in this book.

Conclusion

The nine principles stated earlier and the ten elements of our analytical framework are offered here to help practitioners better appreciate the dynamic nature of social interventions such as youth-led community organizing. Academics, too, benefit from these tools. The nine principles capture a broad arena for the reader. The ten elements constitute the analytical framework that we then use to examine youth-led organizing in the United States. As the analysis moves forward, we will not follow a strict regimen, in which we consider each variable sequentially and separately. Such an approach would be unnecessarily static and too rigid to capture the energy, spirit, and dynamism of youth-led organizing. Rather, these ten elements, like the guiding principles, will be interwoven and revisited at many different points in the chapters that follow. Our goal is to merge a flexible line of inquiry with a sufficient degree of analytical structure to provide a rigorous and systematic study. As noted earlier in the chapter, there invariably is tension between being too descriptive and too prescriptive. Local circumstances must ultimately dictate the interaction between the principles and the framework presented in this chapter.

5

Participatory Democracy

A country where all citizens, young and old,
are informed about and engaged in the issues
that affect their lives. A place where adults
and young people are together at the table—
grappling with problems, crafting solutions,
and deciding how resources are allocated. A
robust democracy where all people, including
youth, exercise their right to select those who
speak on their behalf. Where young people
have an equal opportunity to a sustainable
livelihood. Imagine adults and young people
building their nations from the ground up, and
changing their nations when they fail to meet
their needs.
—*Building Nations, Changing Nations* (2001)

The above quotation powerfully describes a society that is democratic and elects to be inclusive rather than exclusive in who decides what is important and how best to address issues of common concern (Conover and Seering 2000; Sherrod, Flanagan, and Youniss 2002). The concept of participatory democracy has emerged as a vehicle for setting goals and providing mechanisms for increasing participation on the part of all citizens, regardless of their socio-demographic background (Cutler 2002; O'Donoghue 2003). Meaningful participation in decision making about youth matters usually has been accessible only to adults with children (Golombek 2006). Youth essentially have been disenfranchised from decision-making roles in most of the institutions entrusted to serve and educate them (O'Donoghue, Kirshner, and McLaughlin 2002). For example, young people typically have been given only passive roles in most scholarly activities meant to enhance their well-being (Chan et al. 2003).

Democratic principles have been developed exclusively by adults for adults, and youth either have been ignored totally or told that their time will come if they are patient. The emergence of participatory democracy is in many ways a direct attempt to rectify the deleterious consequences of disenfranchisement. The subject of how youth can play a meaningful role in creating a democratic civil society has not suffered an absence of attention and literature (Golombek 2006). There is general agreement, as the reader soon will see, that a vibrant democratic society cannot afford to deemphasize youth and expect them to miraculously become contributing citizens the moment they achieve the magical stage of adulthood (Charles 2005; Checkoway and Gutierrez 2006; Cohen 2006).

Definition and Rationale

Before examining participatory democracy as a central tenet of youth-led community organizing, it is important to define this term and to understand its significance at the level of the general society. *Webster's New World College Dictionary* (Agnes 2000, 384) includes the following definition of *democracy*:

> (1) government in which the people hold the ruling power either directly or through elected representatives; rule by the ruled; (2) a country, state, etc. with such government; (3) majority rule; (4) the principle of equality of rights, opportunity and treatment, or the practice of this principle; (5) the common people, esp. as the wielders of political power.

When one looks closely at the literature on democracy, it is clear that it most often has been conceptualized in terms of a form of governmental rather than as a participatory process through which people pursue their rights, opportunities, and interests by wielding political power either through government or civil society. There are numerous models for democratic government, and they run along a continuum from direct participation (Rousseau 1762), as evidenced in town meetings or kibbutzim, on through a variety of indirect forms, including representative (Mill 1861), accountable (Powell and Bingham 1989), and liberal constitutionalism (Weale 1999).

It is not within the scope of this book to critically evaluate the different types of democratic governments. However, the debate about how much participation in the democratic process is optimal is most relevant to this study. Dahl (1982) raised the problem of scale, pointing out that in a large country, government cannot be "highly participatory," thus limiting how much influence an average citizen can have. His solution was to ensure the existence of "smaller democratic units" (Dahl 1982). But while some theorists and writers have advocated for more decentralization (Jefferson 1824;

Tocqueville 1840; Arendt 1963; Lynd 1967; Hayden 1970), others have argued that there are limits to its desirability (Mill 1861; Nisbet 1953; Fanon 1965; Moynihan 1969; Etzioni 1969).

While there is a clear, positive correlation between decentralization and the degree of possible democratic participation, few writers, including the authors of this book, maintain that participatory democracy is a panacea for societal ills. Nevertheless, it is a central feature of all community organizing, which is characterized by collective action, participatory processes, indigenous grassroots leadership, and "people power" (Staples 2004a). Minkler and Pies (2005, 116) note: "The single most important factor distinguishing true community organizing from other approaches . . . is the active involvement of people, beginning with what they define as the needs and goals to be addressed."

Therefore, it is important to understand the basic nature of participatory democracy and the processes by which it works most effectively. Cook and Morgan (1971, 4) offer a very good working definition for this concept:

> It seems that participatory democracy connotes two broad features in patterns of decision-making: (1) *decentralization or dispersion of authoritative decision-making*, whereby the authority to make certain decisions is to be dispersed downward from remote points near the top of administrative hierarchies or outward from central geographical locations, thus bringing authority closer to the people affected by it; and (2) *direct involvement of amateurs in the making of decisions*. Some participatory-democracy structures drop the representative principle; those that retain it at all require that representation be kept "close" to the people, with amateur representation selected from a relatively small-scale or immediate constituency.

These writers go on to quickly make the point that when referring to amateurs, they "do not use the term in a disparaging sense." Rather, the word is employed to make the distinction between laypeople who "need not carry credentials as formally trained experts or professionals serving in career capacities and are not regularly elected officials" (4). Thus, participatory democracy entails decentralized structures and processes that enable ordinary members of a society or community to be actively involved in making important and authoritative decisions that affect their lives.

What are the benefits of such involvement? It is the protection from "tyranny by dispersion of power" (Cook and Morgan 1971). Left unchecked, power does tend to become concentrated in the hands of a few leaders, a phenomenon that Robert Michels (1949) characterized as "The Iron Law of Oligarchy" in his classic study of organizational behavior. Certainly, direct and active grassroots involvement can be a powerful antidote to centralized power, by holding entrenched leaders accountable to their larger constituency.

However, while participatory democracy involves the will of the majority, the process of arriving at collective decisions often is contentious (Pitkin and Shumer 1982). Indeed, the democratic process may feature challenges to dominant elites when ordinary people take extraordinary action. Attempts to democratize "from below" can result in significant social change (Parenti 2002, 312):

> Many of the struggles for political democracy—the right to vote, assemble, petition, and dissent—have been largely propelled by the struggle for economic and social democracy, by a desire to democratize the rules of the political game so as to be in a better position to fight for one's socioeconomic interests. In a word, the struggle for democracy has been part of the class struggle against plutocracy.

Beyond providing a means for power dispersion, as well as exercising and protecting rights, participatory processes tap into the unique perspectives, wisdom, information, expertise, and lived experiences of community members, interest groups, consumers/clients of services, and others who do not hold positions of leadership in the relevant public or private administrative hierarchies. This additional input usually results in more effective decisions and plans (Cook and Morgan 1971; Burke 1979), although the inherent challenge to the power and prerogatives of professional experts and institutional decision makers often leads them to fiercely resist such democratic contributions. Participatory processes also are notoriously messy, since they usually are more time-consuming and involve additional divergent views than when authoritative experts make unilateral decisions without grassroots input. Nevertheless, taking the time to get it right by involving those most impacted by decisions usually is more efficient in the long run, with the ideas, insights, and initiatives of the "amateurs" transforming both the process and the product of resolving social issues.

Finally, there are arguments that participation provides an invaluable learning experience for ordinary citizens, that it "socializes people into new beliefs, attitudes, and values" (Cook and Morgan 1971). Kieffer (1984) coined the term *participatory competence* in his study of citizen empowerment through grassroots organizing. He presents a developmental model that consists of three intersecting dimensions: (a) development of more positive self-concept, or sense of self-competence; (b) development of a critical or analytical understanding of the surrounding social and political environment; and (c) cultivation or enhancement of individual and collective resources for social and political action. Indeed, active involvement in successful efforts to bring about social change can lead to dramatic increases in perceptions of both self and collective efficacy (Pecukonis and Wenocur 1994).

Elements and Forms of Participatory Democracy

Given the obvious advantages of participatory democracy, what does it look like in practice and what are the mechanisms and means by which it can be implemented? (Westheimer and Kahne 2002). Burke (1979) identified six strategies of citizen participation that still are relevant and instructive today: education-therapy, behavioral change, staff supplement, cooptation, community power, and advocacy. Both *education-therapy* and *behavioral change* focus on making changes in individual participants, with the first approach operating from the assumption that those involved will gain "increased competency in civic affairs," and the second endeavoring to change individual behavior through the powerful experience of group participation. *Staff supplement* is a value-added organizational benefit that occurs when volunteers are recruited to carry out responsibilities and tasks that cannot be accomplished fully by existing paid staff members.

Cooptation is a cynical and manipulative strategy "to involve citizens in an organization in order to prevent anticipated obstructionism" (Burke 1979, 97). The concept was introduced by Selznick (1948) in a classic work in which he distinguished between *informal cooptation,* where some measure of power is shared by a dominant group as a response to pressures from challenging groups, and *formal cooptation,* which "merely seeks public acknowledgement of the agency-constituency relationship, since it is not anticipated that organizational policies will be put in jeopardy" (Selznick 1948, 99). The current catchphrase, *the illusion of inclusion,* helps capture the essence of cooptation. Frequently, individual community participants "are selected as 'types' based on race, ethnicity, gender, age, sexual orientation, income, or other status, rather than as *representatives* of organized groups" and "often turn out to be *atypical* of the very group they are chosen to exemplify" (Staples 2004a, 211). But even when participants are indeed accountable representatives for a larger constituency, cooptation features participation without a significant measure of accompanying power.

Burke's usage of the term *community power* actually refers to approaches that attempt to involve individuals who already have power attendant with their high status. Either such persons seek out particular organizations in which to participate (thereby meeting some of their self-interests) or they are recruited to join. In a sense, this might be characterized as a quasi-elitist strategy, since the participants are of high standing and their involvement either is welcomed or is actively sought by the dominant group.

Finally, *advocacy* operates from the premise that "change . . . can be caused by confronting existing power centers with the power of numbers—an organized and committed mass of citizenry" (Burke 1979, 102). Consistent with current practice in macro social work, we will reserve usage of the term *advocacy* to describe actions taken *on behalf of others* to bring about social change or secure rights and opportunities (e.g., advocates *for* youth). To the extent that *self advocacy* occurs (e.g., youth acting on their *own* behalf), that activity will be designated as *community organizing*. Burke, in fact, describes archetypal social action *community organizing*, which features the creation of "a new center of power" derived from the large numbers of grassroots participants. "This type of organization has the ability to obtain accommodation from existing power centers, both from its inherent strength and from its choice of tactics" (102). Indeed, this book focuses on the strategy of participation termed *advocacy* by Burke, but we continue to refer to this approach as *community organizing*.

Prior to Burke, Arnstein (1969, 216) clearly had articulated the relationship between grassroots power and community involvement in her seminal critique of the federal programs of the 1960s:

> [C]itizen participation is a categorical term for citizen *power* [emphasis added]. It is the redistribution of power that enables the have-not citizens presently excluded from the political and economic processes, to be deliberately included in the future. It is the strategy by which the have-nots join in determining how information is shared, goals and policies are set, tax resources are allocated, programs are operated, and benefits like contracts and patronage are parceled out.

Arnstein (1969, 217) developed a typology of eight levels of participation "arranged in a ladder pattern with each rung corresponding to the extent of citizens' power in determining the end product." Despite the specificity of her analysis and the passage of time, this formulation of *participatory roles* can be generalized and still is relevant to current practice.

Arnstein's eight rungs in ascending order of power are manipulation, therapy, informing, consultation, placation, partnership, delegated power, and citizen control. The bottom two levels, *manipulation* and *therapy*, do not allow for any consequential participation, and they place power holders in the position of educating or reeducating community members. The next three steps—*informing, consultation*, and *placation*—are forms of token participation. Dominant groups do not surrender or share any significant degree of power. Informing processes entail a one-way flow of information, with members of the community hearing but not speaking; while consultation allows participants to speak but not necessarily be heard or heeded. Placation raises basic questions about which participants are heard, since it features unrepresentative, handpicked tokens or types, as described above, who do not reflect the majority view of the community from which they have been chosen.

The top three levels do, in fact, represent degrees of genuine citizen power. *Partnerships* can be structured along a continuum from junior partners to full equals. Many community groups have had difficulty squaring the egalitarian rhetoric of partnerships made with universities, health facilities, schools, local government, corporations, and service agencies or bureaucracies with the reality of relationships experienced more in form than in substance. Nevertheless, where a situation of genuine partnership does exist, an important measure of power has been redistributed. Arnstein (1969, 221) points out that this is most likely to occur "where there's an organized power base in the community." Indeed, Staples (2004a) has built on this insight with his concept of Community Obligated Institutions (COINS); and he lays out guidelines for institutional power sharing with grassroots community organizations (GCOs) in four areas: decision-making structures, operating policies and procedures, programming, and staffing.

When participation has advanced to *delegated power* and *citizen control*, the balance of control has tipped in favor of community members. Arnstein (1969, 222) describes delegated power as "dominant decision-making power" and argues that this occurs when "have-not citizens obtain the majority of decision-making seats, or full managerial power." Citizen control takes participation to its highest level, where community members actually have the right to govern.

In fact, these categories are prototypical ideal types, and Arnstein herself points out that there could be many more levels with less sharp distinctions. She also reminds the reader that neither community groups nor those holding power are homogeneous blocs. The real-world dynamics of community involvement and power-holder responses often feature mixing and phasing of the above participatory forms. The processes may not be so clear-cut, but rather be nuanced and subtle. Nevertheless, this model is helpful for understanding the range of forms and roles that may exist.

Evolution of Civic Participation

While the roots of participatory democracy are firmly embedded in traditional American values and political philosophy dating back to Jefferson, the degree of citizen involvement has increased and diminished at different points in history. In his frequently cited book *Bowling Alone*, Robert Putnam (2000) recounts the steady decrease of civic engagement in the United States following an era of heightened activity during the 1950s and 1960s. His comprehensive study chronicles the decline in social capital and civic participation through an examination of data about social trends. Elsewhere, Putnam (2003, 2) has defined social capital as "social networks, norms of reciprocity, mutual assistance, and trustworthiness."

A brief review of Putnam's findings is in order. Putnam (2000, 41) found sharp reductions in voting, but also decreases in "political participation outside the context of national elections, especially at the local level," including writing letters to the paper, attending public meetings, working for a political party, running for office, attending political rallies or speeches, making a speech, or taking part in a political campaign. Union membership also was dropping during this time and people were less likely to join with co-workers in formal associations. Meanwhile, church attendance has declined, "and the churches we go to are less engaged with the wider community" (2000, 79), since evangelical Christianity is rising while membership in mainline denominations is falling.

Putnam (2000, 338) sees voluntary associations as incubators for social capital, describing them as "places where social and civic skills are learned—'schools of democracy.' Members learn how to run meetings, speak in public, write letters, organize projects, and debate public issues with civility." However, holding office or serving as a committee member in a civic association also has declined, and "active involvement in face-to-face organizations has plummeted, whether we consider organizational records, survey reports, time diaries, or consumer expenditures" (63). Finally, Putnam (2000, 115) observes that:

> [T]he last several decades have witnessed a striking diminution of regular contacts with our friends and neighbors. We spend less time in conversation over meals, we exchange visits less often, we engage less often in leisure activities that encourage casual social interaction, we spend more time watching ... and less time doing. We know our neighbors less well, and we see old friends less often. In short, it is not merely "do good" civic activities that engage us less, but also informal connecting.

Yet, while civic participation may have diminished in many realms, the past several decades also have witnessed increased challenges to the power of professionals in a wide variety of areas, including medicine, human services, mental health, law, public health, and all levels of education (Finn and Checkoway 1998). McKnight (1995) argues that professionalism has expanded at a rapid rate with the growth of a service economy, making the country "ambivalent" and "confused" about the impacts of professional proliferation." McKnight makes a strong critique of the counter-productivity of the service economy, and maintains that "the power to label people deficient and declare them in need is the basic tool of control and oppression in modern societies" (16), and that the various professions have abused this power, expanding their various domains in the process. He cites three antiprofessional arguments: (1) inefficiency—that is, professional service often is ineffective; (2) arrogance born of elitism and dominance; and (3) the iatrogenic negative effects and unintended consequences of professional helping, which have contributed to the backlash against professionals.

Regardless of the causes, during the last twenty-five years of the twentieth century, users and consumers of a broad array of services began to assert their rights to question the judgment and performance of professionals who previously had operated as uncontested experts. At the individual level, the number of lawsuits filed against service providers began to skyrocket; an assortment of consumer advocates suddenly appeared on the scene; and a vast amount of advice was dispensed to service users through every medium (television, radio, books, magazines, newspapers, work-shops, Internet). The expertise of professionals of every type and stripe was challenged, including that of doctors, psychiatrists, psychologists, nurses, social workers, lawyers, professors, and teachers.

At the collective level, there was an explosion of organizing activity including, but not limited to, the self-help movement (Riessman and Gart-ner 1984; Riessman and Carroll 1995), patient's rights, mental health con-sumer rights, student rights, and parent involvement in the schools. These consumer initiatives first began to take shape during the organizing move-ments previously referenced in chapter 3 (civil rights/people of color, wel-fare rights, women's rights, environmental justice, elderly rights, gay and lesbian rights, rights for people with disabilities), and they continue today. This consumer movement has been profoundly democratic, participatory, and anti-elitist. As a result, the gap between professionals and the people whom they serve has narrowed significantly, and a new paradigm of pro-fessional helping has emerged. This new model rests on the conceptual foun-dation of empowerment, which draws from a strengths perspective and an emphasis on client and community resiliency.

There are many different conceptions of *empowerment*, with no univer-sally accepted definition; and there is general agreement that it can arise from many sources (Jennings et al. 2006; Simon 1994). However, a number of common themes and elements can be found in the literature. For exam-ple, empowerment is operative at both the personal and collective levels (Petterman 2002; Lee 1997; Cox 1991; Staples 1990), and it often focuses on oppressed groups with an emphasis on changing the stigmatization and unequal structural relations of power that perpetuate personal and social problems (Boehm and Staples 2004; Itzhaky and York 2002; Moreau 1990; Solomon 1976). This concept refers to both the *process* by which individuals and groups move from relative powerlessness to increased power and the outcome dimensions or *end products*, such as the right to vote, access to in-formation, availability of educational degrees, or increased economic re-sources (Miley and Dubois 1999; Zimmerman and Warschausky 1998; Staples 1990).

The ability to act efficaciously on one's own behalf (or as a group) goes to the heart of this concept; it is not possible for someone to fully empower another person or group (Staples 1999). Empowerment is based on the prem-ise that relatively powerless individuals and groups nevertheless possess capacities, skills, strengths, and assets that can be powerful resources during any helping process or initiative to bring about social change (Tomlinson and Egan 2002; Cowger 1994). Indeed, a "strengths based approach" (Saleebey 1992) is in sharp contrast to a traditional deficit model, which has evolved from medicine and focuses almost exclusively on weaknesses, lim-itations, vulnerability, and pathology. When client/consumer/community strengths are a starting point in any helping process, the individuals and groups being assisted are in a position to take a more active role in that process—a key element in empowerment (Gutierrez 1990). And these abilities and skills also will be further developed and refined when provider professionals actively involve those being served in the helping process (Dodd and Gutierrez 1990).

The concept of *resiliency*, or competency for a variety of adaptive behaviors in the face of adversity, also is highly relevant for empowerment. It has been defined as "the process of, capacity for, or outcome of successful adaptation despite challenging or threatening circumstances" (Masten, Best, and Garmezy 1990, 426). These authors have identified three distinct types of resilience: (1) "overcoming the odds" in spite of being in a situation of high risk; (2) "sustained competence under stress," which entails various forms of coping; and (3) "recovery from trauma," which might include a particularly stressful life event or situation. A number of variables have been associated with resiliency, including both the factors related to external protection and those linked to internal self-resiliency, such as spirituality, cognitive competency, behavioral/social skills, emotional stability, and physical well-being (Kumpher 1999).

Freire (1970, 1973) maintained that *critical consciousness* is an essential element in the development of empowerment. He urged service providers to function as "teacher-learners" and to raise questions ("pedagogy of the question"), rather than simply providing answers for clients and community members. In fact, while empowerment can not be created for another person, it can be *facilitated* through a number of practice principles and techniques that tend to be nondirective and that underscore the need for consumers to make decisions and take initiative (Staples 1999; Gutierrez 1990).

Provider professionals who embrace an empowerment approach essentially operate under a different paradigm of helping (see table 5.1) than the traditional professional model. While the figure employs ideal types, and such pure distinctions may seldom exist in actual practice, nevertheless the fundamental differences in assumptions, principles, methods, and techniques do, in fact, constitute two separate approaches: the traditional model and the empowerment model. We submit that the traditional model has been challenged over the past several decades and that the dominant *paradigm of helping* now is in transition. It should be noted that while these two approaches can be generalized across all the helping professions, the language used is most consistent with human services.

In practice, a provider professional that is operating under an empowerment model commits to actively involving consumers of services and community members in the helping process. Such active engagement is most possible when one starts by identifying and working from the strengths of those being helped. This entails recognition of and respect for expertise, capacities, and skills. No longer is the professional the sole actor working as all-knowing expert; instead, the professional supplements his or her own expertise by drawing on consumer and community assets and resources.

Table 5.1 The Changing Paradigm of Helping

Traditional Model	Empowerment Model
General Approach	General Approach
Deficit Model	Strengths Model
Formal helping systems	Formal and informal helping systems (natural supports: extended families, friends, churches, small businesses, and other nontraditional settings)
Vulnerability	Resiliency
Identify pathology	Identify assets and resources
Treat problems	Prevent problems and promote opportunities
Individual responsibility	Individual and institutional responsibility
Agency-driven programs: Top-down approach	Consumer and community-driven programs: Bottom-up approach
Programs for individuals	Programs for individuals, families, and communities
Categorical, specialized programs	Comprehensive, holistic programs
Success defined by agency	Success defined by consumers/users and community members
Conception of People Served	Conception of People Served
Clients	Consumers/users, community members
Passive	Active
Individuals	Individuals, families, and communities
Relatively helpless, *lacking* capacities, skills, and expertise	People served *do have* lived expertise, capacities, and skills
Role of Professional	Role of Professional
Expert	Expertise, facilitator, enabler, catalyst
"Do to" and "Do for" clients	"Do with" consumers/users and community members
Professional as sole actor	Partnership with consumers/users and community members
One-way relationship	Mutual two-way relationship
Provide answers	Ask questions
Find solutions	Help identify options and choices
Formal	Informal
Distance	Closer relationship (with boundaries)
Protect clients	Challenge and support consumers/users and community members

This new role requires professionals to function effectively as facilitators, enablers, and catalysts; and to establish two-way partnerships in which they ask questions that enable consumers and community members to identify their own options, make their own decisions accordingly, and develop a greater degree of critical consciousness in the process. Providers who use an empowerment approach "do with" rather than "for" or "to" whomever they are serving, decreasing professional distance (although maintaining boundaries), acting more informally, and challenging and/or supporting people who have strengths and resiliency, rather than simply protecting "vulnerable clients."

At the programmatic level, there is not a sole focus on individual treatment, but rather an emphasis on preventing problems and promoting opportunities. Responsibility is lodged with external institutions, which are held accountable to both consumers and the larger community (see discussion about COINS above). Programs result from bottom-up community-driven processes rather than top-down agency agendas. Professional service providers supplement their work with formal helping systems that engage informal networks and settings, including extended family members, friends, faith-based aggregations, small businesses, and other nontraditional resources (Delgado 1996, 1999). Success is defined by consumers and community members, and participatory evaluation methodology is employed (Minkler and Wallerstein 2003; Coombe 2005; Finn 1994).

In short, the empowerment model of professional helping, and the accompanying consumer movement, has been a democratizing force in American society. Participatory democracy has been enhanced by the establishment of egalitarian relationships between providers and recipients of services. As discussed above, active participation is central to the empowerment concept, which is fundamentally democratic and anti-elitist by its very nature. Professionals who adopt this approach emphasize the direct involvement of service users and community members in the helping process.

Linkage to Youth-Led Organizing

Over the past decade, participatory democracy has gained considerable attention in the youth field and its accompanying professional literature (Checkoway and Gutierrez 2006; Ginwright, Noguera, and Cammarota 2006). Foster (1998) makes an impassioned plea to have youth achieve a role as a legitimate constituency of a civil democratic society that is based on their demographic significance and their potential to develop as important contributing members. In order to make such a goal a reality, a society must develop mechanisms for encouraging significant youth participation (Larson and Hansen 2005). The Youth Council for Northern Ireland (Green 2004) notes that it is essential for a democratic society to provide youth with genuine opportunities to use power democratically and responsibly. Such political education serves as the foundation for youth to assume a decision-making role in helping to shape society (Watts, Willams, and Jagers 2003).

The concept of participation is manifested in a variety of ways. According to Youniss and colleagues (2002, 126):

> Perhaps the fairest conclusion is that there is not a definite demarcation between the political and civil realms. Rather there is a continuum between formal political acts such as voting, political actions such as protesting for a moral cause, and performing a service such as working in a rural literacy campaign. Scholarship concerned with young people's preparation for civic participation as adults would be wise to take into account the whole range.

There are various perspectives on how civic engagement and participation can be operationalized for youth (Skelton, Boyte, and Leonard 2002). For example, Bass (1997) advocates for the use of a public-works approach to develop active citizenship. He stresses civic renewal and "new citizenship" that entails service learning through collaborative problem solving among youth and between youth and adults. The Forum for Youth Investment (Building Nations 2001) identified six forms of youth action/civic involvement: (1) service and service learning; (2) voter education and get-out-the vote; (3) governance; (4) youth development; (5) issue advocacy; and (6) youth organizing. Each of these forums can use a variety of methods that take into account organizational and youth goals, and each can cover distinct periods of time, both short and long term. Gil (1998) notes that one of the important lessons gained from studying social-change activists is the importance of differentiating between short-term or emergency measures and long-range goals.

Youth civic participation can also be found on organizational boards, advisory committees, commissions, and task forces, for example (Hohenemser and Marshall 2002; MacNeil and McClean 2006; Stoneman 2002). The 1990s witnessed continued efforts to bring about youth representation in a structured and sustainable manner. This form of youth civic participation has continue to expand during this decade, and all indications are that it is no longer viewed as novel and is slowly becoming institutionalized across the country (Delgado 2002; Frank 2006; Young Wisdom Project 2004).

Watts, Williams, and Jager (2003) advance the concept of sociopolitical development (SPD), or political education, as a process through which youth acquire knowledge, analytical skills, emotional faculties, and the capacity for action. This action, however, must entail struggle against all forms of oppression in a political and social system. As a result, youth participation must address issues of social and economic justice for SPD to occur and reach its potential for youth transformation. Political education provides youth with the necessary language to engage in problem solving and critical thinking—essential components in achieving social change (Roach, Yu, and Lewis-Charp 2001; Stepick and Stepick 2002).

Certainly, participatory democracy and empowerment have been central features in the youth-led field, which is based on an assets paradigm that highlights the potential for positive contributions to society through direct participation, action by young people on their own behalf, youth leadership, and the exercise of political power in the pursuit of social and economic justice (Ginwright and James 2002; O'Donoghue, Kirshner, and McLaughlin 2002; Susskind 2003). If youth are to experience significant empowerment, they must be active participants in the process of social change, not passive recipients (Checkoway, Figueroa, and Richards-Schuster 2003; Gutierrez 1990; Pinderhughes 1983; Rappaport 1981).

Therefore, adults interested in facilitating youth empowerment and participation should use the pedagogy of the question more often than instructing youth about what should be done and how to do it (Freire 1970). Opportunities for decision making and collective action should be maximized, along with chances for developing participatory competencies and skills (Cervone and Cushman 2002; Kieffer 1984). Decision making cannot have significant and long-lasting meaning without corresponding attention to increasing youth knowledge and competencies in the process.

Downton, Downton, and Wehr (1997) conducted a series of qualitative interviews in communities undergoing periods of great challenge (tensions, threats, and violence). Their findings call attention to the importance of youth's making a commitment to the creation and maintenance of a social justice movement. This commitment is fostered over an extended period through meaningful opportunities for youth engagement in collective action. Cowan (1997, 194) specifically ties the concept of youth participation in civic life to community organizing by identifying four key lessons: (1) "the real problem is politics, not young people"; (2) "service leads to service, not politics"; (3) "don't agonize, organize"; and (4) "a new politics begins at home." These lessons, not surprisingly, have tremendous applicability to all spheres of life and are not restricted to social action.

Other research focuses on values, relationships, and organizational culture as important variables that impact motivation to become involved in youth organizing. Scheie (2003) found that youth are more likely to participate in community affairs when their parents hold values of social responsibility. Nevertheless, youth frequently are attracted to community organizations for different reasons from their parents (Costello et al. 2000). While it is a well-established principle in community organizing with adults that the key to participation is immediate self-interest on particular issues of concern, other motivational factors for youth involvement frequently are relevant. According to Stahlhut (2004, 74), "[w]e have learned that, like it or not, prime reasons for youth to be involved in organizing are to get out of the house, do something with their peers that is productive, safe and fun, and get away from their parents (not necessarily in that order)." It is necessary to create multiple points of entry to attract youth with different interests and talents (Beyond Base, 2004; Sanchez-Jankowski 2002).

We have emphasized the importance of building relationships of trust and solidarity in all the successful youth organizations examined in this book. Indeed, it has been noted that "youth organizing provides the very space and social cohesion that many gangs across California afforded" (Pintado-Vertner 2004, 23). Therefore, the organizational culture of youth groups is supremely important. The most effective efforts emphasize having fun, providing social activities, offering relationship building, and suggesting individual development, as well as guiding collective action for social change. Interactive processes are given equal weight with product outcomes. The individuals involved are seen as ends in themselves and are not viewed solely as means toward an end of achieving people power. It logically follows that a key to youth organizing is recruitment through peer relationship networks. Youth who are respected and admired by others have the ability to engage their friends and followers.

Conclusion

Participatory democracy is a central concept underlying youth-led organizing, and there are both challenges and opportunities attendant with it. Certainly entrenched interests and dominant elites can be expected to resist bottom-up participation that threatens their ability to retain and exercise power. And youth continue to hold the status of a relatively powerless group in American society—one that makes it easier for them to be marginalized, demonized, or dismissed. Elitism is antithetical to the egalitarian, participatory ethos that infuses youth-led organizing, and this sentiment often poses a significant barrier to popular democracy.

As discussed in chapter 2, the phenomenon of adultism also is a pervasive and persistent problem in virtually all types of youth work. The dominance and control exercised by adults is fueled by ageism directed against young people. Adultism plays out in practice when youth are not empowered to make their own decisions freely and/or are not trusted to exercise true leadership when taking action on choices that have been made. The restriction of free will, self-determination, and voluntary action is fundamentally undemocratic, and adultism remains one of the greatest impediments in the youth-led movement.

While the subjugation by adultism operates in a manner similar to the other "isms," in fact youth-led organizing disproportionately involves low-income young people of color who also must deal with the pernicious, interactive effects of poverty, classism, and racism. And many, if not most, of the organizing issues related to social and economic justice are products of these other forms of oppression. This constellation of negative societal forces operates at multiple levels and in a variety of ways to challenge youth of color who are poor. Their participation in youth-led collective action may be limited by a broad array of factors, including the need to work multiple low-paying jobs, perceived threats to personal safety, required gang membership, responsibilities to care for younger siblings, lack of adequate housing, health or mental health problems, substance abuse, a great deal of schoolwork, multiple extracurricular activities, and other competing demands on their time. As noted by Lourdes Best, a staff member at YUCA (Weiss 2003), it may be necessary to provide a weekly stipend for core participants, enabling them to avoid having to make the difficult choice between organizational involvement and paid employment.

Earlier in this chapter we discussed the perversion of authentic democracy that occurs when mere participation supersedes genuine power. Under such circumstances a dominant minority elite may employ strategies such as cooptation or tokenism to suppress bona fide participatory democracy. However, another phenomenon, often termed tyranny of the majority, poses a different challenge for proponents of participatory democracy. Essentially, a majority can make a democratic decision that is discriminatory, prejudicial, and disempowering to a minority group by race, ethnicity, gender, class, sexual orientation, age, disability, or a host of other statuses. Cook and Morgan (1971, 14) assert that "the only way to break . . . the 'tyranny of the majority' is to shift toward nonelitist decision-making units that permit a minority to avoid being submerged in majority sentiment and preference." But such an occurrence also underscores the fact that, while participatory democracy usually is a high-order value, there are times when it can be abused, to the detriment of minority constituencies.

Beyond these limitations of participatory democracy as it relates to youth-led organizing, there are particular opportunities associated with this demographic. Certainly, the energy and enthusiasm of young people can feed broad and deep participation in many actions, activities, and events. Youth have the capacity to mobilize more quickly and with greater vigor than many other groups in society. The uniqueness of youth culture also can be a tremendous asset for recruitment, engagement, and collective action. For instance, as discussed in chapter 3, hip-hop can serve as a means of self-expression, a setting for building relationships and networking, a venue for engagement, a free space for developing critical consciousness, a forum for political protest, and a tactic for social change. Hip-hop can best be appreciated and understood from a multifaceted perspective as it relates to youth-led community organizing. Indeed, as part of the tactical repertoire of young people, hip-hop is a prime example of legendary community organizer Saul Alinsky's (1971) dictum to stay within the experience of your own constituency and go outside the experience of the opposition. Additional challenges and opportunities can be expected to arise in the years ahead, but participatory democracy will remain a primary principle and motivating force in youth-led community organizing, for it is at once both a means and an end.

6

Leadership Development

> One part of making the transition from child
> to adult is learning about leadership. Who
> are leaders? What is leadership? Could I be
> a leader? Unfortunately, most adolescents
> answer this last question, "No, I am not a
> leader."
> —Linden and Fertman, *Youth Leadership* (1998)

The quotation by Linden and Fertman (1998) above is quite provocative and of extreme importance to the field of youth-led community organizing, particularly when youth cannot perceive themselves as leaders in this society. This sad state of affairs speaks volumes about how undervalued youth feel and the amount of work that must be undertaken—opportunities as well as support—to rectify this situation. What are the qualities that are essential to make a good leader in this society? The answer to this question goes to the heart of what makes a good youth community organizer and helps to shape how youth-led community organizing must be conceptualized and carried out in the United States.

There is extensive literature on the qualities essential for productive leadership, the best models and modes for leading most effectively, and the processes by which new leaders are identified, recruited, and developed. Much of this literature is adult-centered (MacNeil 2006); indeed, many leadership principles, functions, roles, tasks, and skills can be generalized across dimensions of age, race, gender, and class. Nevertheless, the youth development and youth-led approaches have placed a unique emphasis on employing methods that increase the leadership capacities, critical consciousness, and skills of young people. Consequently, a growing body of knowledge specifically related to youth leadership has begun to emerge over the past two decades (Klau, Boyd, and Luckow 2006a; MacGregor 2005; Smith, Genry, and Ketring 2005). Insight (Turning the Leadership 2003, 2) notes that:

> Youth leadership . . . is fundamental to youth and community develop-
> ment, especially for low-income youth. . . . Equally important, communi-
> ties need to look to youth leadership strategies to ensure that institutions,
> policies, and practices are responsive to the needs of young people and
> their families, and that the principles of democracy are honored and up-
> held.

The youth-led movement in general has recognized the importance of youth leadership development. However, this field has viewed youth leadership through a broad lens, as this chapter highlights.

Certainly, no book about youth organizing can afford to ignore leadership development, and this chapter examines this phenomenon and the particular challenges or tensions inherent in carrying out a social-change agenda while concurrently developing new leadership that can sustain future campaigns as existing leaders age out. A focus on youth leadership development brings youth into a context that serves multiple goals, such as improvement in relationships with peers and adults and engagement in the life of an organization and community (Edelman et al. 2004; Ferber, Pittman, and Marshall 2002; Wheeler 2003).

Leadership development, in essence, is the anchor to hold the attention of youth, thereby enhancing their assets, providing growth experiences, and facilitating identity development. Youth-led community organizing, in turn, brings the critical dimension of shaping the interventions, particularly those involving marginalized youth in this society who have few opportunities to exercise leadership outside of gang membership. Klau, Boyd, and Luckow (2006b) raise important questions about youth leadership that pertain to youth-led community organizing: What exactly is youth leadership? Is it different from adult leadership? How does it differ from productive youth development? Can it be taught? If so, what are the best and worst practices? These and other questions will be addressed in this chapter.

Leadership

It is certainly appropriate to start this chapter with a definition of what a leader is. Using the term *leadership* evokes a wide range of responses, and this result can present a challenge in better understanding its meaning and key elements (Libby, Sedonaen, and Bliss 2006). The context in which leadership is exercised also determines how the word is defined. For example, Libby, Sedonaen, and Bliss (2006) make a conceptual distinction between internal and external youth leadership that is predicated on contextual forces shaping the definition and determining its actions. *Internal leadership* describes youth leadership within formal institutions, generally those institutions entrusted to serve youth; *external leadership* describes youth leadership outside of these youth organizations and in the community instead. The authors argue that both internal and external youth leadership must be fostered and supported.

There has been no conclusive empirical evidence to show that particular innate personal qualities and characteristics are associated with leadership (Stogdill 1974), and the trait approach for explaining leadership has not been viable for several decades. Theories that leadership behavior is a response to different situational variables and external stimuli also have been discounted for many years (Heifetz 1994). Today, leadership is conceptualized as a reciprocal relationship that exists between those who lead and those who follow (Rost 1991; Heifetz and Linsky 2002).

Research on reciprocal leader–follower relations has been conducted according to two distinct theoretical schools of thought. The transactional model (Hollander 1978) views relations between leaders and followers through the lens of exchange theory, with leaders exercising power via their ability to provide rewards or mete out punishment. On the other hand, the transformational model is based on inspiration, emotional appeals, and the leader's ability to communicate a compelling vision (Sashkin 1988; Berson et al. 2001; Haslam and Platow 2001).

Reciprocal relations vary depending on whether leaders hold formal positions and carry out official duties or they simply emerge, based on trust and respect developed with other group members (Gibb 1969). The social power earned by leaders may include social and political support, knowledge, reputation, legitimate power, and the power of personality (Tropman 1997; Zachary 2000). Leaders also differ as to the degree that they focus on accomplishing tasks or concern themselves with intra-group processes and the feelings of members (Bales 1970). While both instrumental and socioeconomic orientations are essential for successful group operations, few leaders are equally attentive or adept in both areas, presenting a balancing challenge for most community-based organizations (Hanson 1972; Burghardt 1979, 1982; Hardcastle, Wenocur, and Powers 1997; Johnson and Johnson 2003; Ephross and Vassil 2005).

The literature on community organizing identifies a variety of functions, roles, and tasks that grassroots leaders are likely to execute, including recruitment, facilitating meetings, problem solving, decision making, action research, strategic planning, direct-action tactics, public speaking, negotiation, internal conflict resolution, team building, media relations, lobbying, advocacy, administration, management, and outcome evaluation (Boehm and Staples 2005; Staples 2004b; R. Sen 2003; Bobo et al. 2001; Kahn 1994). Community organizing also tends to operate from the assumption that leadership abilities and skills can be developed through a combination of direct experience (informal) and formal training in methods and tools

(Aglooba-Segurno 1997; Hollister and Mehrotra 1999; Wheeler and Edle-beck 2006; Zachary 2000).

Kim and Sherman (2006) argue that, despite the impressive role youth played in the social-justice movements of the 1960s and 1970s, little attention was paid to recruiting and training a new cadre of youth leaders, which resulted in a generation gap that had critical implications for the remainder of the twentieth century. A number of explanations can be put forth to account for this oversight; however, conservative political forces succeeded in criminalizing young people (Elikann 1999). The application of super-predator labels to urban youth of color typifies how this political movement manifested itself.

The importance of leadership development in youth-led organizing is difficult to overemphasize, and careful thought and attention must be given to the social context in which this development is conducted (Martsudaira and Jefferson 2006). However, much also depends on how that leadership is defined. Soyun Park, of One Nation Enlightened (ONE), the Colorado Progressive Coalition, notes:

> There's no point in building all these leaders...and none of them can work together.... Sometimes to me leadership development almost does more damage than anything without the group dynamic, without making sure people can work together.... And I think when people don't do well in school or can't participate in society, it's not because they lack, or they've not heard...support for some innate characteristics they've grown up with—which is supporting each other and being part of a broader network. I mean, you don't hear much of that in school. (Leadership? 2003, 2)

Linden and Fertman (1998, 17) provide a definition of *leader* that is consistent with the reciprocal model, yet goes beyond conventional characterizations of this term and has tremendous implications for how youth-led community organizing is conceptualized. They define leaders as:

> [I]ndividuals (both adults and adolescents) who think for themselves, communicate their thoughts and feelings to others, and help others understand and act on their own beliefs; they influence others in an ethical and socially responsible way. For many, leadership is best described as a physical sensation: a need to share ideas, energy, and creativity, and not let personal insecurities be an obstacle. Being a leader means trusting one's instincts, both when doing leadership tasks and being a leader.

Linden and Fertman's definition is the basis for their model, which includes both transactional and transformational leadership. Their model also broadens the concept of leadership to be more inclusive and situational—namely, that leaders can emerge and withdraw depending on needs that are expressed by an action group. A conventional definition of *leadership* would place a leader in that position at all times, regardless of the group's expressed needs. Transactional leadership stresses particular competencies and sources of power that come with *assuming* a leadership role. Transformational leadership entails being the leader one *already* is. The former emphasizes the leader's use of compliance approaches to motivate others to participate based on instrumental considerations. The latter highlights the leader's ability to cultivate member ownership through problem solving and decision making, as well as focusing members' attention on desired outcomes. Linden and Fertman (1998) note that transformational leadership stresses participation and contributions of others while transactional leadership values problem and solution identification.

Various Manifestations of Leadership in Youth-Led/Youth Development

The concept of leadership receives a tremendous amount of attention in society, which is not restricted to a particular age group, although youth generally seem to be missing when the term is used unless the reference is to gang leaders. For example, the "ability to exercise leadership" is a common description used when judging the effectiveness of an individual as a leader, and it is not unusual to find this phrase in performance evaluations. However, it would be a serious mistake to think that leadership is defined similarly across all sectors of this society. Clearly, the concept is highly influenced by socioeconomic class, gender, race, ethnicity, age, social situation, and a number of other factors.

Golombek (2002) notes that commonly accepted visions of leadership are invariably based on research conducted on adults—not unlike research on empowerment, for example. Certainly a nonconventional vision of leadership such as Linden and Fertman's model greatly influences how leadership is viewed and encouraged within youth-led community organizing. The field of youth organizing needs to emphasize three critical elements of leadership: (1) knowledge and awareness, (2) community and collective identity, and (3) shared visions (Beyond Base 2004).

One youth organizer articulated the role of leadership in youth-led community organizing quite well (Transformative Leadership 2004, 22):

We have faith. More importantly, we have a sense of urgency. Special opportunities for reinventing and restoring principled, democratic leadership that is truly reflective of our racial, economic, and experiential diversity lie in the work of this generation. Given the need and the promise, investing in these youth and the different leadership paradigm they aim to uphold is a must.

This perspective, which defines leadership in a democratic and inclusive manner, appeals to youth-led community organizing because it stresses the importance of all participants having opportunities to exercise leadership. This perspective also builds on most visions of youth development programs.

The very nature of leadership within youth-led community organizing campaigns necessitates a broad base of support and participation by members to sustain a social-change agenda. This organizing approach seeks to expand the number of leaders or potential leaders who can set the stage for future, even more ambitious social-change efforts. Leadership is not viewed as an exclusive category, static and monolithic; rather, from the youth-led organizing perspective, all youth are considered leaders (Linden and Fertman 1998).

Youth leadership involves multiple roles and tasks, and it must take into account situational (local) factors. Therefore, no one individual should be expected to fulfill all of the functions. Situations dictate different roles; leadership is viewed as dynamic and subject to the expectations of particular strategies and tasks. Further, given the relatively narrow age range of youth-group members, leaders age out at a more rapid pace than is typically seen in adult organizations. Yet some skills may take years to learn; and often by the time they are mastered, the youth are older and are moving on to other stages of their lives, such as to college or into full-time employment. This presents a challenge for the youth-organizing field: should the focus be on developing leadership skills that meet immediate organizational and campaign needs, or should it be in the development of skills that will manifest themselves well after youth age out of youth-led organizing?

Preparation to assume leadership falls within the responsibility of all youth who participate (Beyond Base 2004). Beyond promoting specific skills, leadership development also entails gaining the ability to critically analyze the inequitable distribution of wealth and power in society, knowledge of the dynamics of oppression, and understanding of collective action as a means to bring about social change. Freire's concept of "conscientization" (1973) best captures the process by which youth leaders actively reflect on their personal experiences, recognize experiences shared by other youth, develop a critique of systematic oppression, and prepare to engage in collective action to challenge and change the circumstances of their lives. Effective youth leaders develop an increased critical consciousness and an enhanced capacity for strategic analysis.

The process of learning how to be a leader and assuming a leadership role can be very complicated and depend on the interplay of numerous factors (Transformative Leadership 2004, 2): "Those who never identified as leaders become immersed in the larger purpose of their work, and suddenly realize that they have become a leader, as a consequence and necessity, not as an end goal." The rewards of leadership far outweigh its challenges and complications in the youth-led field (Kress 2006; MacNeil and McClean 2006).

Tensions and Youth Leadership

Life would be too simple if we could all—practitioner, academic, and youth participants—view the youth-led organizing field and not encounter dilemmas, tensions, and debates. In fact, we would argue that a field without any tension is a field that is irrelevant. *Tensions*, if you wish, provide valuable energy for expansion of a field.

Klau, Boyd, and Luckow (2006b), in examining the field of youth leadership with direct applicability to youth-led community organizing, identify seven core themes that are shaping current discourse and debate: (1) the importance of social justice to the discussion on youth leadership; (2) the differences between inside and outside leadership; (3) leadership as a position of authority versus leadership as an activity for everyone; (4) everyone as a leader versus only a select few serving as leaders; (5) youth as future leaders versus youth as current leaders; (6) the challenges inherent in a youth–adult partnership in leadership education; and (7) clarity and alignment in youth leadership education.

We are certain that these seven themes do not hold any surprises for the well-initiated in this field of youth-led community organizing. Mind you, this is not to say that a comparable list of themes cannot be generated for adult organizing. However, youth bring particular circumstances that highlight the importance of leadership opportunities and support at that particular stage of life. The tensions described earlier in this section take on added significance because of the nature of the work youth-led organizers do. Social action invariably involves activities that cause tension for both the youth and adults involved; this tension adds a dimension to leadership because of the immediacy of a campaign.

Characteristics of Effective Youth Community Leaders

As previously stated, hundreds of research studies have failed to demonstrate the existence of inherent traits for good leadership. Ultimately, leadership is a reciprocal relationship between leaders and their followers; and effective leaders must have the ability to influence and inspire others in a variety of situations. That said, the following characteristics have been identified as important for successful youth leadership. Most, if not all, of these qualities and attributes can be learned and developed through direct experience, mentoring, popular education, consciousness raising, observation, dialogue, reflection, reading, the arts, workshops, conferences, and structured leadership training programs.

Patience

Youth often have a strong desire for immediate gratification, and this is quite natural and to be expected. The energy associated with this desire for immediate gratification adds a dimension to social change that must never be lost in youth-led community organizing. Indeed, this "lack of tolerance," so to speak, can be a driving force in social-action campaigns. However, it also introduces a factor that must be addressed and has both short- and long-term consequences for youth organizers.

A recruiter may look for potential youth leaders who possess patience and a long-term perspective. According to Weiss (2003, 114), "[s]ometimes with young folks, they believe change happens overnight. They get bored. They have trouble realizing the necessity of long-term campaigns." Certainly, patience can be learned, and Freire's (1990) conceptualization of "impatient patience" is particularly relevant and appropriate for many youth leaders. Acquisition of patience helps youth organizers appreciate how time can be turned into an asset. When there's insufficient time to plan and carry out a strategy, rather than the situation being viewed negatively, the limited time can be seen positively as a way for youth to focus and concentrate their energies and other resources.

Open-mindedness

Youth workers must be able and willing to work with emerging leaders to give them guidance in recognizing the bigger picture: raising critical consciousness. It may be unrealistic to expect many youth to already possess a broad perspective on societal issues and to understand their interrelatedness. However, a prerequisite for selecting youth leaders may be their ability to see beyond their immediate problems and to show a willingness to expand their horizons. Open-mindedness is a quality that helps youth organizers expand their visions of self-interest to embrace the community at large.

Also, as noted by Clayborne (Polk and Clayborne 2004), youth must be open-minded about trying new skills such as public speaking and grant writing. Personal development has to be a significant part of any work to change communities. If youth participate but do not benefit personally from this participation, then the goals and tasks of community organizing cannot be considered complete. Clayborne lays the groundwork for youth to enter into a learning contract that systematically builds on their assets but also identifies areas for their growth.

The quality of open-mindedness is multidimensional. Its presence is essential in youth-led community organizing because it not only serves the current cause of social change but also creates personal change. Youth ac-

quire new knowledge and skills, but in the process also assume an attitude that seeks to be inclusive of others and a willingness to venture into
uncharted territory to find new experiences that will benefit them in the
future.

Critical Thinking Skills

The ability to think critically and be able to grasp the seemingly disparate
ideas that connect to create a broader picture is an important asset in youth-
led community organizing. It is also an important quality in adults; however, in the case of youth, it takes on greater significance because of the
marginalized position they hold in this society.

Ginwright's (2003) identification of key topics, and how they relate to
creation of a critical consciousness, clearly has a place in youth-led community organizing. Critical thinking leads to further politicization, which in
turn helps stimulate engagement and action. Youth go through a process, or
take a journey, that invariably entails multiple steps or stages. In essence,
there are no shortcuts. Each youth goes through these stages at his or her
own pace, with some entering the field of youth organizing with a clear
understanding of how societal forces shape behavior and outcomes while
others bring a high degree of skepticism about individual versus society's
responsibility for community conditions.

Desire and Ability to Commit Time to a Cause

Youth must be more than passionate about an issue or cause in order to be
productive leaders and organizers. They also must be able to commit the
time necessary to act on their convictions, in the short and long run. These
two elements transfer to other social arenas in their lives. Since many of the
skills needed for organizing take time to develop, even if some youth initially possess a number of these characteristics, younger individuals will be
able to participate over a longer span of years and are more likely to see a
campaign through from beginning to end.

It is important to add that a commitment to bringing about change
should be rewarded—with funds, whenever possible. Merging commitment with career potential becomes critical when agendas for social and
economic justice are put forth by economically marginalized youth; few of
them are in a position to volunteer their time and effort. However, it is
critical also that a youth's commitment to social change not be supplanted
by a commitment to the paycheck.

There is always tension between commitment to a cause and commitment to earning a wage! One youth organizer stated this very well (Polk and
Clayborne 2004, 5):

One of the biggest risks was youth who would come in for the wrong reasons. They wanted a job or income. Not that it's wrong to want these things, but when money is your only agenda, you're not looking at the overall agenda and what you're supposed to be doing there or how significant it is to the overall product. The other risk was organizations not really expecting youth to do what we said they'd do. If you send youth into that type of environment you can expect negative outcomes.

The tension between making a commitment to the cause and needing a source of income highlights two important, conflicting motivations that must never be compromised in youth-led community organizing.

Anger at Social Injustice

The statement "It is not fair" has often been the rallying cry for efforts to address social and economic inequalities, and it is an idea that often resonates with youth regardless of age (O'Kane 2002). However, it is never sufficient to be aware of social injustice; this awareness and anger must translate into concrete and constructive action. But being able to ground this sense of unfairness is an important first step in creating a goal-focused youth organizer. When youth perceive and react to social injustice with anger and indignation, they set the foundation for action to occur, channeling that resentment into productive work (LISTEN, Inc. 2004; Pecukonis and Wenocur 1994). Youth activists deepen their sense of outrage as they gain direct experience through collective action. Charles (2005) notes that, in the case of African-American adolescents, a faith tradition of giving back to the community further channels this outrage into creative social change.

How the outrage gets expressed is determined by the context (time and place) within which it operates. As addressed in chapter 3, Chang (2003) notes how hip-hop activism reflects this ability for critical thinking and a willingness to get involved in purposeful change by providing space and opportunity for dialogue, in a fashion similar to how the civil rights and black power movements did in previous generations. Thus, hip-hop activism can be considered a natural expression of a post-civil rights generation's desire for social and economic justice. Today's hip-hop activism reflects a shift from the old-guard civil rights organization to present-day civic engagement (Kim and Sherman 2006). However, as noted earlier in this book, this may also be a source of tension.

Belief in Social Justice and the Ability to Effect Change

A fundamental belief in one's ability to create change and the vision that accompanies it are the building blocks for successful leadership in any social intervention, but particularly for social action, as in the following case

(Youth United for Change 2005, 12): "My teacher urged me to join. He knows I'm an outspoken person and I love justice," said Derrick Smith, a blunt and articulate tenth-grader at Olney High. Thus, beyond holding a strong passion for justice, youth must have a sense of individual and collective efficacy—a belief that their efforts can result in progressive social change.

A certain degree of resocialization must transpire to transform feelings of powerlessness or personal inefficacy into a desire for change and a belief in taking part in social action (Pecukonis and Wenocur 1994). This process can be painful, but it takes place within the context of organizational campaigns for social change. In fact, this process or stage of development occurs among most youth, so it becomes only a question of degree and is quite normalizing in youth-led community organizing. Youth who recognized and accept these stages will well serve themselves and any campaigns by developing a greater awareness and understanding of social change at individual and macro levels.

Questioning the Status Quo

A willingness to risk the consequences of questioning the status quo is a quality often found in community organizers and is not restricted to one age group. Yet there is an awareness that questioning, regardless of its legitimacy, is looked at differently if the questioning individual is an adult or a youth:

> Youth who excel as leaders among their peers, in street organizations or street economies, or youth who are seen by adults as troublemakers, often respond to youth organizing even as they remain skeptical of more traditional programs. Youth organizing capitalizes on their street smarts, entrepreneurial spirit, their questioning of authority, and legitimate frustration with things the way they are. (Open Society Institute 1997, 6)

Youth-led organizing is a vehicle for marginalized young people to act collectively with peers to challenge the policies and procedures of mainstream institutions that negatively impact their lives. When youth willing to question the status quo come into contact with other youth with a similar orientation, the personal change is transformative, placing this characteristic in a broader group context.

Ability to Work with Peers and Various Social Systems

Strong interpersonal skills are essential for effective leadership in all types of community organizing, including collective action that is youth-led. The most successful leaders are able to work with other activists as a team, embracing participatory democratic processes, pursuing common goals, and sharing responsibilities, as well as credit for organizational achievements (Staples 2004a). They also are able to navigate their way through different settings and institutions (Tolman and Pittman 2001).

Most organizational activities take place within the context of small groups, where emerging youth leaders develop and refine the interactive skills that are essential components of their leadership tool box. As with the characteristic of willingness to question the status quo, described above, working within a group or team whose members share this perspective helps youth organizers operate within a sociopolitical reality that has not existed in the home or school.

Willingness to Work with Adult Allies

The roles that adults play and their influence on the youth-led movement, including community organizing, invariably results in ambivalent feelings on the part of youth (Jennings et al. 2006). Because adults usually have authority and can considerably influence the lives of youth, they tend to be the prime target for most youth-led organizing efforts. However, it is necessary for youth leaders to be able to work productively with adults and not turn every instance of adultism into a confrontation.

Most youth leaders develop the capacity to work effectively with adults through direct experience in a variety of settings. This ability to work across age groups will serve them well, in both immediate campaigns and in the future, when they are adults themselves. For example, their ability as adults to work with youth and adults older than they are will open up great possibilities for intergenerational organizing campaigns that will yield tremendous benefits across communities. Further, as Halpern (2005) has found, youth, particularly those who are marginalized and live in the inner city, can benefit from positive relationships with adults.

Eagerness to Learn

Eagerness to learn is a quality necessary to any meaningful participation and is not restricted to the young or to youth-led community organizing. This quality manifests in many different ways among young people and also involves a different dimension—namely, the different learning styles of youth. Young people learn a wide variety of skills when they take on leadership roles in community organizing initiatives. As will be discussed in chapter 7, there are numerous ways that this quality can be assessed, particularly during the training phase.

Eccles and Gootman (2002, 299), in their comprehensive review of community programs to promote youth development, conclude that young people need to be provided with opportunities to gain a variety of experiences that will enable them to develop their maximum potential. However, according to Eccles and Gootman, this learning is not limited to academic subjects. Introducing multicultural activities into youth organizing will enhance learning, recruit potential organizers, and inform the at-large community (Checkoway 1998).

The Hazen Foundation, based in New York City, was established in 1915 and seeks to "assist young people, particularly minorities and those disadvantaged by poverty, to achieve their full potential as individuals and as active participants in a democratic society." In 2005, the Hazen Foundation made over $1.2 million in grants to community organizations and youth organizing groups.

A survey of Hazen-funded projects identified five categories of leadership competencies, ranked in order of highest gains: (1) relationship skills (conflict resolution, accountability, mutual support); (2) organizing ability (how to influence school or community issues); (3) communication (listening, public speaking, writing); (4) critical thinking (analytical and imaginative problem-solving); and (5) basic literacy (reading) (Scheie 2003). As the reader will no doubt realize, the ability to learn is integrally related to all of these leadership competencies. Learning, in essence, is a lifelong process, and youth leaders who can embrace this idea and convey an appreciation for learning to the whole group perform a public service that goes beyond an organizing campaign in the here and now!

Willingness to Take Calculated Risks

Community organizing often conjures up images of mass rallies, with participants being arrested. While youth-led organizing activities seldom lead to actual arrests, youth still must be prepared to take risks. In many instances they are challenging established systems, which have the capacity for strong negative reactions. Because of the limited rights youth have in this society, the possibilities for retribution cannot be minimized.

The experience recounted by one youth activist, cited in a California Tomorrow report, unfortunately is not uncommon (Cervone 2002, 13): "It was hard for us to go on campus to do our organizing because [the assistant principal] was always there giving us a hard time. . . . She'd give youth a hard time, calling them 'trouble makers.' Teachers would give us a hard time too." It is important to note, however, that youth who are overly interested in taking risks and engaging in conflict without serious deliberations represent a serious risk to any youth-led campaign, as with risk-taking adults in adult campaigns. The screening and training processes are excellent points at which to assess this propensity in youth and to address it.

Taking *calculated* risks does not guarantee no consequences for youth; in fact, taking calculated risks highlights the challenges associated with relationship-building models of organizing (Sherwood and Dressner 2004). Consequently, it is important for youth leaders to examine the possible consequences of their actions for members of the campaign and to establish a climate in which youths' fears about such consequences can be aired in a supportive atmosphere.

Willingness to Be a Mentor and to Mentor

Youth-led community organizing is an approach to social change that historically has not been taught in academic classrooms. Consequently, training in the field has almost exclusively been through a range of methods such as apprenticeship, advisement, and workshops, conveying the skills and knowledge necessary to effectively undertake community organizing. However, mentoring as a method stands out because of its emphasis on personal interaction and mutual trust.

There is no consensus on a definition of *mentoring*, even though the past twenty-five years have produced a prodigious amount of scholarship on the subject (Hardley 2004). Mentoring can be explained as a process through which knowledge, attitudes, and skills are imparted via a relationship between at least two individuals, one being a mentee and the other being the mentor. Although mentoring very often is specifically designed to impart a set of knowledge and skill goals, it also involves emotional and social elements. Although the definition of mentoring used in this book appears rather simple and straightforward, in reality mentoring is a multifaceted and complex process. Further, mentoring can transpire informally, without explicit expectations, or formally, with an explicit agreement that covers the nature and content of the process.

Hardley (2004) notes that mentoring must bring together critical elements to be effective, including a focus on the young person's needs; recognition that mentoring is essentially about relationships; and an emphasis on the close connection between mentoring and the wider community, whereby effective mentoring both develops and strengthens many levels of community partnerships. Hardley's (2004) assessment of effective mentoring makes this approach conducive to youth-led community organizing and other forms of youth-led interventions. The importance of mentoring, therefore, is such that it cannot and should not be separated from leadership development. The long-term sustainability of movements for social justice, and not just for civil rights and racial justice organizations, very much depends on effective leadership development among young people (Kim and Sherman 2006). The close relationship between mentoring and leadership development highlights the multifaceted way that leadership development can occur.

The field of youth development has addressed the role and importance of mentoring (Saito and Blyth 1995). As with the other concepts covered in this book, there is wide variation in definition and type. Rhodes, Grossman, and Roffman (2002), for example, have identified various approaches to mentoring, such as (1) school-based; (2) work-based; (3) agency-based; (4) religious-based; and (5) e-mentoring (online).

The goals associated with mentoring must not be limited to the inculcation of specific knowledge and skills—in this case, community organizing. Effective youth mentoring must embrace a broad set of goals that go beyond specific knowledge and skills acquisition. It must also address emotional, moral, spiritual, and physical elements that complement cognitive goals (Rhodes, Grossman, and Roffman 2002). Youth mentoring, in addition, is not restricted to one time or one place. In essence, youth mentoring in community organizing often takes place when interactions are happening. These events become teachable or mentoring moments, because they capture the excitement of the event and the time. They also introduce the importance of doing and learning at the same time, which is how most learning occurs. The process of critical consciousness, for example, gets highlighted during these interactions.

One final note on mentoring is in order, and it is the issue of whether to go with established leaders (who soon will age out) when the stakes are high or to give responsibility to untested emerging leaders. Mentoring is an ideal relationship to enhance the leadership skills of youth who show extraordinary potential for playing visible roles in youth-led community organizing. It allows for the transfer of critical knowledge (cognitive as well as emotional) from the mentor to the mentee. But mentoring relationships can prove quite labor-intensive, because every effort must be made to facilitate close contact between the parties. Strategic decisions must be made as to the amount of emphasis and resources to be spent on one or several youth leaders, and at what cost to other youth organizers. It is essentially a zero-sum decision, one that must never be made without serious deliberation because of its implications for an organization. It may be tempting, for example, to focus on an immediate campaign, with the perceived value of achieving significant results. To achieve these results, several youth leaders may be singled out for attention. However, from an organizational perspective, emphasizing the present may mean sacrificing the future. This dilemma is not restricted to a particular region of the country or type of social action.

There is little question that the field of youth-led community organizing, like its adult counterpart, cannot ignore the subject of leadership without realizing serious consequences. The field of youth-led organizing must contend with all of the benefits and detriments associated with embracing any definition and philosophy of leadership. The tension between immediate success and long-term greater good is inherent in any form of social action; however, it takes on greater significance in the field of youth organizing because of the inevitable aging out of its leadership.

Conclusion

This chapter has provided the reader with a broad perspective on youth leadership and has done this against the backdrop of youth development. The qualities that indicate good leadership potential outlined in this chapter should not be viewed from an either/or perspective. The proper perspective is that all youth have potential leadership qualities and it is just a question of degree as to who will serve the field best and will capitalize on youth assets in the process. Some readers may argue that leaders are born and not made. We subscribe to the theory that some may be born leaders, but most are made leaders through opportunity.

7

Recruitment, Chapter Screening, Preparation, and Support of Youth-Led Community Organizers

> Social change does not come easily, and involving young people won't make it easier. But it will make it better.
> —Wheeler, *Maximizing Opportunities for Young People* (2005)

The sustainability of youth-led organizing is tightly tied to the ability of sponsoring organizations and organizing leaders or facilitators to recruit, screen, train, and support young people in their roles as organizers. Failure to perform these roles adequately increases the likelihood that the goals of youth-led organizing either will not be met or will be carried out only partially. The success of a social intervention never rests on a single phase of the endeavor. All aspects must receive attention and resources. For example, it never is advisable to omit a particular stage for the sake of expediency or with the intention of dealing with it later, when time permits. While this observation does not mean that practitioners may not have their favorite phases, we contend that attention must be paid to all parts of a social intervention. Therefore, this chapter focuses on four essential areas that should be addressed when new youth community organizers are selected, developed, and sustained.

Although leadership in youth organizing has been discussed in chapter 6, this concept takes on dimensions additional to those associated with adults, especially since the role of leader-organizer (Staples 2004a) is typical in so many youth organizations. This model combines both leadership and organizing functions in the same individual, who usually holds a paid staff position. Therefore, the field of youth-led organizing embraces a definition of leadership that is multifaceted, transcends traditional views, and prepares young people to assume roles as community organizers, including recruiters, motivators, counselors, agitators, consolidators, facilitators, fundraisers, strategists, and tacticians. However, as with adults, most youth cannot be expected to discharge all of these duties with equal ability and enthusiasm. These roles must be performed adequately in order for a youth-led organizing campaign to achieve success. But how these responsibilities are balanced, who carries them out, and what supports need to be in place to do so vary according to local circumstances (Walker 2003).

There is a rich body of knowledge and set of skills to help individuals function effectively in the role of organizer. If a person does not possess the requisite information and expertise at the beginning of an organizing experience, she or he eventually must learn it, as is the case for any other fields of practice. The qualities that determine effective youth leaders, outlined in chapter 6, are the foundation upon which to develop the knowledge and skills necessary to be successful organizers in the youth-led field. Organizational resources must be allocated to assess the assets of potential young activists as well as their aspirations and needs. Then youth organizations must provide sufficient opportunities for these young activists to achieve personal growth and professional development.

The capacities and competencies of youth-led organizing often contribute to a leader's personal development as well, and even can shape ultimate career choices. Unfortunately, as noted by Mizrahi (1993), community organizing is not a well-known career choice for many potential organizers. This lack of awareness seriously limits the potential pool of applicants who seek this field as a career choice. In spite of this, community organizing is a viable career option that embraces a variety of job titles, educational qualifications, and functions (Mizrahi 1993).

The field of community organizing is not for everyone. As a career choice, it may be viable for only a select number of young people who become involved in youth-led projects. Nevertheless, even for those not interested in a long-term career in organizing, the skills and knowledge that are learned can be transferred to other occupations. Youth-led organizing as a form of civic participation can be especially fertile ground for those who eventually choose to work in other aspects of public service (Wheeler 2003).

The W.K. Kellogg Foundation (2000, 14), in a comprehensive assessment of the field, identified a series of strategies for recruiting, training, and supporting youth:

Understanding how young people will benefit the organization
Giving young people real, significant things to do and holding them accountable

Actively recruiting young people
Connecting directly with young people's experiences and concerns
Letting young people know what is expected of them
Letting young people know they are making a difference
Investing in training and ongoing support for young people for the
    long term.

This chapter addresses these recommendations and others that are intended to ensure that youth-led organizing gets the necessary support to carry out its vision of achieving social and economic justice. Two of the topics (recruitment and preparation) have received considerable attention when compared to another (screening). This reflects the great variability in screening methods that is a consequence of allowing local circumstances to dictate what is important for an organization. We believe there is considerably more literature on recruitment and preparation because there is less variability in the field.

Recruitment

The importance of effective recruitment to any form of social intervention should not be underestimated, and youth-led community organizing is no exception, especially because it is fueled by the power of numbers. Both the for-profit and not-for-profit worlds have come to realize the importance of effective recruitment strategies (Charles 2005; Cutler 2002). This intervention phase involves a wide variety of activities and competencies, as well as a clear vision of the qualities that young people must possess in order to become effective organizers. When recruitment specifically targets youth who essentially have disengaged from mainstream arenas such as school, structured recreational activities, employment, and even families, it takes on added challenges and reaps additional rewards (Besharov 1999; Kim and Sherman 2006).

One very experienced youth-organizing leader mentioned a different dimension of recruitment, one that can be found throughout the country (Youth Organizing 1998, 5): "A significant challenge for youth organizing is the fluidity of an inherently changing constituency. How do you build structures while recognizing that particular individuals might change from project to project or from year to year, so there is some sense of accountability about kids coming back?"

Murphy and Cunningham's (2003, 82) perspective on recruitment fits well with youth-led community organizing:

Serious recruitment takes time, sincerity, respect, good listening, and patience as well as discrete care to ensure diversity of the membership. The organizer looks for a latent receptivity in each person being recruited and seeks to provide an "appropriate incentive" to motivate the person [youth] to accept an invitation offered.

These authors also stress, and we strongly concur, the importance of engendering and spreading a vision (mental picture) of a transformed community that embraces all within its boundaries.

Goals of Participation

Only recently has civic activism focused on themes of change for social and economic justice related to youth development, but in doing so, it has important implications for recruitment (Wheeler 2003, 195):

> While theory supports the merging of civic activism and youth development practice, the truth of the matter—capacity at the community level—is that they have tended to be ships passing in the night. Civic activists and youth development practitioners, with some notable exceptions, rarely collaborate or share strategies. Moreover, adults need to serve as youth development practitioners, while youth and young adults prefer to participate in civic activism.

Wheeler (2003) makes an important distinction—namely, that young people generally are more comfortable with an activist approach than are adults. Adults may well prefer a traditional view of development for both youth and community. As a result, youth-led community organizing has a distinct advantage in recruiting marginalized urban youth over more conventional youth-development programs that stress individual change at the expense of community capacity enhancement.

LISTEN, Inc. (2003) raises a number of key elements that aid in the conceptualization and implementation of targeted recruitment strategies that benefit disenfranchised youth by connecting their public and private lives. For example, youth organizing allows young people to find companionship, structure their lives, and discover a critical framework for analyzing and understanding their world, as well as developing collective power in the process.

The recruitment phase should be considered both strategic in nature and labor-intensive in effort. Effective recruitment, as any experienced practitioner would agree, is never a mystery. It necessitates a multi-prong campaign that gets the right message out in compelling language to the target population with the proper personnel carrying out the effort. Although youth-led organizing projects use various methods to achieve this aim, good recruitment invariably involves person-to-person contacts with young people and possibly their families. Face-to-face interactions are particularly necessary during the development of a new program or initiative, as are efforts to reach newcomer communities, when personal contact is necessary to obtain buy-in from parents. However, the recruitment of youth organizers does not have to be exclusively carried out within the neighborhood or in the institutions that typically serve the community, such as schools. For example, Youth Force actively recruits in juvenile detention centers (Alexander 2001).

Local circumstances or local context exerts a tremendous influence on recruitment and development strategies, as in the case of Youth United for Community Action (YUCA):

> YUCA discovered that many membership recruitment and development strategies work only for a particular context, community and constituency. In Los Angeles, for instance, offering in-house academic and tutoring support are effective, as few services are available to supplement an under-resourced, overcrowded public school system. Lee notes, however, that the strategy is not relevant for East Palo Alto, where students are bused to more affluent neighboring cities with relatively well-financed schools and a nearby university supplies a plethora of tutoring programs. (Weiss 2003, 83)

Pancer (2001) notes that youth participation and engagement is best conceptualized in three distinct stages, with each phase presenting a unique set of rewards and challenges for an organization:

1. The initiation stage (recruitment and exploration), characterized by a set of youth expectations and activities that result in youth exploring the benefits of participation.
2. The sustainment stage, characterized by an extended period of time during which youth actively participate after the initial experimentation stage.
3. The post-termination phase, which attempts to keep youth involved after their contract period of participation is completed.

Clearly, each of these phases is critical and necessitates staff with different skills and varied activities to ensure accomplishment of the goals. Each stage also involves different time periods and requires development of particular resources. These phases, of course, are influenced by local circumstances and the organization's history of sponsoring youth organizing programs.

Challenges

To say that the initial or recruitment phase simply takes care of itself would be a serious mistake on the part of the organization sponsoring the activity. Recruitment in youth-led organizing is equal in importance to its adult counterpart; however, it brings challenges and rewards usually not associated with adult-led campaigns. Some in the field would argue that this phase is the most critical because it ultimately decides who will receive valuable organizational resources and who will not. Also, if recruitment brings in candidates who do not have the potential to assume effective organizing roles in social action campaigns, then turnover will be inevitable. A pattern will develop whereby greater resources are used up in the initial phases of organizing, creating a shortage of resources for equally important phases that follow. And this misallocation of resources will prevent the later phases from occurring in a deliberate and strategic manner.

Recruitment of youth organizers is a labor-intensive process, and this is to be expected regardless of the region of the country or whether the locale is urban or rural. One organizer gave the following advice:

> Visit local hangouts and places that youth go, good or bad (schools, parks, basketball courts, liquor stores), to talk about your program. Know what you're talking about. Don't dominate the conversation. Ask youth for their opinions, and listen. Be well prepared—bring flyers, brochures and signup sheets. Follow through. Send letters to every person you contact inviting them to a meeting. Call those who don't show up to let them know they were missed, and let them know about upcoming meetings and events. (Alexander 2001, 6)

Alexander's (2001) description of this multifaceted, interactive method of finding potential youth organizers certainly does not fit well with those who hope to recruit simply by putting up posters and sending letters to organizations that can feed youth to them. That approach may be successful if young people already are connected to organized groups, although we have our doubts if that is ever the case. However, this book focuses on youth who are disconnected, and in order to attract these individuals, recruitment must have an educational quality that can be offered only through personal discourse and all of the other elements associated with this type of activity. The relationship-building process continues through all of the other phases of youth-led organizing.

Methods

Staples (2004a) strongly suggests that an organizing committee be formed to lead and coordinate any systematic recruitment effort. An organizing committee (OC) is a working group (typically twelve to fifteen people) who provide direction and leadership for the general recruitment effort or organizing drive. The committee gives visible legitimization to the organizing effort, actively recruits new members, helps neutralize potential opposition, begins to define the first issues, and provides an initial leadership core that works together with the organizers to build the new grassroots community organization (GCO). It is critical for committee members to develop a true sense of loyalty to and feel ownership of the organization. They should have an ego investment in its success, actively promote the effort, and defend it if questioned or challenged by various opponents.

Once an organizing committee is in place, a variety of recruitment methods may be employed depending on the particular circumstances of the community. In addition to the types of street outreach that should be done wherever young people tend to congregate, as described by Alexander above, face-to-face recruitment may be carried out through knocking on doors, home visits, one-on-one meetings, house meetings, and talks to captive audiences—that is, gatherings where youth already are present (Staples 2004a). Presentations to such assemblies have the advantage of reaching a large number of potential participants with a minimum investment in time. However, the quality of such interactions usually is minimal, given both the limited degree of engagement and the brevity of the contact. Nevertheless, this problem is easily remedied by using sign-up sheets to secure the names of attendees interested in finding out more about the organizing effort. Follow-up recruitment then can take place through subsequent home visits or one-on-one meetings that provide an opportunity for in-depth conversation.

House meetings are small meetings (typically five to fifteen attendees) that may be held at someone's home or in some other familiar, accessible, and agreeable space where participants feel welcome and comfortable. These low-quantity meetings provide an opportunity for high-quality interactions to take place, since there is extensive discussion about the organizing initiative and an opportunity for those in attendance to ask questions and express their opinions. Getting people to the house meeting can involve street outreach, knocking on doors, captive-audience presentations, networking, electronic communications, word of mouth, invitations from organizing committee members, and other means. Further, house meetings provide an opportunity for training emerging leaders as well as serving as a forum for discussing and testing new ideas (Staples 2004b).

Focus of Recruitment

What types of young people tend to join youth organizing campaigns? Why should they join such a campaign? These certainly are fundamental questions, and the answers are as wide-ranging as there are social-change initiatives, as is noted by one evaluator (Murashige 2001, 12):

> When we interviewed the participants, the list of reasons they gave for checking out their organizations was long and varied. Some joined programs to escape the boredom of school or a particularly nasty teacher. Some had older siblings that had been involved before them. And still others were actively looking for something "political" to do, having been motivated by a teacher or adult earlier in their lives.

Youth who have a spark about them tend to be present at these programs. This profile is true, even for young people who may not be doing well academically and may feel trapped in their school or community by lack of viable options (Sherwood and Dressner 2004). One Boston youth organizer, when asked who joins and stays in youth organizing programs, noted (Sherwood and Dressner 2004, 53):

> The ones who are most likely to stay engaged over the long term are the ones who are the most needy. The ones who are having the hardest time in school are also the ones who have the most family problems. They see and understand opportunities that are there for them and take advantage of them. They have potential but have never been engaged in their schools. The bottom line in what we do is about power—how to achieve it and reach it and create it and shares it. The ones who come in feel powerless, and then understand that they can have power; it clicks for them.

This young Boston organizer touched on a host of instrumental, expressive, and informational needs that are met by participating in youth organizing. Clarity and an understanding of the factors that motivate young people to become engaged become very important during the screening, training, and support/mentoring phases of a youth-led organizing campaign. When youth feel good about their involvement, they spread the word and become key contributors to an organization's recruitment drive. The legitimacy that young people bring to this phase plays a crucial role in convincing others that becoming an activist can be a win-win situation for them, their families, and their community. Participation rates in grassroots community organizing do not differ significantly by age. According to Staples (2004a), it is a realistic goal to involve 10% of potential activists in most community organizing efforts.

And, mind you, most young people who participate in community organizing will not select this field as a career. Such an expectation is unrealistic for any age group, and it would be unfair to apply it to youth. A different perspective is in order: every youth who gets involved will benefit personally and also will become a more informed and active member of society. Thus, the engagement of young people in community organizing is a win–win proposition from society's perspective! Some youth not only will display a talent for this activity but also will develop a strong commitment to work that promotes social and economic justice. For them, this field represents an unlimited potential for involvement, particularly when they focus on marginalized groups in society.

Based on an extensive evaluation of the Youth Leadership for Development Initiative (YLDI) funded by the Ford Foundation (Wheeler 2003), research found that civic activism was a successful approach for recruiting and engaging young people who had disconnected from conventional youth-development programs. The chance to reflect on their lives, having space to focus on better understanding their culture, and realizing vocational and leadership opportunities all became attractive options conducive to participation. Youth-led organizing is one, highly visible choice that combines possibilities for personal growth with opportunities to achieve positive community change (Cutler 2002; Huber et al. 2003).

Wheeler (2003) and others are quick to point out that paying stipends or wages to young people for their participation is considered an important element in recruitment. Essentially, this practice "professionalizes" their roles in the group. It also helps organizations to hold youth organizers accountable for their actions in a fashion similar to how adult staff members are answerable for their organizational functions. Although some in the field would argue that paying young people to participate effectively enables the sponsoring organizations to control their actions, the benefits of payment far outweigh the potential downside from a youth and community capacity enhancement perspective.

The youth development field has been quick to recognize the potential role that communications technology (see chapter 8) can play in recruiting young people while also providing competencies that can transfer to school and career arenas (Delgado 2002). Beyond its actual use as a recruitment mechanism, communications technology can be an attractive inducement for engagement. For example, young people may be drawn to an organization for its opportunity to use and learn technologies that may not be readily available in school or at home.

Ultimately, most organizers, regardless of age, agree that addressing the salient issues for youth is the best recruitment strategy (Staples 2004a). What makes a good organizing issue? Good issues build organizations by attracting participants. They must appeal intensely to the self-interests of a significant number of people, and in order to do so, they need to meet several criteria.

Perhaps the best test of a self-interest issue was established by Saul Alinsky (1971), who argued that the issue must be *immediate* enough for people to care deeply, *specific* enough for them to grasp, and *winnable* or realistic enough for them to take the time to get involved. To the extent that an issue can meet these criteria, it will have a strong *self-interest* draw with the potential to attract large numbers of people. The most compelling issues will have wide *breadth* of appeal while also engendering a significant degree of *depth* of interest and emotional intensity. Therefore, it is crucial that issues be framed or cut in a manner that maximizes their attraction.

It is necessary to create multiple points of entry into an organization in order to attract young people with different interests, talents, and backgrounds (Beyond Base 2004). Successful organizing campaigns need a team of organizers with complementary talents, interests, and abilities. Of course, maintaining this team balance requires that special attention be paid to recruitment. Given the fact that turnover is inevitable in any organizing effort, *especially* in youth organizing where activists age out on a regular basis, recruitment should be carried out almost as a full-time organizational activity to maintain the requisite flow of potential youth organizers to fulfill the multiple roles associated with social action.

Screening

Screening, like recruitment, necessitates that sponsoring organizations take a broad approach to determining who should play a role in youth organizing and what that role ideally should be. The primary functions of a screening phase are to ensure that organizations select youth candidates who best meet organizational needs and to highlight the candidates' strengths and areas for improvement. How these functions get assessed varies widely depending on local circumstances (organizational and community).

Variability is certainly the name of the game in youth-led community organizing. However, as London and Young (2003) note, certain considerations, such as heavy reliance on written applications or formal interviews, must be taken into account regardless of local variability. These methods can effectively screen out potential participants because of past negative experiences with such formal mechanisms. Further, reliance on a minimum grade point average can be a barrier: using grades as a criterion may effectively eliminate good leaders who have not done well in school for a variety of very good reasons. As a result, rigid screening criteria are never advisable. Flexibility, however, requires that those who do the screening have clear ideas about who is it that they seek to involve in their campaigns. Different types of campaigns may require different youth competencies. The screening function is just as important as the recruitment one because it sets the stage for preparation. Lack of clarity in this phase makes the preparation phase all that more difficult.

Screening is best viewed as consisting of nine categories, depending on the goals of the group: (1) youth goals and motivation; (2) emotional maturity; (3) time and geographical availability constraints; (4) potential contribution to the campaign; (5) interpersonal and relational skills; (6) social-demographic profile to balance the organizing team; (7) time commitments and length of participation; (8) leadership potential; and (9) age and length of time before aging out of a youth role. The weight placed on any of these categories will vary according to organizational and local circumstances. Nevertheless, all of these categories must be taken into account during the screening process, in addition to other possible considerations unique to the sponsoring organization.

There certainly is no model for screening youth organizers that enjoys universal acceptance. Generally, the screening process consists of three stages. The initial stage attempts to assess the candidate's experiences, expectations or goals, assets, and needs. The second stage usually involves a group interview consisting of youth members of the organization and it provides an in-depth assessment and insight into the candidate's group-relationship skills. This meeting can involve multiple candidates; it is not uncommon to have about one-third of the group members being potential recruits, with the remainder consisting of ongoing members. Youth interpersonal skills in a group context are very important because they are so much a part of any group effort during training, as well as in the field, carrying out organizing projects. The third and final stage may take anywhere from 10 to 15 minutes, with the major emphasis usually on a group interview, although in some cases the process may be one-on-one. An individual interview is usually in order as a means of answering questions that were raised in the group interview, as well as giving the potential new member an opportunity to clarify points that he or she did not feel comfortable raising in the group context.

Preparation

It is artificial to view each of the stages described in this chapter as isolated from one another (Wilson et al. 2006). One stage influences the other, and this interactive effect continues throughout the organizing process (Carlson 2006; Wang 2006). LISTEN, Inc. (2003) highlights this important point when examining the role of communication skills in the recruitment process through outreach and recruitment. In their view, young people can develop their communication skills through one-to-one interactions, peer-to-peer outreach through social and family networks, schools, and other institutions, and the use of arts and cultural events, such as hip-hop shows and youth festivals, open community forums and events, and community tours and service-learning projects.

Content

A commitment to social and economic justice as a guiding philosophy and set of values helps young people develop a politicized sense of their world and the issues that impinge on their lives. Nevertheless, it is important for youth activists to understand how other groups beyond the young are oppressed in this society as well and are systematically deprived of their rights and opportunities to contribute to the general welfare of all.

Although the following comments by Wheeler (2003, 496) relate to youth development, they also are relevant to youth-led community organizing:

> Presenting these young people with opportunities to express how society has thwarted their development often helps them to move forward in positive ways. Dealing with these difficult topics of gender, class, sexuality, and race has major implications for the content of youth development programs, the method of program delivery, staff training and

development, and the creation of a safe environment that encourages all
youth to act on and explore their own truths.

This journey of self-discovery has been labeled in a variety of ways, with
identity support having the greatest currency in the organizing field.

The mere mention of social and economic justice among young people
elicits responses addressing adultism, sexism, racism, and classism. However, other issues such as homophobia, ableism, body image, xenophobia,
anti-Semitism, and intolerance of other religious groups may not be raised
as frequently or with such intense emotional reactions. Some would argue
that until youth are able to confront all forms of oppression, the youth-led
movement cannot progress and become a force for progressive change in
this society.

Undoubtedly, knowledge of other forms of oppression surely will emerge,
offering a sad commentary on the lives of youth who are marginalized
along ethnic and racial lines—that is, those with minimal knowledge of their
own cultural history may need to be educated in that history before they are
in a position to appreciate the cultures of others. This content can be delivered in highly creative ways, including music, art, storytelling, and oral
history projects. Various methods also facilitate the integration of this material throughout the experiences with youth-led organizing.

Youth organizers being prepared to engage in collective action must be
exposed to an entire range of social and economic issues. This obligation
places a tremendous onus on the facilitator and group. Journeys of experience such as these invariably bring tensions and pain to group members
because any process of discovery often leads to an in-depth exploration of
subjugation, from the perspectives of both the oppressor and the oppressed.
For example, the latter exposes prejudices that we may or may not be
cognizant of (Martinez 1996).

Content related to sexually marginalized youth also must be included in
any training program. An inclusive and affirming climate in youth-led organizing, by definition, cannot be limited to socioeconomic class, race or
ethnicity, and gender, although these are critical factors in the lives of urban
youth of color. It also is extremely important that gay, lesbian, bisexual,
transgendered, and questioning youth find a home in these social-change
efforts. Youth Solidarity Summer (YSS) is a fine example of this situation:

> I think in YSS we definitely prioritize the space as safe as possible for
> queer people. I think that we're lucky to be able to do that, since it's a
> space that we define and it's not in a community. It's easier to kind of set
> these ground rules and have this kind of discussion. Also there are a lot of
> queer people in our organizing collective, and I think that it's good in the
> sense that it's changed the way in which we've dealt with sexuality and
> the idea of queerness.... There are a lot of people without any support
> network and one thing that YSS at least tries to do is connect them with
> South Asian queer movements. (Malick and Ahmad 2001, 7)

Failure to conceptualize oppression as including these young people means that an important opportunity has been missed to give voice to marginalized youth, and the result is that these groups have to create their own campaigns rather than join existing ones. When a separate youth network is necessary, this signals the broader community that the minority group's voice is not important in the creation of a just and equitable society. Consequently, training must include content related to sexual marginalization and must raise the consciousness of youth about how oppression divides groups with common concerns.

Needless to say, such content never should be relegated to a unit of training that, once addressed, is not revisited. Instead, it warrants a prominent place, as well as an ongoing and highly integrative presence throughout the organizing experience. The problem of sexual marginalization is so important that it necessitates its own unit in addition to its infusion throughout the preparation process. However, this does not mean that youth organizers must undertake a broad-based campaign to address every form of oppression; young people can still focus on one or a couple of these forms of injustice. This selection of a focus, nevertheless, should be made within an analytical framework that examines the interaction of multiple forms of oppression. Awareness of the complexity and dynamics of these interrelationships is an important lesson for youth and adult organizers alike.

Social-change organizing efforts can assume a wide variety of approaches, such as direct action and civil disobedience, issuing of publications and media production, lobbying, boycotts, and research (Weiss 2003). A broad and multifaceted orientation for community organizing necessitates that different strategies be discussed in training sessions and that the roles for youth participants be clearly identified. The following are typical subjects to be covered in a training program. Their applicability undoubtedly will vary across regions and because of local circumstances, and this listing of topics is in no particular order of importance:

Working with the media	Solving problems
Building relationships	Resolving conflicts
Identifying and researching community issues	Analyzing political situations
	Conducting a force field analysis
Building recruitment	Developing strategies and action plans
Using communication technology	
Working across cultures	Conducting direct-action tactics
Working with adult allies	Developing negotiating skills
Developing public speaking and other communication skills	Expanding group skills
	Evaluating leadership
Producing newsletters and videos	Chairing and facilitating meetings
	Handling success and failure
Performing in street theater productions	Knowing when to seek help and guidance

Identifying personal and community assets

Developing personal goals and
portfolios

Working with local community-
based organizations

Maintaining a balanced life

The list of content areas is a sampling of what typically may be covered when training youth organizers. However, not all young participants are expected to undergo training in each of these topics. Readers well may argue that this material is not restricted to youth and also applies to adults; nevertheless, these topics have particular meaning for youth because of the limited opportunities young people have to obtain such knowledge and skills in an affirming and empowering atmosphere.

Also note that training does not have to be "front-loaded"—that is, before a campaign starts. There is no denying that training offered during the initial stages provides an opportunity for project leadership to assess new activists. There also is the possibility that young people who do not share the group's expectations may be asked to leave during this phase. Nevertheless, youth training is best thought of as an ongoing activity, shaped by the ongoing experiences of the young participants. While a training agenda is necessary, it must be sufficiently flexible to take into account local events and unexpected circumstances.

Methods

The need for youth-friendly methods to engage and prepare young participants is well recognized in the field (Otis 2006). Although there certainly is no consensus on which tools and techniques are the most effective, there is general agreement on what they should *not* be. Every effort must be made to provide a training experience that is *qualitatively different* from what most young people encounter in school, where adults are in charge and adults determine what is essential. Furthermore, in school, high-stake tests that have little meaning to marginalized youth increasingly dictate the material that is considered essential.

Conventional methods for imparting knowledge usually demand that young people be passive recipients rather than active participants, although there certainly are exceptions to this practice (Eyler and Giles 1999). Ginwright (2003) addresses the potential benefits of education using a service learning approach, but also issues cautions that have implications for the training of youth organizers. However, this form of learning rarely integrates themes of social and economic justice or offers analysis of social problems in a community context. Further, outside of school, service learning in marginalized communities limits who can participate because of familial or work responsibilities (Murphy 1995).

It is strongly suggested that the training format be varied to help ensure youth engagement. Diversification of format and scheduling increases the receptivity of young people to learn the content (this is true when training adults, as well). Role plays, discussions, question-and-answer periods, videos, and field trips are some of the most common methods, although didactic sessions also may be employed when deemed necessary and the participants are receptive to this approach. One method found to be particularly attractive to young learners is hands-on immersion in and exposure to history through the use of visualization and role-play workshops; these exercises enable participants to have a visceral appreciation of social and economic issues (Wheeler 2003). In fact, Wheeler concluded that, though workshops require a high degree of emotional and physical safety within the group, they facilitate awareness of issues than more typically didactic approaches do not.

Collective solidarity also is fostered through group exercises and discussions at the same time as individual mentoring takes place. For example, team-building exercises are highly recommended because they not only encourage the development of group identity but also introduce fun into the training experience. Rewards that promote cooperation instead of competition help develop cohesion, bringing an added dimension to group activities.

Periodically, celebratory activities should be included to mark milestones in the training program; pizza parties and movies are common examples. These fun-filled occasions take on symbolic and substantive significance for marginalized youth, because typically their educational institutions do not see such celebrations as warranted. Additionally, a graduation ceremony of some kind should be held, and certificates of accomplishment be issued at the end of the first major training period. Sadly, such attestations of achievement may mark the first public recognition of success that these young participants have ever received. Families, friends, and stakeholders should be invited to these ceremonies, as well as the media.

Excellent training programs are well crafted, with tremendous attention to detail—especially to the characteristics and backgrounds of youth participants. No two groups are ever the same, and therefore no two trainings ever should be identical. Group dynamics must always be taken into account. For example, trainees with limited literacy skills should not be expected to participate in activities that require strong writing and reading skills. Training activities should be sufficiently flexible to take into account a number of such factors.

One training activity that sometimes is addressed implicitly or explicitly in organizations that sponsor youth-led organizing is what is commonly referred to as praxis, or critical reflection:

> Although reflection can feel indulgent in the face of this urgency [life and death], it is also important for strengthening your work. Have the courage and the foresight to make time for reflection. Reflection processes create space . . . to step back and critically examine your work. (Youth in Focus 2004, 5)

At first glance, praxis seems rather straightforward, a relatively easy activity for which to set aside time. However, in reality, this reflection can be a painful journey for young people (as well as adults). This is true because praxis forces the participants to tie emotions, history, and theory together in order to develop a composite picture of their own lives, as well as the life of the community in which they reside. When accomplished well, praxis represents a time for healing and for taking stock of individual and group accomplishments—and this can be very rewarding!

On a final note, it is imperative that youth-led organizing provide opportunities for promising young people to receive the proper training and a chance to work their way up the organizational ladder to high-level positions. One experienced youth organizer, Henry Fernandez, of the Open Society Institute, made this very point (Youth Organizing 1998, 10):

> While youth organizing seeks to be non-hierarchical, in good youth development programs youth can be pulled through the hierarchy in an individual development process so they can eventually have skills to be good managers. Hierarchy allows the program to set expectations for young people, so they can see where they are going. . . . I wonder if youth organizing groups should have the ability to build institutions which can focus on young people as they develop during different stages.

Structure

With any form of training, the structure and size of the group play an influential role in helping shape the training experience. Usually, a cohort size of approximately ten is ideal for most training sessions that place importance on the quality of interaction in the group. This limited number enables participating trainees to better understand the role and influence of group dynamics, and it also may approximate experiences that they will have during collective actions and events. Other structures for training exercises divide participants into two's or three's so that they can go into the community and undertake activities focused on identifying community issues and assets.

When activities require trainees to report back to the group, every effort should be made to ensure that each participant has an opportunity to do so. Some young people will show leadership qualities and want to report back whenever they have a chance. It is important that trainers rotate the group reporters in order to give each participant an opportunity to exercise listening, group facilitation, and public speaking skills.

Attendance at local, regional, and national conferences, although expensive, provides young activists with important opportunities both to learn and to share experiences with youth leaders and organizers outside of their immediate neighborhood. Wheeler (2003) recommends that activities be developed that encourage young people to make global connections through international exchanges, visits, and interactions. When finances are limited, the young people who attend local, national, and international conferences should be expected to assume training or facilitating roles upon their return. Leadership skills are developed through these experiences, and those who have the privilege of attending are placed in positions of increased power and additional responsibility.

Trainers/Facilitators

The role of trainer/facilitator is critical in any form of social intervention, and youth-led community organizing certainly is no exception (Wilson et al. 2006). The age, gender, sexual identity, experience, and other socio-demographic background factors of the trainer/facilitator also will play a role in his or her ultimate effectiveness. Ideally, the best trainer/facilitator is someone who is from the community and who has worked his or her way up through the ranks. The individual brings the legitimacy of expertise (educational/training and experiential) and is a role model for young people, even though he or she may not feel comfortable in that role. The less social-cultural distance between the trainer/facilitator and the group, the higher the likelihood that training will be successful.

It is best to conceptualize trainers as a team rather than as one person because there are so many different facets to training that it is unrealistic to expect a single individual to meet all of the group's needs. Some courses of instruction may lend themselves to teaching by one or two trainers, while others will necessitate more than two. The concept of a cadre has emerged in the literature, and this is generally a nucleus or core group of participants who stay with an organizing campaign over an extended time (Murphy and Cunningham 2003). Members of a cadre make excellent candidates to assume the roles of trainers in youth-led campaigns.

What are the qualities that make someone a successful trainer? There certainly is no magic package of traits. However, a successful youth organizer trainer is someone who: (1) has had extensive experience in the field and can share war stories; (2) is a great listener; (3) has excellent verbal and nonverbal communication skills; (4) feels comfortable with youth; (5) knows the community from an experiential perspective; and (6) has the knowledge and skill sets that can be tapped by youth.

Practitioners may argue that the above list of qualities makes the position difficult to fill, even for adult organizers. In truth, effective trainers and facilitators must be developed by sponsoring organizations. As noted in chapter 4, intermediary organizations often have the resources to conduct training for youth organizers at their own facilities or by sending staff out to local groups to provide instruction, consultation, and technical assistance. Although it always is ideal to have the expertise in house, this sometimes is not possible, particularly in the case of organizations that have been in existence for a short time or have limited resources. Under such circumstances, assistance from intermediaries is appropriate. However, regardless of where they are situated, ineffective trainers and facilitators can cause a great deal of damage to any youth-led campaign; this role cannot be compromised without increasing the likelihood of failure.

Support

The role of ongoing support once a participant becomes part of an organization and engages in social action has received a fair amount of attention because of its critical importance (Walker 2003). Ongoing support also provides campaign leaders with opportunities to help youth reflect on their experiences, learning in the process. Ongoing support for youth organizers goes far beyond providing technical assistance. It also encompasses help with the pain that young people feel as they gain a perspective on the history of oppression that they have experienced (James 2005). In more extreme situations, a referral to outside help may be in order.

LISTEN, Inc. (2003, 13) specifically identifies these types of support when facilitating the participation of marginalized young people:

> In addition to political development, youth organizers are increasingly assuming responsibility for supporting young people through the stresses of daily life. Youth organizing groups often work with youth who are at risk of incarceration, in danger of dropping out of school, or are disconnected from family. Managing the diverse and sometimes life-threatening needs of these young people can be overwhelming. Oftentimes, youth organizing groups establish partnerships with existing social service agencies in order to refer young people for formal intervention such as health services, literacy, and tutoring. In the absence of such partnerships, many youth organizing groups find the lack of resources and expertise within their organization—or within the community at large—an obstacle to maintaining youth participation.

As a result, finding the right source for potential counseling support is of critical importance before young activists even start a new project. As noted by LISTEN, Inc. (2003), academic support also must be available whenever tutoring or educational guidance is offered; and this feature must be fully integrated if these efforts hope to be sustained. In essence, successful youth organizing depends on taking a holistic approach, identifying the assets and needs of young people. Failure to embrace a broad view of support is to deny the reality that many marginalized youth face in their daily struggles.

Peer-Group Supervision

Supervision in youth-led organizing provides leaders with an opportunity to impart practical knowledge, helps participants grow personally and professionally, and presents valuable information to project staff about how participants view their experience and how to enhance their learning. At times common themes emerge out of individual supervision/mentoring that can serve as a basis for peer discussions, further training, and guidance for future activities and organizing efforts.

Individual Supervision/Mentoring

Many labels are used to characterize the situation in which one person provides guidance and feedback to another. Typically, this relationship is referred to as *supervision*. However, the direct encounters that young people may have had with supervisors, along with the similar experiences of family and friends, will color their expectations and perceptions. If supervisory interactions are positive, then young people will enter this relationship with hope for a positive outcome. However, when previous encounters have been negative, such as associated with micro-management, supervisors/mentors will have additional work to do to prepare participants for new and more positive associations.

On a final note, it is highly advisable that organizations develop mechanisms for maintaining contact and support among alumni. The important work of attaining social and economic justice cannot necessarily be confined to immediate or ongoing organizing programs. It also takes place in other settings and may well be integrated into the fabric of life of former participants. The South Asian Youth Action (SAYA) has recognized this group and attempted to address the importance of connectedness. They use alumni reunions, for example, to facilitate the arduous process of achieving social change, providing a forum for reconnecting with those who have aged out of youth organizing and moved on to adult-led social-change efforts (Malick and Ahmad 2001).

Conclusion

Clearly, the preparatory stages examined in this chapter are critical to meeting the overall goals of youth-led initiatives. The reader can argue that these steps are labor-intensive and thus quite costly; however, any form of social intervention, particularly one that stresses civic participation on the part of marginalized youth, will be labor-intensive. This certainly is the case when that participation is oriented toward social change and possibly entails conflict!

Furthermore, one learns to expect the unexpected because, for many of these young participants, this organized activity may be their first formal involvement in civic life and offer a new experience playing an active role in shaping their own futures. The opportunity for youth to be proactive, rather than reactive, brings with it its rewards and challenges. If youth-led organizing is conceptualized as community capacity enhancement, then the financial costs and time involved in preparing young people for roles as civic activists who enhance community capacity are not excessive. Clearly, the long-term benefits result in empowered individuals who are willing and able to help empower their communities.

8

Crosscutting Theoretical and Practice Themes

> Social change does not come easy, and involv-
> ing young people doesn't make it easier. But it
> does make it better. It adds new depth and
> perception to the challenges and opportunities
> that face the community. It can result in a
> campaign that engages broad sectors of the
> community itself.
> —Innovation Center for Community and
>   Youth Development, *Creating Change* (2004)

Youth-led organizing takes place within a context as do all other forms of social practice. It can occur in a variety of settings, but most typically it is found in schools and communities. It addresses a multitude of issues and concerns as it attempts to bring about positive social change. Goals include capacity enhancement for both youth participants and the larger community (Williams 2003). However, regardless of the particular youth-led organizing focus, there are important similarities with other organizing campaigns. These crosscutting themes provide both practitioners and academics with a means for recognizing commonalities in the field of youth-led organizing across the nation, even though particular initiatives and projects are re-sponding to local concerns and issues.

Research Informing Crosscutting Themes

The discussion of crosscutting themes addressed in this chapter, as with the guiding principles addressed in chapter 4, was influenced by the authors' experiences and empirical research from the field. Findings from research studies, some similar to the ones cited in chapter 4 and others, helped us select these themes and shape them. As noted in chapter 4, the researchers drew upon findings from a variety of fields, most notably youth development, community organizing, and youth-led organizing. These sources, along with the themes we have identified, are as follows:

- Innovation Center's *Youth Leadership for Development Initiative* (2003) resulted in a wealth of qualitative and quantitative data about youth experiences and organizational challenges in the field (themes 1, 3–6, 8, and 13–15).
- The senior author's book on youth-led research, *Designs and Methods for Youth-Led Research* (Delgado 2006), raises a number of key issues regarding the youth-led field and the research that youth must be willing to undertake in leading community organizing efforts (themes 1, 3–8, and 10–15).
- The Carnegie's Young People Initiative's (Cutler 2002) research report *Taking the Initiative—Promoting Young People's Involvement in Public Decision Making in the USA,* based on findings from over forty youth programs across the country, focuses on a wide variety of youth civic-engagement manifestations (themes 1, 2, 4, 6, 8, and 12–15).
- Eccles and Gootman's (2002) book *Community Programs to Promote Youth Development* examines the field and research on facilitating and hindering factors in carrying out youth development-focused and inspired initiatives (themes 1, 3–6, 8, and 13–15).
- A report for the Edward W. Hazen Foundation (Scheie 2003) titled *Organizing for Youth Development and School Improvements* raised important issues and made recommendations for youth organizing involving education (themes 1–3, 5, 6, 8, 10–12, 14, and 15).
- Lerner and Benson's book (2003) *Developmental Assets and Asset-Building Communities* provides data on youth and community development (themes 1, 3–6, 9, 13, and 15).
- The Philanthropic Initiative for Racial Equity's multi-level study *Changing the Rules of the Game: Youth Development and Structural Racism* (Quiroz-Martinez, HoSang, and Villarosa 2004), based on sixteen youth development organizations, focuses on themes related to social justice in the field (themes 1–3, 5, 6, 8, and 11–15).
- The Movement Center has produced three reports that have direct applicability to youth-led community organizing. The first report

(James 2005), in *Bringing it Together: United Youth Organizing, Development and Services for Long-term Sustainability*, based on an analysis of six community organizing sponsoring organizations, provides important lessons for intergenerational and youth-led youth organizing (themes 1, 3, 6, 8, 9, and 11–15). The second report (Quioroz-Martinez, HoSang & Villarosa 2004) is *ReGeneration: Young People Shaping Environmental Justice* and it presents important lessons and themes related to youth organizing, intergenerational and youth-led from an environmental justice perspective (themes 1–6, 8, 11, 12, 14, and 15). The third and final report is *Making Space, Making Change: Profiles of Youth-Led and Youth-Driven Organizations* (Youth Wisdom Project 2004). It offers many critical lessons for maximizing youth leadership in organizations (themes 1–3, 5, 6, and 10–15).

Crosscutting Themes

We have identified fifteen crosscutting themes and devoted this chapter to examining each in turn. These fifteen themes fall into four categories: (1) purpose of organizing; (2) recruitment and support; (3) group structure; and (4) youth and adult roles. Within these four categories, there are several subcategories, as follows:

1. *Purpose of organizing*: empowerment through inclusive democratic participation and ongoing recruitment; multifaceted organizing goals; and positive social change for individuals and community.
2. *Recruitment and support*: importance of planning; leadership development as a central feature; learning; importance of fun; funding of project; family as a facilitating and hindering force; role and importance of communication and information technology in youth-led organizing.
3. *Group structure*: autonomous, locally based, unaffiliated, streamlined structures; age-related issues shape target systems; youth culture shapes the organizing process.
4. *Youth and adult roles*: youth in decision-making roles; and adult roles in support.

These themes reflect some of the major advances made in youth-led organizing, as well as some of the challenges that remain. Several of these topics are covered in greater detail in this chapter, while others receive only a broad overview—not because of a lack of importance but because they have already been examined in other portions of this book.

Purpose of Organizing

1. Empowerment Through Inclusive Democratic Participation and Ongoing Recruitment

Young people are a relatively powerless group in our society, and the central goal of community organizing is collective empowerment for social change. The concept of empowerment, while overused and abused, is used in youth-led community organizing (Checkoway, Figueroa, and Richards-Schuster 2003; Young Wisdom Project 2004). Empowerment is sought at both the individual and collective levels—a critical point that is revisited in several of the themes that follow. And youth empowerment is consistent with the fundamental belief that young people are assets to their communities, with the potential of making significant contributions to bettering the lives of others (Checkoway, Figueroa, and Richards-Schuster 2003).

Community organizing generates power through its large numbers of participants, or people power. Indeed, the youth-led model emphasizes inclusiveness and participatory democracy, as examined in chapter 5. But the distinction between *participation* and *power* is germane here. It is insufficient to have a voice through simple participation; *power* implies the ability to bring about desired changes, even in the face of opposition. Organizing challenges the entrenched interests and the dominant elites, who can be expected to resist attempts to alter existing power relationships. Their responses may include cooptation, deceptive and diversionary counter-tactics, or outright repression (Ginwright 2006).

Youth-led organizing initiatives attempt to change and democratize institutional policies and procedures using the power of numbers; the capability of quickly mobilizing a large, energized, and activist base of constituents is a major strength of this form of social intervention. Therefore, recruitment of new participants is a high priority, and the methodology for doing this was discussed at some length in the previous chapter. Given that the membership constantly turns over as older youth age out and younger ones join, recruitment is an ongoing activity. Since youth-led organizing seldom uses a model whereby an overarching organization of pre-existing youth groups is formed, direct membership recruitment is most appropriate (Staples 2004a). Young participants are recruited on a one-by-one basis, through a variety of techniques including street outreach, knocking on doors, home visits, word of mouth, one-on-one meetings, house meetings, and presentations at other gatherings where significant numbers of youth are present.

2. Multifaceted Organizing Goals

Ideally, youth-led community organizing embraces multiple goals that are both short term and long term depending on their probability of success

(Charles 2005; Scheie 2003). And these goals are not just externally oriented but also include personal development. As with their adult-led counterparts, the success of youth organizing initiatives very much depends on how the issues are conceptualized and framed. As discussed in the previous chapter, good issues to organize around should meet all three criteria: (1) be specific; (2) be immediate; and (3) be winnable (Alinsky 1971; Staples 2004a); it does not suffice to meet just one or two of these criteria.

Being able to achieve the group's immediate ends will do wonders for young people who previously have not experienced significant success in their lives. When achievements are accomplished within a group context, positive feelings are intensified. The process that youth activists have undertaken to arrive at shared goals then takes on immense importance, because ultimately the group must own its common ends and those ends must have true meaning to their lives. Consistent with adult-led initiatives, the goals for youth-led organizing are unlikely to be embraced if imposed on the group by an external source.

Breaking long-term organizing goals into incremental mid- and short-term goals makes it possible to measure progress. This practice also helps prevent young activists from becoming overwhelmed by large issues, helps them maintain a sense of momentum as regular headway is recognized and recorded, and facilitates the necessary adjustments that have to be made along the way. Remember, social-action campaigns are best thought of as dynamic and flexible; unforeseen circumstances (both opportunities and barriers) can arise to alter goals as well as strategies. This is normal or typical, and the valuable lessons gleaned from this experience apply to life goals as well.

3. Positive Social Change for Individuals and Community

Positive social change must be considered from a multifaceted perspective to fully appreciate the ramifications of a change campaign. The simplest view of this focuses on the individual organizer and the goal of the campaign. However, a more encompassing view necessitates examination of the immediate circle (family, friends, and neighbors), as well as the unintended community changes. This broader and deeper analysis makes evaluation more challenging, but it likewise is more rewarding and empowering from a change perspective, and also is more consistent with the way youth-led community organizing should be envisioned (Simpson and Roehlkepartain 2003).

It would be tempting to focus on individual behavioral changes and the acquisition of personal competencies when considering youth organizers. Certainly, there is evidence of growth in positive attitudes and improved self-esteem in the youth development and youth-led literature (Charles 2005; Perry and Imperial 2001; Ramphele 2002). What makes youth-led

community organizing so different and powerful is that the field has conceptualized the importance of change at *both* the individual and the community levels. These two goals are not mutually exclusive! One of the more
serious criticisms of youth development has been its exclusive focus on
individual gain, rather than placing that advancement within a broader
context of valuing both individuals and their communities.

Recruitment and Support

4. Importance of Planning

It is relatively easy to think of community organizing as a method unto itself,
in similar fashion to management or planning and program development.
However, it would be foolish to believe that successful youth-led organizing
does not require good management and planning skills. True, management
and planning may be the backdrop rather than the foreground when community organizing efforts are underway; however, they still are part of the
picture! This section highlights the importance of careful planning for social-
action campaigns and explains how these skills can be transferred to other
youth-focused arenas.

There are at least six essential elements to planning: (1) a commitment to
do so; (2) time; (3) resources; (4) careful crafting of goals and objectives; (5)
implementation and contingency planning; and (6) evaluation. Each of these
elements brings with it a set of perspectives, rewards, challenges, and conflicts that must be acknowledged and addressed for youth-led community
organizing to succeed.

Murphy and Cunningham (2003, 154) highlight the importance of planning in organizational and community development: "Both organizational
planning and community planning require patience, flexibility, the ability
to meld disparate interests and ideas, persistence, hope and a positive outlook, and confidence that the job can get done. Both are grounded in maximum resident participation producing locally grown and rooted plans."
The authors' named qualities inherent in planning apply also to community
organizing, whether youth led or adult led. Also, these qualities bare striking similarities to the qualities of youth-led leadership that were identified
in chapter 6.

It should be noted that, for youth-led community organizing, the importance of planning is not restricted to social-action campaigns; it also is
necessary for strategic organizational planning. However, youth organizers
may not be familiar with a strategic planning process and the organizational
development terminology can be confusing and intimidating. Young people, as a result, can benefit from coaching or consultation from adults (Young
Wisdom Project 2004), but they must have a central role in carrying out this
type of planning.

5. Leadership Development as a Central Feature

Chapter 7 is devoted to leadership development while much of chapter 6 examines the roles for and recruitment of leader-organizers; this coverage indicates the importance of this concept in the youth-led organizing field. Indeed, as previously noted, both the youth development and overall youth-led fields give leadership development the highest priority. In both of these instances, however, the focus is on development of personal competencies and individual skills. Gambone and colleagues (2004) found that, when compared to youth development organizations, youth organizing agencies are characterized by youth having more meaningful experiences with leadership, decision making, and community involvement.

Youth-led organizing additionally places young people in decision-making roles, as noted in the previous crosscutting theme. However, it also requires that they develop other abilities and skills that enable them to function effectively in multiple leader and staff roles in a collective context, as discussed in chapters 6 and 7 (e.g., recruitment, facilitating meetings, problem solving, action research, strategic planning, direct action tactics, public speaking, negotiating, internal conflict resolution, team building, media relations, lobbying, advocacy, administration, management, evaluation).

It also entails development of critical thinking skills, as examined in multiple chapters of this book, as well as learning from veteran leaders and others who provide mentoring and role modeling. In fact, in the youth-led organizing field, consciousness raising to understand the causes and consequences of oppression often is given equal weight to skill development. And this political awareness is linked to collective action as a way to alter existing power relationships in pursuit of a social and economic justice agenda.

The fact that youth leaders age out at a rapid rate necessitates ongoing processes to develop replacement leadership without loss of organizational momentum and continuity. While qualities and characteristics such as patience, open-mindedness, interactive skills, commitment to social justice, questioning of the status quo, willingness to take risks, and ability to work with adult allies may be more or less present in some individuals before they become involved in a youth-led organizing project, these attributes can be developed and sharpened through training, direct experience, mentoring, coaching, consultation, technical assistance, observation, readings, films, street theater, conferences, role playing, and other methods and techniques. And the predominant democratic, inclusive ethos in youth-led organizing (Transformative Leadership 2004) is consistent with the notion that there are multiple forms of (and needs for) leadership that transcend any one particular function, personality, or skill set (Staples 2004a).

6. Learning

Emphasis on the opportunities to learn is a crosscutting theme not restricted to youth-led community organizing, and it should be an integral part of any social intervention, organizing or otherwise. Learning can be achieved in numerous innovative and participatory ways. Youth-led community organizing has managed to use many forms of informal education during the process of bringing about social change, and in a manner that is affirming, relevant, and fun. Social action campaigns, after all, are not just about bringing about change at the community and macro level; they also transform the lives of the individuals who participate. That is, young activists have profound learning experiences when they engage in social-action campaigns that challenge existing patterns of institutional power relationships.

It is essential never to lose sight of how important youth learning is during any process that emphasizes achieving goals for social change (Beyond Base 2004, 2):

> To do so, youth learn to hone their analytical skills through political education and analysis, research, reflection and evaluation. With the support of adult allies, they also develop skills through the overall development and functioning of organizations—making decisions, fundraising, facilitating meetings, recruiting members and other tasks to strengthen the institution. This experience trains young organizers to think critically, be unafraid to ask hard questions, and most importantly, apply these skills to achieve palpable change. One young person said he learned to be critical and analytical, but "not just to be critical, but to be critical so that we could do something about it."

The problem-solving skills that youth acquire in their organizing roles will serve them well later on. Furthermore, knowledge acquired regarding communication, relationship building, exercising power, and history can be of great use in academic pursuits. In short, young people learn a great deal about themselves that will become a basis for future decisions and actions. Unfortunately, the subject of learning has acquired a negative connotation for many marginalized youth in this country, and mere mention of the word can be off-putting for some. Nevertheless, learning must play an instrumentally explicit and implicit role in youth-led community organizing.

Finally, any initiative that places youth in leadership positions must take into account the time and resources needed to facilitate learning and reflection (Gambone et al. 2004). Gambone and colleagues cite the tension that is inevitable when goals for social change conflict with those for individual growth. Both are important for youth-led organizers, and attempting to balance the two is not easy. Youth leadership requires an even greater expenditure of time and resources; however, the long-term benefits make this expenditure of resources worthwhile.

7. Importance of Fun

What does fun have to do with social change? After all, social change is about addressing issues of oppression and their associated pain. However, to relegate fun to the margins of youth-led community organizing would be a serious mistake, for both the young participants and the sponsors of this form of social intervention. Fun-related activities and a fun-filled atmosphere contribute the balance youth organizers need in their lives. Fun easily can be equated with edginess and being cool (W.K. Kellogg Foundation 2000). These labels can go far in helping organizations recruit young people and attract badly needed funding.

McLaughlin (1993, 66) addresses this need for balance, also noting the important role adults play in this quest. "Enabling inner-city youth to find balance in their lives comes down to enabling trust in and positive involvement with adults. Leaders with fire in their belly are an ingredient essential in constructing the environments in which such trust can be nurtured and sustained." Adult organizers who have managed to keep that "fire in their belly" while balancing fun, learning, and personal and familial relationships are excellent direct and indirect role models for young activists, who otherwise might lose their sense of proportion and equilibrium. The Young Wisdom Project (2004) also identified the need for self-care and balance in the lives of youth organizers because young people face multiple life-defining issues and are making important decisions about their lives. It's not considered extraordinary for organizations to include self-care packages in their benefits for employees, including counseling, life planning support, alternative health care and massage, among other offerings.

There is universal acknowledgment in the youth-led/youth development literature that activities must provide meaning, learning, and fun in order to attract and engage young people (Delgado 2000). Cultural activities also can be a way to introduce fun into youth organizing while infusing important content. For instance, young people can express their ideas and frustrations in a "cultural space" that otherwise has brought them to the table in a more overtly political way (Weiss 2003).

It is possible to learn, produce results, and have an enjoyable time in the process. This multifaceted approach does not take away from the importance and seriousness of the work of achieving social and economic justice. No job will prove rewarding if it has no element of fun—and this observation takes on even greater significance when youth are involved. The manner in which fun is introduced and sustained can vary, of course, according to the methods and styles of the organizations involved. Nevertheless, the high stakes and emotionally charged nature of social-action campaigns require that organizers have a sense of humor and a broad perspective; they must be willing and able to laugh and enjoy the moment whenever possible.

8. Funding of Projects

As noted throughout this book, funding for youth-led community organizing projects is a crosscutting issue and a perpetual challenge, although
this field of youth practice slowly is taking center stage, with many funding
sources (Quiroz-Martinez, HoSang, and Villarosa 2004; Scheie 2003; W.K.
Kellogg Foundation 2000). In fact, it is rare not to have the subject of funding
addressed as a major challenge and recommendation in the field, as evidenced in the countless research studies cited in this book.

Lack of adequate funding for youth-led community organizing has far
reaching implications for both individual programs and the field in general, including (1) chronic staff shortages; (2) inability to take advantage of
the latest technology; (3) missed opportunities to learn from other youth
programs; and (4) short funding cycles (one to two years), combined with
increased expectations on producing measurable changes (W.K. Kellogg
Foundation 2000). These and the other challenges discussed below effectively limit the potential of this field to make the advances that normally
would be expected of such a dynamic and ever expanding field of practice.

The Young Wisdom Project (2004) comments on the difficulties that are
unique to fund-raising for youth organizing, since many young people do
not have fund-raising experiences, and potential donors may be skeptical
and mistrustful of young people's managing money. In addition, youth need
to understand what a fund-raising cycle is, what relationship development
with funders is, how to develop a fund-raising plan, and the importance of
employing different fund-raising strategies. Sources of funds for social interventions that challenge the established sociopolitical order as a central
goal often are limited. Not surprisingly, government—a prime sponsor of
youth programs—often is not a viable source of funds for youth-led community organizing. Furthermore, youth-led organizing programs can require more funding than conventional youth-orientated organizations because of their emphasis on learning and leadership development. Gambone
and colleagues (2004) found that youth organizing groups often have a low
staff-to-youth ratio. This ratio facilitates intensive staff work with a relatively
small cohort of youth, also making youth organizing programs less com-
petitive than conventional youth programs and more expensive to fund.

Sherman (2002, 27), in a rare in-depth analysis of funding challenges encountered by youth who lead community organizing campaigns, identified
five funding practices that undermine these activist endeavors and must be
systematically addressed by organizations that sponsor youth-led organizing:

1. Issuing specific funding as opposed to multi-issue, multifaceted
   funding.
2. [Showing a]n obsession with nonpolitical, bipartisan, 'beyond ideology' approaches to social change.

3. Failing to provide general support grants that allow for the building of organizational infrastructure as opposed to short-term projects and programs.
4. Failing to provide multiyear grants that allow for planning and program development; and
5. [Sponsoring] too many under-funded grass-roots nonprofits disconnected from one another and from a national political agenda.

Sherman's (2002) insightful assessment raises important theoretical, philosophical, and operational issues for the field of youth-led community organizing. When youth-led organizing initiatives totally or almost entirely depend on one funding source, invariably there are concerns about whether and how the funder might pressure organizers to tone down content strategies in favor of educational campaigns and collaborative efforts. Funding never is given without strings (Staples 2004a). The question is whether those strings are huge, like tugboat rope, or so small that they can be seen only in the right light, much as a spider's web.

The Applied Research Center (Weiss 2003) found that foundations are much more interested in funding youth development programs that emphasize individual-focused goals that do not challenge institutions or attempt to redress the balance of power, yet, of course, collective action to alter existing power relationships goes to the heart of youth-led community organizing initiatives. This finding substantiates those of Sherman (2002) and underscores the importance of securing financial resources for social and economic justice campaigns through creative funding initiatives that ensure the independence of these projects. In the late 1990s, no youth-led community organizing campaign in the country had an operating budget of more than $400,000, while at the same time many youth-development programs were working with multimillion dollar budgets (Youth Organizing 1998). One report identified this issue back in the late 1990s, and it persists today, although not to the same extent.

Even when a foundation is receptive to supporting a youth-led community organizing campaign, there still may be bias toward funding youth development because of the impressive numbers of young people who can be involved in the latter programs. Furthermore, in situations where youth are in leadership positions within the organizations, foundations may raise concerns about those organizations' ability to sustain that leadership (Youth Organizing 1998). Consequently, what is a central mission and goal in youth-led organizing becomes a limitation from the perspective of many funders. Organizations that sponsor youth-led campaigns often are left scrambling to find creative ways of minimizing these biases.

Funding resources that emphasize family (see next section) may be an innovative source of support for youth-led community organizing, as reported by Scheie (2003, 27):

A final area where Hazen might find allies is among funders of family concerns—particularly since Hazen finds ways to highlight how parents and other family elders contribute to youth development and engagement, and how youth organizing contributes to stronger families and more family-friendly communities. (Research shows that parents' values of social responsibility play an important role in whether young people participate in community affairs, for example.) Families are an issue receiving broad, mainstream support; if Hazen could influence even a small percentage of that field to support youth (or intergenerational) organizing, the influx of resources to youth organizing could be quite large.

Sherwood and Dressner (2004), in their study of fourteen youth organizing groups, reported on the potential of AmeriCorps volunteers to become involved in youth-led organizing initiatives. However, this program is not intended to support political organizing, thereby limiting how these volunteers can be deployed to youth-led organizing initiatives. Organizations from the broader community can assist youth-led organizing groups by providing supplies, transportation, space, volunteers, and other in-kind donations; and the process of obtaining such contributions is an important way for youth-led programs to maintain a community base of support. However, this source of funding is unpredictable and labor-intensive, making it difficult to plan major social-change initiatives when youth-led organizing depends on whether these resources can be acquired.

YouthAction (1998) specifically recommends that grants be given directly to community organizations undertaking youth-led community organizing, without the need to go through typical channels or intermediary organizations. Youth-development focused organizations often are in an advantageous position when compared to those groups that sponsor youth-led organizing because of the former's track record of obtaining funding from foundations and other sources. For example, employing grant development directors is a luxury that few youth-led organizing sponsors can afford, while such positions may exist in many youth-development-oriented organizations (Weiss 2003). Thus, it is essential that funders take into account the specific challenges facing youth-led community organizing when comparing it to more conventional youth-development and youth-led initiatives.

Diversification of funding sources is a necessity in this field, particularly when compared to youth development. Grassroots fund-raising can generate money through sponsorship of a wide range of community-based events and activities, such as concerts and dances, car washes, local business donations, raffles, talent shows, theatrical productions, bike rides, road races, sponsored walks, individual donors/sponsors, art exhibitions, conferences, a speakers bureau, consultation with other organizations, and membership dues recruitment drives (Weiss 2003; Staples 2004a). A dues system can use a sliding fee scale that takes into account the ability of members to afford the costs, with some expected to pay as little as 25 cents per week or month. This money is symbolic and will not generate sizable organizational income; however, the value of such symbolism should not be minimized in any effort to achieve greater social and economic justice. When members commit to paying regular dues, they generally have a greater sense of ownership and make a bigger investment in the organizational mission.

9. Family as a Facilitating and Hindering Force

There are countless factors that can be considered facilitating or hindering forces when discussing youth-led community organizing, and the family systems in which youth organizers have been raised and continue to develop certainly are among the most influential variables (Charles 2005; Scheie 2003). The subject of family is one that generally is not encountered in adult-led community organizing unless it is central to the issue being addressed. Yet whether and how family either facilitates or hinders the participation of young activists is a critical matter in youth-led community organizing.

This important topic is only now starting to get the attention and recognition that it deserves in the literature. Indeed, most acknowledgment of and information about family systems as a contextual factor in youth organizing initiatives have been furnished by reports from the field rather than through scholarship. Family, incidentally, plays a critical role in youth-development programming as well, particularly in the case of refugee and immigrant youth from backgrounds where parents wield tremendous influence on whether their daughters and sons participate in outside-of-school activities (Delgado, Jones, and Rohani 2005).

Recruitment of young people for community organizing projects can involve reaching out to parents and working through those who have histories of social action. Parents who have had positive experiences in these collective efforts usually make the process of recruitment much easier. The following case examples illustrate two of the many ways in which an intergenerational organizing experience may occur (Baxter and Crockett 2002):

1. Lisa Rodrigues, age 17. "Lisa got involved with the Chicago Youth Council when her mother brought her along to a rally. 'I was really loud and everyone was like wow, you should come join the group,' Lisa said. So she did" (1–2).
2. Ales Boykins, age 19. "Ales Boykins . . . was first exposed to activism in 1997 by her mother, who was involved with a program within the Progressive Leadership Alliance of Nevada (PLAN)" (93).

For young people, the role of the family is of central importance because they need permission to become part of any school or after-school program. Family issues and concerns can motivate youth to undertake an organizing agenda (Cervone 2002, 93):

Of course, the causes that attract the passions of the Bay Area's young organizers carry their own fuel. "The issues kids care about most," says Rachel Jackson of Books Not Bars, "are the ones that hit them and their friends and family the hardest. Just about every young person involved in Books Not Bars knows someone who's been affected adversely by the (in) justice system and found themselves on the "prison track" in school and unable to get off." Explains a youth with OLIN, "the reason we've had as many as a thousand youth come to our events is that our push for ethnic studies hits home with thousands of students who can't find their race or language anywhere in the curriculum."

When families are involved in social-change campaigns or young people witness injustices, particularly relating to their parents or other loved ones, such experiences serve to bring a family focus to organizing campaigns. Two more case examples follow, highlighting the importance of family in helping to motivate offspring to engage in organizing.

1. Genevieve Gonzalez, a youth organizer with the School of Unity and Liberation (SOUL), Oakland, California. "I grew up in Chula Vista, California, near the Mexican border. I was in high school during the time when border enforcement and a lot of anti-immigrant legislation were happening, and I saw a lot of blatant racism against my community. My mom was born in Tijuana and my dad was born in the United States, and I remember one time when we were returning from visiting family in Mexico, the border patrol harassed my dad in front of all of us—you know, asked him how he learned how to speak English so good and to prove he was a U.S. citizen. I was so pissed off! I think that is when I really got interested with trying to change things" (Ginwright 2003, 10).

2. Murashige (2001, 16), also based in California, illustrates a way that youth can get motivated by social and economic injustices per-petrated on their family: "We were involved in youth issues, Prop 21. Basically our stuff was oriented toward getting youth to have a voice and speak out for themselves, not to have to worry about being ashamed of what they have to say, what they feel, and our message was to get that across. Don't be afraid that if you see something wrong, don't just hide it, but be positive and have a voice and an opinion...The fact is that we are all about what happened and it affects us when we get older and then it affects our little brothers and sisters when they grow up older, and they ba-sically go through the same things."

Pittman (2002) highlights the importance of *collective responsibility* when reviewing the comparative research literature on adolescent views of social activism, particularly as it relates to their families and school. As noted early in this book, young people who had witnessed the injustices carried out in the South frequently participated with their parents in the civil rights movement in the 1950s. Youth are also committed to serving their communities, preserving the environment, and assisting those with great financial and social needs.

Finally, Martinez (1996, 30) brings another dimension to family and youth organizing by stressing the need for young people to be able to join with parents and others in position of authority:

> Although it began as yet another defensive action, the campaign taught several valuable lessons. A crucial one: the value of youth working closely with parents and teachers in their communities, projecting not only opposition to the curfew but also the need for resources like a youth café or center. Older people came to recognize that the people most affected by a problem—in this case, youth—can be in leadership solving it.

Martinez goes on to take note of young Latino youth activists:

> The second striking fact is Latino youth's basic grasp of "the system." They can break down ruling-class deceptions and double-talk articulately, brilliantly. Even junior high or elementary school students can take your breath away. Like other activist youth they express a profound cynicism about the government, electoral politics, and official institutions, especially as regards racism. Possible reasons for this are having *movimiento* veterans as parents or older siblings, and the presence of universities with a tradition of activist struggle. (1996, 30)

However, family also can be a hindering force in a number of different ways, including the following:

1. Time and scheduling considerations can influence when young people will have time to organize, especially when parents may be working more than one fulltime job.
2. Negative experiences of parents who have been involved in past social change efforts, such as newcomers who have left countries with a history of dictatorships and oppression, can lead to fears of retribution and reluctance to risk the "safety" of their children.
3. Family finances may be such that young people are expected to seek employment for after-school hours as a means of contributing to basic economic support.
4. Cultural attitudes, particularly conservative behavior involving girls, may severely limit their participation in outside-of-school activities.
5. The undocumented status of parents may curtail youth involvement for fear that their participation in high-profile social-change activities will bring unwelcome attention on the family and possible deportation.
6. Parents may have concerns that their daughters' and sons' involvement in campaigns will take time away from their studies and thereby limit their options for further education.

The reader probably has concluded that family is a factor affecting all facets of a youth-led community organizing campaign, depending on local circumstances to a greater or lesser extent. However, young activists whose parents have positive organizing experiences can offer a support system and a legacy of social justice work that will prove of immense value to any campaign. The field will advance in qualitatively significant ways when programs recognize the role and importance of family and, as a result, gather information on this dimension as part of a process-oriented evaluation of youth-led campaigns (Youth in Focus 2004).

10. Role and Importance of Communication and Information Technology in Youth-Led Organizing

There is consensus that technology has shaped modern-day society in ways that few visionaries could even imagine twenty years ago (Schon, Sanyal, and Mitchell 1999; Tacchi 2004). In fact, there is no aspect of life that has escaped the reach of technology, as evidenced in the worries generated by the onset of the millennium just a few short years ago. For our purposes, *information technology* and *communication technology* are used interchangeably in this book.

Certainly, one area where youth often have a decided advantage is in the use of technology. Much has been written about the impact of electronic technology on participatory democracy, for example. There are arguments that there is growing potential for popular engagement and influence "from below." Smith (2004, 177) notes:

> [T]here are unmistakable signs that the Internet has opened new possibilities for citizen involvement in public life. Leaving aside the vast amounts of information available on the Internet and dealing only with the interactivist phenomenon, we find that Net organizers have been remarkably successful in their recent efforts to involve millions of people in national and international political debates. Innovative organizations like MoveOn.org—which has skillfully utilized electronic mail, online petitions, local meet-up opportunities, and small-donor fundraising drives to raise the volume of progressive voices—have made it easier and more rewarding for citizens to reenter the public sphere.

The field of community organizing has not escaped the influence of information technology, which, when applied to efforts to bring about social change, has been given a variety of labels, including terms such as *electronic advocacy*, *Internet activism*, and *online organizing*. In fact, the first book solely devoted to community organizing and technology was published in 1991 (Downing et al. 1991). Over this past decade, technology has become more accessible through the reduction of costs and its availability in public settings, such as libraries and schools. Recently, there has been increased attention to the question of how technology can help organizations and communities bring about social change. The broader accessibility has increased the options for residents in marginalized communities to participate in the workings of government and society, both nationally and internationally (Ogbu and Mihyo 2000; Wilhelm 2000).

The importance of technology in a technological age is evident, and not just for adults. Katz (2004, 1) effectively ties together youth, the use of technology, and social activism when noting the increased access of young people to information that previously was available only to the privileged:

> Children are at the epicenter of the information revolution, ground zero of the digital world. They helped build it, and they understand it as well or better than anyone. Not only is the digital world making the young more sophisticated, altering their ideas of what culture and literacy are, it is connecting them to one another, providing them with a new sense of political self. Children in the digital age are neither unseen nor unheard; in fact, they are seen and heard more than ever. They occupy a new kind of cultural space. They're citizens of a new order, founders of the Digital Nation.

Norris and Curtice (2004), in a study of the Internet as a vehicle for strengthening democratic participation, social capital, and civic engagement in Britain, but with implications for the United States, found that the potential impact of the Internet on democratic participation is influenced by the type of activism under comparison. New technologies such as the Internet are expected to benefit new social movements, transnational policy networks, and single-issue causes. Another recent study found that most youth working with public health nurses in a school-based community development project "perceived that using computers and the Internet reduced their anxiety concerning communication with adults, increased their control when dealing with adults, raised their perception of their social status, increased participation within the community, supported reflective thought, increased efficiency, and improved their access to resources" (Valaitis 2005, 2).

Bass's (1997) concept of new citizenship, first addressed in chapter 5, identifies information and communication technology as vehicles for connecting individuals and organizations and for facilitating the exchange of information for achieving positive community change. Carpini (2003) advocates use of the Internet as a vehicle for increasing civic engagement among the young, helping them to find their place in public life in the process. The creation of an ethos that politics matters is one direct manifestation of youth engagement. This also has served to connect young people to intra-, inter-, and transnational political movements, thereby giving them a broad view of political matters that transcends a focus on purely local issues.

On the other hand, concerns also have been expressed that electronic technology is not sufficient to remedy the structural inequality that contributes to the lack of participation by large numbers of disempowered citizens (van Dijk and Hacker 2000, 210): "No technology is able to 'fix' a lack of political motivation, lack of time, effort and skills required for full participation in democratic activities. No technology can dissolve the social and material inequalities that appear to be so strongly related to differences in participation."

Technology never should be viewed as a replacement for the labor-intensive work of community organizing (Roberts-DeGennaro 2004). However, technology can make organizers more productive and able to reach a wider constituency in less time, even though organizing remains an intervention founded on face-to-face, interpersonal relations (McNutt 2000). Toward this end, McNutt (2000) identifies six ways that technology can help initiate and sustain an organizing campaign:

1. Coordinating activity and community with stakeholders
2. Use of online databases and discussion groups to gather tactical and strategic information
3. Using mapping/GIS programs, community databases, and statistical packages to analyze data
4. Advocacy Web pages
5. Online fund-raising and volunteer/member recruitment
6. Automating office and administrative tasks

The above uses of technology require a range of resources, hardware, software, and skills. Again, one size does not fit all circumstances.

In a review of the Internet and community organizing, Stoecker (2002) found that the Internet has had a "crucial and positive" impact on the scale of community organizing projects. Historically, organizing typically has been conducted on a small scale, such as at the neighborhood level. However, the Internet has facilitated multi-locational organizing by exploiting the potential of the Information Highway. Nevertheless, there are concerns about using this informational source for creating social change. Stoecker (2002), like Spector (1994), raises questions about how "e-democracy" can be subverted by corporations. Limited content in languages other than English also severely restricts this technology's reach to communities that historically have been marginalized and not enjoyed access to language-specific information attentive to their social conditions and local circumstances.

Information technology comes in a variety of forms that lend themselves to particular uses during different facets of an organizing campaign: cell phones, conference calls, transmittance of images, text messaging, organization Web pages, video equipment, word processing, financial spreadsheets, e-mail, list serves, chat rooms, Internet information and resources, storage of data sets, computer programs, especially software for producing flyers, letters, and presentations. Flexibility with access to and use of these technologies can be quite appealing when launching an organizing campaign involving youth. Lomardo, Zakus, and Skinner (2002) argue that informational and communication technologies can and do provide opportunities for dialogue between diverse communities, and this offers young people valuable opportunities to engage in collective action across ethnic and racial communities.

The present generation of youth grew up with these technologies, and this is particularly the case for youth from privileged backgrounds. Nevertheless, youth from lower income backgrounds also are familiar with information technology. Flanagan and Galley (2001) comment that technology has placed many young people in the position of helping their parents and other adults navigate this new terrain.

It certainly should come as no surprise that information technology is an important component in youth-led community organizing. The attractiveness of technology to the young and their familiarity with it make it a natural for inclusion in community organizing. Youth can learn about growth opportunities within and outside of their immediate community. Further, technology knows no geographical boundaries, facilitating young people to interact and learn from their counterparts around the world (Golombek 2002).

Golombek's (2002) observations about the pervasiveness of technology in youth organizing offer an intriguing glimpse into a world with unlimited potential. The appeal of information technology in youth organizing is strong, indeed. Technology facilitates the process whereby young people transcend the geographical boundaries of their communities and expose themselves to a world normally not within their reach. Engaging in exchanges of information with peers at a transcommunity level promotes and inspires both learning and service. In essence, young people go from being global consumers to global citizens, increasing the likelihood of their engagement in global activism, with a shared vision of social and economic justice (Taylor 2000; Youniss et al. 2002).

The term *cyber-participation* has been coined to capture both the practice and potential of electronic communication to increase community engagement (Golombek 2002, 71):

> If used appropriately, communications technology lifts geographic and cultural boundaries, makes time zones irrelevant, and can be used as a vast educational resource. With these qualities in mind, how can technology make youth participation efforts more effective? It can offer young people the possibility of sharing effective practices, exchanging contacts and resources, and most importantly creating an awareness about a global community of youth seeking social change.

Potential use of communication and information technology in social-action interventions cannot be ignored, and in fact, these technologies can be important tools for recruitment, as well as capacity enhancement. Technologies such as cell phones (instant contact), e-mail (informal use and quick spreading of messages), and computers (offering acquisition of valuable marketable skills) hold special appeal for young people.

Although the potential for these technologies is yet to be fully realized, it is important to note that youth-led community organizing, or even adult-led organizing, is not without its limitations, with access being one of the most prominent ones. There seems to be broad agreement that electronic technology is a supplement to rather than a substitute for face-to-face, grassroots community organizing (Roberts-DeGennaro 2004; McNutt and Hick 2002). This sentiment has been captured by Smith (2004, 190), who observes: "while the new interactivists may have opened the public sphere to new voices, without additional offline grassroots initiatives, we may unintentionally exclude the very voices that have always had the most difficulty being heard."

Access to information technology is not a universal phenomenon, particularly when examined from a social-class perspective: many marginalized young people do not enjoy these benefits (Beamish 1999; Sanyal and Schon 1999). Much attention has been directed to what is referred to as the "digital divide," a line of demarcation that marks differential access to a computer and the Internet (Kitlan 2004; Tardieu 1999). The higher the socioeconomic level of the family, the greater the likelihood of access to computers and the Internet at home, school, and other community settings. However, Hargittai (2002) has explored this digital divide and focused on online skills (the ability to find necessary content online and the time needed to complete these tasks). Findings suggest that age is negatively associated with competence level, that experience with the technology is positively related to skill, and that differences in gender do not explain variance in abilities. As a result, youth are in an advantageous position regarding technology when compared to adults.

Golombek (2002, 15) notes that as the digital divide has diminished, the potential of the Internet for youth-led community organizing has grown considerably:

> The websites are often the virtual arm of organizations, which find in technology a vehicle to scale up their youth participation efforts. A common objection to the reliance on technology to increase youth involvement is that lack of access to that technology . . . is an impediment to young people's participation. This cannot be denied. However, there are indications that technological innovations are emerging to narrow the digital divide (such as setting up a computer with Internet access in a rural community center or the increasing number of distance learning programs). Even language barriers are beginning to blur due to translation software packages. These resources are still in their preliminary development stages, but given the pace of technological change it can be expected that their quality will improve.

Thus, once access is provided, and young people are trained in how best to obtain needed information, the Internet's potential is quite promising for use in youth-led community organizing. However, Golombek (2002, 14) goes on to provide a good illustration of how information technology in service to social action gets operationalized differently, depending on the socioeconomic class of youth:

> Two massive non-violent demonstrations in 2001 in the Philippines, known as EDSA II and EDSA III, reflect the high level of youth's awareness regarding their right to participate. However, these two phenomena are also a manifestation of how youth participation greatly differs between social classes. A clear example of this difference is the communication channels available for each group. While upper class and middle class youth exchanged text messages to recruit participants and arrange where to meet to express their sentiments on EDSA II, poor urban youth relied on "word of mouth" and even alleged financial motivation.

Technical skills are intrinsically associated with media skills, and these abilities can be transfered to other arenas, such as leadership and communication capacity development (McGillicuddy 2003, 3):

> The details, responsibilities, and opportunities are enormous: organizing community forums and school assemblies, educating residents door-to-door, writing one's own stories and creating one's own media (such as newsletters, CDs and videos), educating and cooperating with journalists, organizing meetings with city officials, testifying at public hearings, integrating cultural expressions into outreach (open mics, spoken word, graf, and slap tags, etc.).

Information technology is here to stay, so it only becomes a question of how this tool will influence youth-led community organizing and other forms of social intervention. As a result of technology, youth-led community organizing has connected across the globe and become a worldwide movement. How this technology can be made available to marginalized youth in this country will become the subject of greater and greater attention in the coming decade.

Group Structure

11. Autonomous, Locally Based, Unaffiliated, Streamlined Structures

Many youth-led organizing programs are connected to adult-led organizations that provide fiscal sponsorship, administrative support, technical assistance, or physical space (Young Wisdom Project 2004). However, as the term youth-led organizing implies, and crosscutting themes 2 and 4 show, a high degree of autonomy is the hallmark of this approach. In essence, there are structural implications.

Regardless of whether they are located in school settings or neighborhoods, youth-led organizing initiatives tend to be locally based. Consciousness raising about overarching forms of oppression frequently is linked to agendas of large-scale social and economic justice issues, and communication and information technologies enable young activists to reach out to those in similar programs around the country or even internationally; nevertheless, the organizational structures within which these bodies function typically are relatively small and restricted to a limited geographic area. This is largely a function of modest operating budgets (see theme 8 above) and the scarcity of statewide, regional, national, and international youth-led organizations or support networks. While electronic technology has facilitated informal communications between youth-led organizing initiatives, this contact usually is idiosyncratic and sporadic, not systematic. Most youth-led programs do not have structural linkages to one another and they remain unaffiliated with larger entities.

Fluidity of membership, meager budgets, and the quick pace of organizing all serve to promote streamlined operational structures. Youth-led organizing projects are nothing if not dynamic in methodology and style. They customarily are disposed toward short-term ad hoc committees, rather than permanent or standing organizational bodies. These temporary committees "provide structural access points through which newcomers can become active" and thereby help to keep "a steady flow of fresh 'new blood' flowing into the organization" (Staples 2004a). New leadership emerges to take on roles of responsibility within these work groups, thereby helping prevent the concentration of power by entrenched veteran leaders. These committees also require less staffing and readily can be dissolved once an issue has been resolved or a campaign loses momentum, thus helping prevent a do-nothing or fossilized organizational structure from becoming locked into place.

12. Age-Related Issues Shape Target Systems

It should come as no surprise that the agenda for youth-led organizing is driven by age-related issues. Both internal and external target systems are shaped accordingly. For example, potential youth participants *are internal targets* of strategies and tactics for recruitment and engagement. Typically, recruitment is done around issues that are deeply felt, and this activity usually is carried out where young people can be found in community and school settings. In chapter 2, we listed the sixteen key issues identified by Wikipedia (2006), each directly related to age. These issues currently have the greatest self-interest draw for young people across the country, providing the most favorable odds for an organization's securing buy in and involvement.

Youth-led organizing campaigns attempt to persuade or pressure *external targets* to agree to act in a certain manner or to alter or halt their current activities. Most often, the issues flow from perceived injustices related to institutions dominated by adults. Common targets include public or private schools, local police departments, the criminal and juvenile justice systems, municipal governments, and businesses. As discussed in the previous chapter, youth-led organizing programs tend to incorporate social justice issues that impact sexually marginalized young people. Recently, there has been an increase in youth organizing around environmental justice issues and also for immigrant rights.

13. Youth Culture Shapes the Organizing Process

All community organizing draws on the unique assets and strengths of the constituency that is being mobilized. The creativity, enthusiasm, and high energy of young people are infused with aspects of youth culture attendant to any community where youth-led organizing takes place. The particulars may vary, and "youth culture" can encompass a broad range of scenes. For example, the hip-hop activism of street-smart kids, the high-tech games of computer geeks, the service learning projects of middle-class suburban students, the sports competition among high school jocks, the violence of urban gangs, the music of metal heads, and the religious activities of evangelical Christian youth are but a few examples of youth culture. And certainly not all elements of youth culture are actively engaged in youth-led organizing.

However, as discussed in chapter 3, culture profoundly shapes the political content of youth-led organizing, as well as the recruitment methods, leadership styles, structural factors, nature of collective gatherings, media forms used, patterns for conflict resolution, strategic choices, and tactics employed. Regional differences and local circumstances certainly alter the ways in which youth culture influences the organizing models, methods, and modes of projects, but a common pattern of cultural infusion is evident, with typical elements including music, film, fashion, style, art, dance, theater, photography, poetry, and prose. While rap, graffiti, murals, and street theater may be central features in one organizing initiative, heavy metal, video production, and newsletter publication may characterize another. Similar to the social work axiom of "starting where people are at," youth culture has the power to engage and activate young people through familiar media where they feel valued and validated, as well as most free to express themselves.

Youth and Adult Roles

14. Youth in Decision-Making Roles

It is sad that the young rarely are placed in decision-making roles in the very organizations that society has established to educate and support them

(Cutler 2002; Huber et al. 2003). Consequently, the youth-led movement has "front and centered" young people in the process of deciding how social interventions are to be conceptualized, implemented, and evaluated. This empowering experience, in turn, has helped create a cadre of youth activists who eventually will assume responsible adult positions in society. And when they do so, they will be predisposed and prepared to create even more opportunities for young people to be decision makers in the pursuit of a progressive agenda that embraces the principles of social and economic justice.

It is important to acknowledge that the field of youth development has played an influential role in encouraging community-based organizations to create decision-making roles for youth (W.K. Kellogg Foundation 2000; Young Wisdom Project 2004). However, from an operational standpoint, the fields of youth development and youth-led community organizing are light years apart in this regard; the latter places much stronger emphasis on putting young people in positions of power. Nevertheless, at this time, significant efforts are underway to help bridge this gap.

Having youth in decision-making roles does not mean that adults cannot or should not help them when requested to do so, or that only young people will make the "right" decisions throughout their involvement. We never would expect that of adults, and we should not demand it of youth, as well! Instead, it is useful to visualize a "ladder of leadership," whereby young activists step up to increased authority as they gain experience, develop their knowledge base, learn new skills, and exercise their newfound power. Eventually, they may even be promoted to the top position in an organization or program initiative.

The field of youth services has numerous frameworks that address a course of action placing young people in decision-making roles. Some of these models stop just short of making young people the ultimate arbitrators, while others do not hesitate to put them in the highest position of authority (Delgado 2006). Not every youth can and should be expected to assume total leadership. (The same also can be said of adults.) Nevertheless, every young participant must be given opportunities to exercise decision-making skills and to learn from the successes and failures. Anything less would be simply unacceptable.

15. Adult Roles in Support

Mention of the youth-led movement generally conjures up images of initiatives run totally by and for youth, with no adults in sight. Nothing could be further from the truth. The most successful youth-led initiatives have adults involved in numerous capacities, and organizing is no exception (Yohalem 2003). The majority of the research cited in chapters 4 and 8 note the critical role adult allies and mentors play in encouraging the field of youth organizing, including youth-led efforts. Adult allies bring with them access to resources (informational, expressive, and instrumental) needed by young activists in order to carry out their responsibilities in their campaigns (Nygreen, Kwon, and Sanchez 2006; Rhodes and Roffman 2003).

Adult allies also benefit from involvement in youth-led initiatives (Young Wisdom Project 2004): "As allies, adults learn new ways of relating to young people as partners and peers. They learn how to shift to a coach and mentor relationship, supporting young people's full potential. In turn, they are challenged to continue their own process of learning and developing." A good learner is someone who can recognize new lessons to be learned in a variety of situations, regardless of the age of the individual imparting the wisdom. Thus, adults can and should be receptive to learning from youth. Unfortunately, most young people have been socialized to think about knowledge as only worthwhile when imparted by adults. As a result, adults must be willing to be resocialized to view young people as a source of knowledge.

Within the youth-led model, the role and extent of involvement by adult allies is determined by youth (Delgado 2006). Young people decide when and how adults are to be involved, and under what circumstances they are not welcomed; however, a "good" adult ally almost always is accepted. Consequently, it is important that youth-led community organizing be thought of as a form of coalition, with youth in positions of leadership and adults playing behind-the-scene roles, entering and leaving the joint effort as required by youth leaders.

Conclusion

The fifteen crosscutting themes identified in this chapter highlight both what makes youth-led community organizing unique to this group and the elements they share with their adult counterparts. These crosscutting themes are by no means the only that can exist. We are sure that the reader may disagree with the selection of some of these themes and undoubtedly has his or her own themes in addition. This is expected and even encouraged. Age-related issues, the role of family, the importance of fun, and the use of technology have distinctive characteristics that highlight how youth-led community organizing differs from its adult counterparts. We believe the crosscutting themes identified here are salient topics for understanding the field of youth-led community organizing. Ultimately, which themes will emerge as the most significant, and which will die a lonely death through lack of attention, no one can predict. However, debate about crosscutting themes will continue as long as the field of youth-led community organizing is growing and venturing into new and exciting social arenas, in this country and internationally.

Part III

A View and Lessons from the Field

The reason why I say organizing is the best model of youth development is you're not just focusing on one specific area. You want to develop a young person . . . in a very holistic way and at the same time really raising their consciousness so that they're not just an individual. They're not just one person that's becoming better and then they can better their lives—but that for them to better themselves they also need to better the community as well. [Youth organizing] really changes the concept from an individual to a collective and I think that's really important to the person's development.
—James, *Bringing it Together* (2005)

9

Youth First in Jackson Square!
¡Jovenes Primero!

Case Study: Boston, Massachusetts

> We will do a disservice to all young people if
> we do not find ways to create a public idea
> of youth as change agents: one that starts
> rather than concludes with the engagement
> of young people whose lives and communi-
> ties are most in need of changing.
> —Pittman, *Balancing the Equation* (2000)

Case studies can help practitioners see how theoretical concepts can be applied to actual, real-life situations. Practitioners then may be able to apply these principles and methods to their own work. However, local social-change activists must determine which aspects of a case study are transferable, or universal in nature, and which must be modified to meet local considerations. Practitioners often criticize social theories by saying that they fail to take into account local circumstances, such as geographical region, demographic differences, cultural features, political climate, and characteristics of nontypical participants. As with other forms of social intervention, change initiatives must be contextualized and modified to allow for a wide range of ecological factors. This chapter uses a case study from the field to show one of a multitude of ways that youth-led community organizing can be done and how local circumstances help shape these efforts.

Unlike case material cited in previous chapters of this book, this case has been developed fully to illustrate a particular youth-led community organizing effort. The case integrates key themes and principles discussed earlier in the book, in the hope of providing readers with an opportunity to witness the translation of basic concepts into everyday practice, as accomplished by organizations sponsoring youth-led community organizing.

We made every effort to select a case study that represents diversity in terms of ethnicity, gender, goals, and focus. Youth First (¡Jovenes Primero!) does this. In addition, the case was also selected for a variety of additional factors: (1) the relationship between the authors and the organization; (2) the degree of documentation available for the process; (3) the easy geographical access for the authors; (4) the multifaceted and prominent dimensions of youth-led community organizing in this social-action campaign; and (5) the richness of detail concerning the rewards and challenges that youth organizers face in conducting campaigns.

Additionally, this case study is used in one of our macro-practice classes at Boston University School of Social Work, and it has been regarded by our graduate students as an excellent learning tool. At the end of the case study, we offer commentary and analysis that uses the ten principles presented in chapter 4 for assessing grassroots community organizing (Staples 2004a), making comparative analysis easier.

Background

Hyde/Jackson Square is a community viewed as the bridge between the neighborhoods of Jamaica Plain and Roxbury. Running along a stretch of Centre Street and separated from Roxbury by Columbus Avenue, Hyde/Jackson Square also borders the affluent communities of Brookline and West Roxbury. Two major housing developments—Bromley-Heath and Academy Homes—are within the immediate area. The community of Hyde/Jackson Square has a population of 48,000, many of whom pass through the Jackson Square Metropolitan Boston Transit Authority (MBTA) subway and bus transit station daily.

This area has been described by the Boston Redevelopment Authority and the United Way of Massachusetts Bay as one of the most densely populated minority-youth concentrations in the city of Boston. Thirty-one percent of the population is under the age of 20, and more than 12,000 youth and children under the age of 18 live in the neighborhood (Jackson Square Coordinating Group 2003). Over 6,000 students attend Boston Public Schools within the immediate area of the Hyde/Jackson Square community (Boston Public Schools 2004). Sixty percent of the households with children are headed by single parents. The estimated per capita income is only $17,253, and more than 40 percent of area households earn less than $25,000 per year (Jackson Square Profile Report 1998). Thirty percent of the adult population has not completed high school, and only 27 percent has attained a college degree.

History of the Hyde Square Task Force

Hyde/Jackson Square has been an immigrant community for more than fifty years. Heavily concentrated with Latino immigrants from South and Central America, the community has maintained the authenticity of its culture, despite the wave of gentrification taking place in other parts of Jamaica Plain and Roxbury. Many credit the efforts of a core group of activist residents and organizations that have dedicated the past twenty years to making this area a better environment for the families and youth who call it home. One of the leading organizations is the Hyde Square Task Force, Inc.

Located in the heart of Hyde/Jackson Square, the task force has been serving this community for more than fifteen years. The organization first took shape in 1988, when a group of community activists came together because they were fed up with the gang and drug violence that dominated the neighborhood (Tangvik 2004). In the 1980s, Hyde/Jackson Square was known as the "Cocaine Capital of Boston" by the Boston Police Department. Abandoned properties and unclean streets were the scene of constant shootings among rival gang members and drug dealers.

Tired of being scared to live in their own neighborhood, community activists formed the Hyde Square Task Force as a subcommittee of the Jamaica Plain Neighborhood Council, a local governing body that serves as an advisory group to the city of Boston (Sheffield 1998). The task force members were community residents, local business owners, and representatives from the local churches. The group met with city and state politicians, including Mayor Raymond Flynn and State Representative Kevin Fitzgerald, to discuss the severity of the drug and violence problems (Lupo 1989). In addition, with the closest police station in West Roxbury, they voiced their frustrations with the lack of police presence in the neighborhood and urged these officials to invest more time and resources in this long-forgotten community (Schoberg 2001).

The group organized community meetings where residents voiced their fears and concerns about the deteriorating condition of the neighborhood. Realizing that many of the problems were the result of a lack of resources in the community, the Hyde Square Task Force was incorporated in 1991 as a 501(c)(3) nonprofit organization to facilitate tax-deductible contributions (Tangvik 2004). The new group took on the mission of bringing in more opportunities, programs, and services for the neighborhood's families and youth.

The organization faced an immediate challenge when the shooting of Manuela Baez took place in October 1991. Ironically, Baez, a mother of four, was caught in crossfire in broad daylight, during a rededication ceremony hosted by the city of Boston at Mozart Park, a troublesome local playground (Seamans 1991). The shooting left her paralyzed and the event outraged the community. This high-profile tragedy put Hyde/Jackson Square on the map as one of Boston's most dangerous neighborhoods.

The newly established Hyde Square Task Force, along with other local activists, began hosting vigils to advocate for peace in the community. They also met with city and state officials to discuss strategies to stop the violence that was leaving many families devastated (Seamans 1991). Finally, in 1993, the shooting of Alex Reyes, a 16-year-old student at English High School, forced Mayor Ray Flynn to promise immediate changes in the community (Dowdy and McGrory 1993). Crack-downs on gang activities and drug busts began to take place regularly, and the local police force became more visible through routine patrols of troubled areas. In 1996, with the increasing need for more street patrols, the Boston Police Department finally reopened the E-13 District Police Station in Jamaica Plain to serve the immediate area (Schoberg 2001).

While the work of improving community safety was under way, the Hyde Square Task Force began approaching the local elementary school to discuss the possibility of establishing educational and recreational programming for the local youth (Delgado 1994). The lack of community resources had left many young people with no place to go when school was not in session, and increasing numbers were getting into trouble. So, the Task Force worked through its Safe Neighborhood Program to convince the school officials to open space up for the organization's first educational program, the Evening Tutorial. The program, run entirely by community volunteers, provided a place for young people to go after school and left the community wanting more youth services.

At the task force's 1995 annual meeting, neighborhood youth and families gathered to advocate for similar youth programs as a positive effort to take back the community. Over the next few years, the area began to turn around, and the Hyde Square Task Force became a visible and respected leader in the revitalization process. During this time, the organization's programming increased to serve both youth and parents through after-school and English-as-a-second-language education. As the organization's membership grew, the need for more space and resources became obvious.

In 1998, the Hyde Square Task Force's board of directors appointed Claudio Martinez, a long-term community resident and activist, as the new executive director (Tangvik 2004). With a background in community organizing and economic development, Martinez immediately began a strategic planning process. He called on residents and young people to envision the future of the Hyde/Jackson Square community, and the creation of a youth and family center was a unanimous response. Hyde/Jackson Square was the only residential neighborhood in the city of Boston without a full-service family center, and such a project could bring much-needed resources into the community (Tangvik 2004).

Under Martinez's leadership, the task force took the initiative and led the fight to turn the vision of a new community center into a reality. After much discussion and serious consideration, the group identified vacant land across from the Jackson Square MBTA Station as the future home of the youth center. This marked the official beginning of the Hyde Square Task Force's involvement in the Jackson Square Development Area.

History of Jackson Square Development

The Jackson Square Development Area comprises the acres of empty land located around the corners of Centre Street and Columbus Avenue and consists of several different size parcels. The area has been the center of the community's attention for years. In the 1950s, many families who had been displaced from other parts of the city for economic reasons moved into the Jackson Square community in search of affordable homes (Gail Sullivan Associates 2001). However, the lack of resources to maintain the aging buildings in this historically industrial neighborhood led to rapidly deteriorating conditions. By the 1960s, many buildings and properties had been abandoned by their owners, and the remaining residents struggled to keep the neighborhood safe and livable.

In the meantime, the state began major demolition projects in the area in preparation for construction of the Southwest Expressway (I-95), which was projected to run straight through the community (Gail Sullivan Associates 2001). Properties that stood in the way of this project were acquired by the state and demolished under eminent domain. As a result, many existing businesses began to relocate outside of the neighborhood, leaving even more buildings and properties abandoned.

In an effort to take back the neighborhood, many community groups from Hyde Square and Egleston Square began working together to voice their discontent with the city and the state's disregard for residents' needs. They organized spirited protests against the proposed expressway and demanded that the project be stopped immediately. Community opposition ultimately led the state to reevaluate its transportation plan and change its priorities. With agreement from the residents, the Southwest Corridor Project was initiated to relocate the MBTA Orange Line; as a result, the Jackson Square MBTA Transit Station was born.

After the Jackson Square Transit Station was constructed, the Economic Development and Industrial Corporation (EDIC) of Boston began a city-wide focus on industrial job opportunities within the city in order to increase and enhance existing properties and businesses. In 1987, the EDIC entered an agreement with the Jackson Square Station Area Task Force to plan usages for the MBTA-owned lands that surround the station, with the goal of revitalizing the immediate area. Local organizations, including the Academy Homes Tenant Council, Bromley Heath Tenant Management Corporation, Dimock Health Center, Jamaica Plain Neighborhood Development Corporation,

Urban Edge Housing Corporation, Oficina Hispana, and Southwest Corridor Community Farms, were included in the planning (Gail Sullivan Associates 2001).

The new collaboration between local representatives and the city led to development priorities that would benefit the community. In 1992, the EDIC presented an Economic Development Plan that included projects designed to create more employment opportunities and improve the area's physical appearance (Gail Sullivan Associates 2001). Even though much of the plan reflected community needs, the suggestion of a recycling plant was widely opposed by the neighborhood. Ultimately, EDIC's plan never was implemented, leaving the future of Jackson Square in limbo.

The Urban Edge Housing Corporation made another attempt in 1995 to develop the area through its Jackson-Egleston Strategy Proposal (Gail Sullivan Associates 2001). Urban Edge, a local community development corporation (CDC), has a long track record of community-oriented developments in Boston. Primarily focusing on housing, it has become well known for its aggressive and successful approach to revitalizing traditionally forgotten communities. Prior to its attention to Jackson Square, Urban Edge had successfully rebuilt the nearby Egleston Square by developing neighborhood-focused projects, including a community center, affordable housing, and space for commercial use. Hoping to bring the same success to Jackson Square, the corporation began an elaborate planning process that included many community meetings and workshops. Hundreds of residents became involved, hoping to contribute to the future of Jackson Square.

In 1997, Urban Edge published its first draft of the Egleston-Jackson Square Strategy, emphasizing priorities for affordable housing, economic development, commercial space, and facilities for youth and resident services (Urban Edge 1998). Unlike the EDIC's plan, this one included heavy involvement from the community. As a result, the Boston Redevelopment Authority promised that the city would support and provide resources for development that reflected the community's vision (Urban Edge 1998). For the first time, the future of Jackson Square Development seemed to lie in the hands of the people who lived and worked in this community.

"No to K-Mart, Yes to Youth": Birth of the Youth First in Jackson Square Initiative

The Hyde Square Task Force was one of the most active organizations involved in the planning for the Jackson Square Development Area. Youth and families worked to ensure that their needs for better resources would be a priority. While the task force began to envision its own future through the 1998 strategic planning process led by new Executive Director Claudio

Martinez, Urban Edge met separately with various interested developers and investors (Gail Sullivan Associates 2001).

One of the potential investors was the K-Mart Corporation, which was beginning a nationwide inner-city initiative. Representatives from K-Mart approached Urban Edge to discuss the possibility of opening a store in the Jackson Square Development Area. The large parcel of vacant land in an inner-city setting was ideal for the store's new initiative, and representatives promised the new store would bring jobs and local economic development (Faircloth 1998).

K-Mart's interest in Jackson Square became public during Urban Edge's Jackson Square community forum, held on September 23, 1998. The organization presented a drawing of the Jackson Square Development Area that included a K-Mart store and a large-scale entertainment complex (Y. Miller 1999). Representatives from K-Mart attended the meeting and assured community residents that the store would generate employment opportunities, boost the local economy, and provide a more affordable and convenient shopping option (Faircloth 1998).

The plan to include K-Mart as a part of the Jackson Square Development Area upset many community residents and organizations that had been involved in the planning process for years (Bearse 1998a). Local merchants expressed concerns about the effect that a large store like K-Mart would have on their longstanding businesses, while other community residents feared the increased traffic a large-scale store would bring to an already congested Jackson Square area. People were outraged most by Urban Edge's failure to include community input in the negotiations with K-Mart (Bearse 1998b).

Community groups, including the Hyde Square Task Force, Hyde/Jackson Square Main Street, City Life/Vida Urbana, Jamaica Plain Neighborhood Council, Hyde/Jackson Square Business Association, Hyde/Jackson Square Merchants Association, and Egleston Square Neighborhood Association, began working together to oppose Urban Edge's plan to bring the store into the area. An editorial written by Claudio Martinez and Ken Tangvik (1998b), two of the task force's founders, urged the community to focus once again on the needs of youth when envisioning the future of Jackson Square.

Despite widespread opposition from the community, Urban Edge announced in December 1998 that they were in negotiations with K-Mart to sign a letter of intent about possible development in Jackson Square (Bearse 1998). With the drafting of the letter of intent in the works, community members became furious, and they immediately stepped into action. Leading organizations, including the Hyde Square Task Force and area business associations, met with city and state officials and wrote letters to Mayor Thomas Menino strongly opposing the plan (Hyde Square Task Force 1999). These stakeholders suggested that it was extremely inappropriate for Urban

Edge to negotiate any plan regarding Jackson Square without consulting the community, and they questioned the motives of this community development corporation. Accusations were made that the plan to partner with K-Mart was strictly profit driven, rather than community focused (Lupo 1999a).

In January 1999, with the plan under attack, Urban Edge agreed to cease negotiations with K-Mart until they received further input from the community (Bearse 1999a). A coordinating committee made up of more than seventy community residents and business owners was formed to address the issue. Urban Edge stated that they would hold off any action until the coordinating committee met and delivered its feedback. In the meantime, community residents voted against the K-Mart plan during the Jamaica Plain Neighborhood Council meeting (Bearse 1999a).

In March 1999, after meeting with community residents and youth, Jamaica Plain City Councilor Maura Hennigan organized a special city council hearing on the future of Jackson Square development (Bearse 1999b). During the hearing, held at Roxbury Community College, hundreds of residents voiced their strong opposition to Urban Edge's plan. Youth leaders from the Hyde Square Task Force held signs with the powerful messages SCHOOL IS OUT. WHERE DO I GO? KMART? and WE MUST BE A PART OF THE PROCESS! They spoke in front of the city councilors about their desire for more youth services and a place to go after school (Hyde Square Task Force 1999). The community's voice was delivered clearly that night and city officials took notice.

Immediately following the meeting, the Boston Redevelopment Authority, under orders from Mayor Menino, stepped in to monitor the planning process of the Jackson Square Development Area (Lupo 1999b). As a result, the Jackson Coordinating Group was established in June 1999 to represent the community's voice during the process (Gail Sullivan Associates 2001). The Hyde Square Task Force was among the thirty organizations identified as part of the Jackson Coordinating Group. In fact, youth leaders from the task force were designated to represent the interests of young people in the community and therefore were considered to be an entity apart from the rest of the task force. Every Jackson Coordinating Group member was given one vote; the Hyde Square Task Force and the Youth Organizing Team were given their own vote.

While the city-monitored process began to pick up the pace, the task force hired its first youth community organizer, Caprice Taylor, to lead a team of fifteen youth organizers. The ultimate goal of the Youth Community Organizing Team was to lead and empower other young people in the community to advocate for more resources, including a much-needed youth and family center (Tangvik 2004). During the Hyde Square Task Force's annual meeting in November 1999, the organization formally featured the fifteen Youth Community Organizers (YCOs) as a team and launched the "Youth First in Jackson Square" campaign in front of hundreds of residents and young people, as a declaration of the battle to bring a youth center to the community. It was considered one of the most significant moments in the history of the Jackson Square Development project because neighborhood youth finally were given a voice to represent their own needs.

Take Back the Land

While the Hyde Square Task Force prepared to launch the "Youth First in Jackson Square" campaign, Urban Edge announced its plan to conduct a "shopper's survey" during November 1999 as a way to gather more information on the needs of the community (Mason 1999). The shopper's survey was a four-page questionnaire developed by an independent firm; it featured questions to identify participants' current shopping habits, as well as their preferred shopping environment. The plan was to administer the survey at the local transit station and to announce the results by early 2000.

The shopper's survey immediately was attacked by the same people who opposed the K-Mart development. Many suggested that the survey was just another expensive tool used by Urban Edge to push the K-Mart propaganda. The Hyde Square Task Force, skeptical of the motives behind this plan, invited several professional statisticians to evaluate the survey and the process by which it would be administered. All of these experts suggested that the survey was no more than a marketing tool to push a specific agenda (Friar 2000; Terrin 2000). They stated that the questions were formulated so as to guide the participants to provide biased answers; furthermore, it was considered statistically unsound to administer a questionnaire about residents' shopping habits during the holiday shopping season.

Despite opposition to the survey from the Hyde Square Task Force and other community stakeholders, Urban Edge carried out the project and publicized the results in March 2000. As expected and feared, by both the activists and the professionals who evaluated the survey, the results suggested that residents would much prefer a large-scale store similar to K-Mart (Daniel 2000). Announcement of the survey results once again outraged the community; many could not believe that Urban Edge was still considering K-Mart as a possible development project for Jackson Square (Kahn 2000).

To fight back, the Hyde Square Task Force and its YCOs hosted a community meeting in May 2000, to which they invited guest speakers Al Norman and Tony Barros to better educate the community about the negative effects of a K-Mart in their neighborhood (JP Council 2000). Al Norman, a well-known advocate for the nationwide anti-K-Mart movement, spoke about the K-Mart Corporation's unfair labor practices, as well as their disengagement from the community. And Tony Barros, president of the Hyde/Jackson Square Business Association, pleaded for the community to continue supporting local businesses that had been in the area for many years.

In June 2000, soon after the community meeting, youth leaders from the Hyde Square Task Force and representatives from Urban Edge attended a community forum where the two groups engaged in heated discussion about the future of Jackson Square (I. Sen 2003). The tension continued to build during the summer, until tragedy struck the community once again. On August 5, 2000, 15-year-old Cedric Ennis was stabbed near the Jackson Square Transit station (Bombardieri 2000). The wounded teenager crawled from the station, across the street, through the vacant lot that everyone had been fighting over, and finally collapsed and died in front of his friend's house on Columbus Avenue.

The death of Cedric Ennis saddened a community that had longed for the day when there would be no more violence against young people. Many argued that if the vacant lot had not remained empty for so many years, things might have been different (Bombardieri 2000). In an effort to turn this tragedy into constructive community change, the YCOs organized a march on October 21, 2000, to take back the community (Miller 2000).

The march began at the vacant lot, where hundreds of young people showed up and participated in the clean-up of this long abandoned property. The group, joined by other community residents and city officials, then marched through the surrounding area chanting "Youth First in Jackson Square! ¡Jovenes Primero!" Eventually, they returned to the vacant lot, where they placed a banner, symbolically claiming the land as their own and as the future site of the youth and family center.

The march, attended by well over 200 people, delivered the youth's message loud and clear, and the idea earned the support of city officials (Miller 2000). Immediately following this action, a representative from Urban Edge wrote an op-ed in the local newspaper thanking the task force youth for organizing the march and promising the organization's support in building a new youth and family center (Stoddard 2000).

Youth and Family Center: No Longer a Dream

In December 2000, Jamaica Plain Neighborhood Council member John Demeter proposed lowering the voting and membership age in the council to 16 years (Lombardi 2000). Demeter, a board member of the Hyde Square Task Force at the time, stated that he was inspired by the work of the task force's youth and proposed that young people be given authority to make official decisions in their own community. The Jamaica Plain Neighborhood Council unanimously voted in favor of the proposition and lowered both the voting and membership ages to 16 years. In the summer of 2001, Kimberly Chacon and Oscar Vega campaigned for office and became the first youth leaders to be elected as council members (Two Teens 2001). This so-lidified the organization's status as a highly respected and effective model for youth organizing.

Following the council election, the youth of the Hyde Square Task Force began working pro-bono with architect Dan Dilullo to come up with their vision for the youth and family center (Rudavsky 2002). Simultaneously, they developed and administered a youth-focused survey to gather infor-mation about what young people desired and needed in the community. With assistance from Jesus Gerena, the newly appointed community orga-nizer of the Hyde Square Task Force, these young activists increased their skills for advocacy and community organizing. Gerena guided them through the analysis of community power and training for basic organizing, in-cluding public speaking and media advocacy, in preparation for a long fight to bring the much-needed youth and family center to this community.

During a press conference in November 2002, this group of young leaders presented their vision for the new center, as well as their needs for more youth development services and programs. Their consistent partici-pation in hundreds of hours of meetings hosted by the Jackson Coordi-nating Group paid off when their vision was incorporated into the overall development of Jackson Square (Rudavsky 2002). With support from the community, as well as city and state officials, the youth and family center finally seemed within reach.

During the final Jackson Coordinating Group planning meeting on Oc-tober 2, 2003, young people once again publicly demonstrated their support for the new center, marching into the meeting chanting "Youth First in Jackson Square, ¡Jovenes Primero!" (MacDonald 2003). After the meeting, community residents approved the development priorities set forth by the group to include a youth and family center, affordable housing units, and small-scale commercial space. The Boston Redevelopment Authority gave its approval and a request for proposal (RFP) was released, soliciting in-terested developers to finally begin the revitalization of Jackson Square (Ruch 2003).

Future of Jackson Square

With many interested outside developers waiting for release of the RFP, local grassroots organizations realized that they needed to come together once again to make sure that the community's needs and visions would be addressed and implemented. In the spring of 2004, two major local CDCs—Jamaica Plain Neighborhood Development Corporation and Urban Edge—began discussions on collaborating as developer. Several months later these two organizations officially announced their collaboration, under the name of Partners for Jackson, and became one of the potential developers for

Jackson Square (Ruch 2005). The partnership of these two CDCs was viewed as a symbolic reunion in a community no longer divided and now working toward a common goal. Soon after, the accomplishments and dedication of the young activists and the Hyde Square Task Force were formally recognized when the organization became the third member of the Partners for Jackson Development Team.

After release of the RFP on July 2, 2004, three potential developers, including Partners for Jackson, began preparing proposals that would include a youth and family center, mixed-market housing, and commercial space for small businesses. In January 2005, two developers—Partners for Jackson and Mitchell Properties, LLC—submitted their proposals, each hoping to become the future developer of this long-neglected project (Ruch 2005). During a community meeting in February 2005, hosted by Roxbury Community College, hundreds of community residents gathered to hear both developers present their visions of a future Jackson Square (Ruch 2005). The night was symbolic and sentimental for many, because approximately six years before they had been in the same room protesting the K-Mart to be built in their community. As they listened that night, they realized that their dream for Jackson Square now was within reach.

The final twist in the Jackson Square Development saga came a few days prior to announcement of the Boston Redevelopment Authority's decision to name the developer. Partners for Jackson and Mitchell Properties had decided to combine resources and present themselves as a unified front for the development of Jackson Square, with Partners for Jackson taking the lead (Jason 2005). At a June 1 ceremony, symbolically held on one of the vacant parcels waiting to be developed, young people, community residents, and city and state officials gathered to witness the moment when this combined team was designated for development of Jackson Square (Jason 2005).

This was a major victory for the community, particularly the youth and their advocates who had been fighting for years. Knowing that there still is a long way to go, they remain optimistic and passionate about the youth and family center, commercial and recreational space, and 400 units of mixed-income housing that soon will call Jackson Square home. As Mayor Menino and other public officials spoke about the history of Jackson Square, the young activists from the community were recognized for their hard work and strong contributions.

Throughout the six-year process, the youth of the Hyde Square Task Force attended every major community meeting and forum on the development issue. Their presence represents the power this community and its youth hold. Needless to say, the young people of the Hyde Square Task Force have won the battle. They have accomplished what many adults could not, and they established themselves as visible leaders in the community. They will continue their work to achieve the goal of bringing more resources to their community, and they will carry on the fight to make their voices heard. Soon enough, they will be able to lead the fight from the youth and family center that they helped build!

Commentary and Analysis

The ten principles for examining youth organizations, introduced in chapter 4, are helpful when analyzing this successful case example (participation, leadership, staffing, structure, goals, target systems, strategy and tactics, finances, allies, communications). The campaign to establish a youth and family center arose from the context of a traditional *turf*-based organizing effort by the Hyde Square Task Force that initially focused on gang and drug violence. As neighborhood residents joined together to gain greater control over the redevelopment of the area, the need for a youth center surfaced through a true "bottom-up" community-driven strategic planning process initiated by the task force's executive director. Once it became clear that youth programming was an essential priority, and large numbers of young people became directly involved in the action group, strong elements of *identity* organizing based on age also emerged.

Participation by both neighborhood youth and adults was broad and deep through the many phases of this organizing campaign, which ultimately was successful owing to effective use of people power. Hundreds of residents—young and old—attended numerous community meetings and workshops that were part of the strategic planning process. A large number of other community groups were engaged in the fight to stop the opening of the K-Mart store. Indeed, the coordinating committee that led this part of the effort included more than seventy community residents and business owners. According to Gian Gonzalez, one of the youth leaders interviewed from the campaign, "You could easily turn out 100 people a night."

The initial involvement of many youth was more for social than political reasons. As Gian explains, "A lot of it at the beginning was friends, to come and socialize." A strong bond developed among these youth, whose ages ranged from 13 to 17. "This became a second family away from the house, kind of, because I would see them most of the time—two or three times a week, sometimes four times a week. So, through the process of doing all that, I got really close with the people—I made a whole new group of friends."

Leo Peguero, another task force youth leader, adds, "I guess the longer we were here, the more we liked it. And we never expected to be here as long as we were. I did not expect to graduate from high school. . . . The longer you were here, the longer you wanted to stay. It happened, you know, that we'd gone off to college and still come back."

Over time, the active participation of youth activists began changing some of the negative perceptions about teenagers that were held by many adults in the community. Leo explains, "Before that, me and my brother and my friend, we were seen as trouble makers; and once you start doing stuff like this, you start to notice that people actually change the way that they look at you. They start to give you a little more respect and expect more things from you and better things from you. You do feel good about yourself." There was a growing recognition that youth could make a positive contribution to the community. According to Leo, "Like we started to get a lot more teenagers and it was just like when teenagers are given a chance, they become something really good."

Participation in community organizing activities enabled these young leaders to gain skills, confidence, and a sense of self-esteem. Gian explains:

> So after that, talking to everybody and everything, I broke out of a shell of being quiet and not being able to talk to people. I got to express myself a lot more than I would have if I'd stayed home. By public speaking and talking to people, I've gained more experience in speaking. I gained more confidence. The task force has really helped me a lot finding what I was good at.

This positive experience contributed to their continued involvement over time, despite the many hours of work entailed. Leo adds, "It's very addictive once you start feeling good about yourself—and it's the main thing that I got from this place—this place makes you feel good."

Youth leaders entered the fray in earnest at the Roxbury Community College public hearing on the K-Mart development proposal, attended by Boston City Councilors and several hundred people. And their efforts were recognized when they were officially designated as representatives for young people and awarded one of the thirty organizational member votes as part of the community's voice on the Jackson Coordinating Group's activities. The team of fifteen YCOs was introduced at the Hyde Square Task Force's annual meeting with hundreds in attendance, and these youth activists set in motion the Youth First in Jackson Square campaign.

Overall, more than two hundred youth were directly involved in the action group, with large-turnout events at another community meeting to oppose K-Mart, the march following the death of the 15-year-old who was stabbed, and the final Jackson Coordinating Group planning meeting. But a hallmark of this campaign was the steady, consistent participation of young activists in hundreds of hours of community meetings to envision, plan, strategize, and negotiate for the new youth center. Gian describes it: "We would go everywhere. That's how we got to be known so well, was that we were at every meeting all the time. Basically, put it this way, every time there was a meeting that had to do with that plot of land, wherever it was—we were there." This regular involvement over the course of several years—often through protracted and difficult discussions—clearly demonstrated the commitment, perseverance, and follow-through of the core group of youth leaders.

The fifteen YCOs provided both *leadership* and *staffing*, functioning in the role of organizer/leader that is so typical in youth-led organizing. They performed a number of staffing roles, including recruitment, designing and administering the youth survey, and gathering factual information about various aspects of the campaign. Gian elaborates:

> The whole organizer thing was really, really new to me and I didn't know what I was getting myself into. I started gaining more knowledge about what it was that they were doing. We got a lot of projects where we had to go out and meet with people, talk to people, having them come to meetings that we were having and stuff like that to let them know what we were about. That's how we started by letting people know who we were and what was the difference that we were trying to bring to the community.

And they also functioned as leaders, representing their constituency at numerous community planning meetings and serving as visible spokespeople at marches, rallies, and large public events. Leadership was not vested with one or two youth; rather, it was shared and collective throughout the campaign. Leo says, "Well, at that point we were not separated into different levels of organizers, but definitely in a group." This de-centralized leadership model has enabled the group to deal effectively with the challenge of young leaders aging out, replacing them through an orderly process. Gian adds, "So now there's a whole new group, pretty much nobody from the original group is in the YCO now. They are all pretty young and trying to learn, like the history, and trying to go on their own."

Individual development of both leadership and staffing skills was a product of both structured training sessions and learning through direct experience over the course of the campaign. The workshops on power analysis, public speaking, media advocacy, and basic community organizing were classic components of a leadership training curriculum. However, this more formalized instruction served only to supplement the rich on-the-job education gained through participation in this extensive community struggle. "To put your point across was kind of hard. Sometimes, when it comes to being a kid, it's harder to have them listen to you. So when you're a kid, you have to have the point straight," Gian explains.

Actually, *financing* for the youth community organizer staff positions was quite minimal. At first there was no money at all; later, team members were paid a very modest $50 every two weeks by the Hyde Square Task Force. As this book went to press, youth team organizers were paid at the hourly minimum wage; but consistent with their past track record, these organizers/leaders continued to donate large numbers of uncompensated hours. Leo says, "At that point, we used to be here for a lot more hours, getting a stipend really didn't matter. . . . We used to go from school and stay here [at the task force office] the whole time and put in a lot of hours."

The YCO team was an outgrowth of the Hyde Square Task Force *structure*, and the task force has remained the host agency for this locally based youth-led organizing effort. However, the external structural recognition achieved by the YCO when it was treated as a separate entity from the task force and allotted an organizational vote on the Jackson Coordinating Group was unusual and quite impressive for a newly formed youth group. The lowering of the voting and membership ages to 16 years for the Jamaica Plain Neighborhood Council also was striking and enabled the YCO to play an active and equal role with adults in this larger area of Boston, transcending both traditional age and spatial boundaries.

The *goal* of opening a new youth and family center was part of a larger reclamation program for the Jackson Square neighborhood that also included affordable housing and small-scale commercial space. The YCO used the youth-focused survey to identify the need for a youth services facility and then worked with a pro-bono architect to create the actual vision for the center. Once this goal was firmly established, a number of interim *objectives* were set and met as important steps in the overall campaign. Certainly, the most significant and challenging objective was to stop the development of a K-Mart store on the very parcel of land envisioned as the site for the new youth center. Neutralizing Urban Edge's backing of this retail store and winning their support for a new youth facility were critical pieces of this objective.

There were multiple *target systems* tied to the YCO's ultimate goal and secondary objectives. Initially, the mayor and city council were targeted at public meetings in an effort to involve the city of Boston directly in the redevelopment of Jackson Square. There was a positive resolution when the mayor directed the Boston Redevelopment Authority to take responsibility for monitoring the redevelopment process, and the Jackson Coordinating Group was established to represent the interests of the community. Leo adds, "It's really cool when you see changes that you can do here."

While there was fierce and broad-based community opposition to the opening of a new K-Mart store, the corporation was less a target than Urban Edge, which was the sponsor of the redevelopment plan that included this large business enterprise. Clearly, the youth-led action after the stabbing death was the turning point for Urban Edge, as evidenced by the CDC's publication of a local newspaper op-ed supporting a youth and family center immediately after this high-profile community event. And finally, the Boston Redevelopment Authority was successfully targeted by the entire Jackson Coordinating Group as an acceptable request for proposal was generated and developers acceptable to the community were selected.

A mix of *strategies* and *tactics* were employed, depending on whether relationships with the various target systems required collaboration, persuasion, or adversarial contest (Warren 1975). Obviously, this community organizing effort featured *community development*, but vintage social action strategies and tactics also were brought to bear on target systems that exhibited a range of resistance to community members' vision for accept-able redevelopment and change. Essentially, a persuasive campaign approach was used to win over city officials and the Boston Redevelopment Authority, and once consensus had been established, relations and inter-actions between community members and municipal decision makers ten-ded to be collaborative.

The large and vocal turnouts at the different public meetings effectively convinced elected officials and institutional leaders to heed the wishes of community members who opposed the establishment of a K-Mart store. The YCO team carried signs and spoke passionately about the need for youth services in the community, and the youth-focused survey data supporting this position were presented with great tactical skill. Use of the Youth First in Jackson Square campaign slogan dramatically conveyed the essence of this youth-led organizing initiative and captured the general public's imag-ination. The YCO also employed the media effectively, presenting their vision for a new youth center compellingly at a press conference. Overall, the Jackson Coordinating Group, including its youth representatives, fol-lowed through conscientiously throughout the entire planning process, presenting a unifying and unswerving voice from the community.

On the other hand, a more adversarial approach was taken vis-à-vis Urban Edge, as community members pressured with tactics designed to force the CDC to drop support for developing the store. Youth activists were involved in heated exchanges with Urban Edge leaders during the early stages of the campaign. Leo explains: "We always had somebody—an adult—who would try to make a statement by a teenager sound stupid." Within ten weeks of the much publicized and tragic stabbing death, the YCO organized a march to take back the community, cleaned up the aban-doned property near the MBTA station, and symbolically claimed this plot of land as the site for the new youth facility.

Certainly, the violent death of the 15-year-old was a traumatic and profoundly sad event that had deeply wounded members of the Jackson Square community. However, the YCO used this tragedy as an organizing handle to leverage constructive change, channeling positive energy into unifying direct action and hope for the future. This tactic was broadly supported by the community and won the respect and support of city officials. It also compelled Urban Edge to abandon plans for building a K-Mart and to make a commitment to open a new youth center on this emotionally charged vacant parcel of land.

An extensive list of *allies* from other community organizations—the small business community, neighborhood health centers, tenants councils from public housing developments, community development corporations, hu-man services agencies, area churches, municipal departments—and selected city and state officials supported this campaign. The action group also was able to enlist the services of a pro bono architect, an advocate from the nationwide anti-K-Mart movement, and several professional statisticians who evaluated and critiqued Urban Edge's severely flawed survey of shoppers.

Perhaps most impressive was the strong positive working relationship between young people and adults that was exhibited throughout the campaign. Indeed, the YCO team was accorded equal status with adult groups in the Jackson Coordinating Group, and the Jamaica Plain Neighborhood Council took the unusual step of lowering the voting and membership ages to 16 years in order that youth could participate fully in official community decisions. The election of two YCO representatives broke new ground for youth–adult partnerships in Boston, helping set the tone for the collaborative and productive inter-generational relations that were a centerpiece of this community organizing initiative. Gian concludes: "I think that the best part is actually having people—adults—agree with me... having people see where I'm coming from, actually listening to my point of view of things."

Finally, the youth organizing team used a mix of *communication* techniques to recruit participants from within the community and to carry their message beyond the immediate neighborhood. The most prevalent and effective form of *internal* communication was through face-to-face contact. Recruitment was done through street outreach in places where young people were most likely to hang, such as the MBTA station, schools, playgrounds, parking lots, grocery stores, and street corners. The YCO team also systematically knocked on doors. Gian gives the details:

> Basically, when we talked to people, we had them write down their names and numbers—stuff like that. "If you're interested and you want to help us out." That's a lot of the way we kept in contact. We had a really long list of people that we came in contact with who actually supported us in what we're doing, so when it came time to have a meeting we just took those lists and we did a number of letters where we would fold, stamp, lick envelopes.

Flyers were used to publicize meetings and actions, while posters prominently carried the messages SCHOOL IS OUT. WHERE DO I GO? KMART? and WE MUST BE A PART OF THE PROCESS! at the public hearing before city councilors. The powerful chant "Youth First in Jackson Square! *¡Jovenes Primero!*" resounded at public events. This was very much a grassroots effort; various electronic media were not utilized to a significant degree for recruitment purposes.

As mentioned above, results of the youth-focused survey were presented at a formal press conference as a mechanism for *external* communication. The YCO also published a special newsletter detailing the results of the survey for youth. Youth leaders proved to be accomplished spokespeople at numerous public meetings and events, both large and small. While not part of the YCO's external communicative and tactical repertoire at the time of the youth center campaign, popular theater now is a staple of the group's organizing approach. The central themes are improving relations between local police and neighborhood youth, and preventing sexual harassment in both school and community settings. And, of course, according to Leo, "We're still working on getting our Youth Center."

In summary, the overall change strategy employed in this campaign met the three criteria for success listed by the Innovations Center for Community & Youth Development (2003), as discussed in chapter 4: (1) organizational leadership was able to inspire action and partnership among all members of the community; (2) they were able to develop the capacity of their organization to plan, implement, and achieve its social change goal; and (3) the changes created were effectively sustained and supported over an extended period of time.

10

Challenges Inherent in Youth-Led Organizing

> Sustaining social justice must be a core value and strategy to promote systemic reform. We must articulate a collective progressive strategy that sustains a social justice legacy by promoting youth engagement, analysis, voice, and leadership.... Youth organizing develops a critical pipeline of thoughtful, innovative and strategic leaders who are impacting policy, building institutions, transforming practice, and changing culture.
> —Garrett, *Greetings!* (2006)

All forms of practice bring with them their rewards and challenges, particularly those associated with social change; youth-led organizing is no exception. Some practitioners and academics would argue that a field without challenges is a field that is dead and therefore insignificant! Challenges, in effect, serve to focus attention and bring solutions to practice dilemmas that can take on a variety of forms, from ethical to methodological. They, too, represent focal points at which academics, practitioners, and communities can come together to engage in dialogue and move the field forward, as is the case at hand.

The field of youth-led community organizing has its share of challenges to be met and obstacles to be overcome in order for progress to occur. For example, Williams (2003) identifies four key barriers to youth organizing that present the field with incredible challenges: (1) the need to seek immediate gratification; (2) recognition that attempts at social change can result in failure; (3) the shifting priorities of youth as they grow older; and

(4) the adultism that can undermine youth creativity, drive, and energy. Williams's list is an excellent starting point; however, it is far from exhaustive. Morsillo and Prilleltensky (2005) also acknowledge the barriers to youth engagement in social action, noting that most avenues available to young people are ameliorative in nature and that social change is not always the top priority for adults.

Kim and Sherman (2006, 4) bring another challenge to the table, this one directed at society in general: "The role of youth in the emerging diverse social justice movements of the 1960s and 1970s has been widely celebrated. However, little attention was paid to intentionally developing the next generation of social justice leaders. Many competing explanations have been offered, but the result was unanimous: a deep generational gap." The importance of recruiting, preparing, and sustaining youth leaders is beyond dispute, from our standpoint. The question becomes, How can we as a society ensure that an adequate number of youth leaders—in this case, those who are organizers—address the challenges and surmount the barriers to success, both now and in the future?

This chapter provides a comprehensive view of the considerations and challenges found in all phases of the organizing process. However, in the case of youth organizing, particular attention is paid to how age and gender become both facilitating and hindering factors in campaigns for social change. Some of the challenges discussed in this chapter have been discussed in various ways earlier in this book; however, we believe that they are important enough to the field to be revisited.

Need for Immediate Gratification: "You Can't Always Get What You Want"

Delay of gratification has been found to be a powerful indicator of self-regulatory behavior (Wulfert et al. 2002). Self-regulatory behavior, in turn, gives young people the opportunity to engage in actions that do not offer an immediate payoff, allowing them to opt for achieving more significant change and gratification at a future date. Social change never is simple, immediate, or guaranteed, as any experienced organizer can attest. Thus, young activists who enter this field with the need for immediate gain will have a difficult time as agents for social change.

According to Hanh Cao Yu, youth participants must contend with this reality:

> Thus, while "events" and "actions" can be exciting, the *lead up* to such events involves a lot of hard work. The implication of these results is that youth involved in organizing may not feel consistently challenged and

engaged. Program staff stated that they continually remind youth of the larger purpose of organizing and try to create definable wins so that youth can connect their daily experiences with broader community improvement goals. Additionally, organizing teaches youth patience, commitment and focus, and that change takes time. (Turning the Leadership 2004, 8)

YouthAction (1998) identified a series of challenges in youth organizing, one of which is how to balance achieving significant long-term social change with committing "serious" resources for immediate leadership and skills development? "When change does not occur as quickly as anticipated, youth run the risk of becoming bored and have a hard time embracing the necessity of long-term campaigns" (Weiss 2003, 98). Thus, it is not unusual to see tension between those organizers focusing on long-term goals and those focusing on short-term achievements. Similar strain can be found with regard to differences in individual goals; some achievement of personal growth can be expected immediately, while long-term goals in this regard require the passage of time.

Failure and Success As an Integral Part of Organizing: "Keep on Keepin' On"

Is success ever *guaranteed* in community organizing? No! This should never be the case. However, even when failure occurs, there can be much personal gain as a result. Of course, gain surely comes from success; however, young people must be able to assess both achievements and defeats, seeking to make progress in all areas that need improvement. When young people develop the ability to evaluate both their strengths and weaknesses, and learn from both, they will be more effective in future campaigns and more capable mentors, as well.

Formal evaluations of youth-led campaigns often are the preferred means to gain these insights; however, young people must be clear about what constitutes success and failure. For example, awareness of position must never be confused with objectivity (Youth in Focus 2004, iii):

Every system of evaluation is based on assumptions about what is important, what is measurable and what the information is for. Make those assumptions explicit. Social scientists sometimes see assumptions as a limitation or a bias and strive for an illusion of objectivity. Good evaluation does not try to achieve objectivity but makes clear positionality: who is driving the process, what are their assumptions and what are their goals and where are they coming from. The illusion of objectivity can do nothing but hide the real power relationships in an evaluation process.

Although this analysis by Youth in Focus (2004) specifically refers to evaluation, it also applies to the need for young people to have a clear sense of what their campaign objectives were and to what extent, if any, they were accomplished. Evaluation is usually associated with programming, but it also has applicability for better understanding the outcomes of community organizing. Rarely will a campaign result in clear success or failure. As a result, youth must be able to honestly identify strengths, weaknesses, accomplishments, frustrations, and areas for improvement.

Growing Up and Out of a Youth Organizer Role

Aging out of youth roles and moving into the world of adults is inevitable for young people, and anyone familiar with the field of youth organizing is quick to acknowledge this point and its consequences for organizational development. Indeed, the implications are significant (Sherwood and Dressner 2004, 56):

> Their "workforce" is expected to leave almost as soon as individual "workers" have mastered the skills needed to be good at their tasks. Consequently, not only do youth organizing groups need to have systems and methods to ensure that each young member receives the attention and support needed for his or her learning and personal development, but groups also need to have systems and methods to ensure that every young member is replaced, smoothly, so that the organizing work goes on and, ideally, so that successes build over time into a long-term vision of and progress toward fundamental change. This type of thinking, planning, and juggling is demanding.

There are other, less obvious effects of the aging-out phenomenon. First, and one that often is overlooked, is the loss of institutional memory when youth organizers leave their organizations (Weiss 2003). Their wisdom, experience, and knowledge depart with them. High turnover and transitions in leadership necessitate that important institutional resources be devoted to constant recruitment and training, as has been discussed elsewhere in this book. Second, finding staff positions for new-adult organizers within and outside of the programs can be challenging, time-consuming, and stressful for all concerned. As a result, viable avenues for leadership transition are important in youth-led organizations and initiatives (Young Wisdom Project 2004, 18):

> Like other nonprofits, there is often pressure on leaders of youth-led organizations to be in the public limelight, especially with funders. If the organization's reputation becomes too connected with a single charismatic

young adult leader, it can undermine the leadership potential development of others in the group. Setting up clear structures to develop and transition leadership within the organization is essential.

What are useful and fulfilling roles for young activists as they move out of a youth cohort? Alumni of youth-led campaigns are excellent facilitators to ease the transition of new graduates who have just aged out (YouthAction 1998). For example, they can act as consultants, advisors, and trainers/facilitators. This enables the graduates to tap the knowledge of alumni and, in turn, they can give back to their former group in a manner that is capacity enhancing and facilitative.

Adultism Is Alive and Well

As already noted in chapter 5, adultism is an insidious process, similar to other forms of oppression. However, unlike other types of subjugation, it is seldom acknowledged and not well recognized in society. Furthermore, it can take on many forms, all of which undermine youth decision making and leadership, rendering young people ineffective and likely to blame themselves when failures occur. The best intentions of adults often mask the pervasive nature of this form of oppression. While intergenerational relationships offer great potential for those involved, a tremendous amount of reeducation must occur on the part of adults for the potential of youth to be fully realized (Young Wisdom Project 2004).

This is not to say that adults have no role in youth-led community organizing. YouthAction (1998, 25) poses the question: "How much decision-making power do you give to young people, while also finding appropriate roles that respect the experiences and wisdom of elders?" This query is important and provocative, especially when considered with adultism as a backdrop. Mokwena's (2000, 4) observations bring this matter to the forefront:

> While accepting the important role played by adults, many youth activists in Latin America also sounded a word of caution about the potential for adult manipulation. They were also quick to criticize those adults who only used them as tokens and pawns. Some were deeply suspicious of adults in government, who often attempt to manipulate and placate them. Young community activists drove this point home from COVORPA in Oaxaca. They argued. "Youth have the power to do things for their people and for themselves. We have problems with the state but we don't negate participation with the state, however, we cherish our autonomy."

Competing Demands on Time

Youth-led community organizing, be it urban or rural based, requires that a multitude of individual goals be accomplished in addition to achieving positive change. As a result, time and timing are critical in youth-led campaigns as compared to adult-led organizing efforts. Decision making must consider the learning curve for determining how decisions are made (process), as well as the content necessary for developing an immediate, specific, and winnable campaign.

Although organizing often occupies a central place in the lives of many young activists, it still is an add-on to their busy schedules. For example, school, home chores, part-time employment, assisting younger siblings with homework, after-school activities that may include sports—all compete with organizing for youth's time. As a result, learning how to balance competing demands for time becomes either an implicit or explicit goal for many young participants. Adults also must learn to balance multiple responsibilities that vie for their attention; however, youth typically have much less control over their obligations, which very often are dictated by adults.

Importance of Getting Paid for Organizing

Many organizations and foundations that support youth-led organizing emphasize the importance of paying young activists who take on the organizer/leader role. However, YouthAction (1998, 25) broadened the challenge: "How do you create a lifelong passion for social justice, and simultaneously attempt to meet the economic needs of young people who are seeking gainful summer and/or full year employment?"

Economic status may or may not allow children to forgo working part time. For example, YUCA's practice of paying a weekly stipend to youth participants in the Higher Learning program highlights a critical problem faced by many organizations, especially those with a constituency that need to work to survive. Staff member Lourdes Best explains that YUCA pays its organizer/leaders because they should not have to choose between organizing and getting a paying job.

Burning On, Not Out

Engagement in community organizing can be an exciting, emotionally charged, and exhilarating experience. It also can be a draining, discouraging, and disheartening one. The adrenalin rush and euphoria that accompany and follow a successful rally, march, or direct-action protest can soon be supplanted by a profound sense of failure, misery, and despair when the next plans go amiss and the next social-change campaign falters or fails. Righteous anger can turn inward, resulting in self-blaming explanations for defeats and the onset of depression. Both the need for immediate gratification and the inability to learn from mistakes can lead to the loss of motivation, enthusiasm, and optimism that is associated with the term *burnout* (Pines and Maslach 1978; Harrison 1980). However, burnout also can occur at the same time activists are successful with organizational goals for change, as they become overwhelmed by competing demands for time and financial pressures, as well as a host of other problems, including lack of recognition, feelings of isolation, difficulties getting along with colleagues, poor or no supervision, limited job promotion opportunities, inadequate organizational resources, cramped working conditions, too much work, and absence of a compelling organizational vision and mission (Karger 1981; Maslach 1982).

There is extensive literature on both the causes and the cures for burnout (Cherniss 1980; Jayaratne and Chess 1984; Arches 1991), and we do not revisit this important but well-traversed terrain. However, it should be noted that youth activists, especially those with lower income backgrounds, are particularly susceptible to burnout owing to age and income, including a relative paucity of experience and maturity; the degree of difficulty attendant to many of the change efforts they undertake and adult-led institutions they confront; the scarcity of resources in so many youth-led organizing programs; financial and family stressors; marginalization, especially for youth of color; unwillingness of mainstream media to provide news coverage of positive youth actions and activities; absence of professional trainers; and disconnection from other youth-led organizing programs and larger support networks.

Since so many of these factors are deep-rooted, intractable impediments, burnout will remain a challenge in youth-led organizing for years to come. Certainly, antidotes include a broad range of personal and organizational supports, such as mentoring, strong supervision, high-quality training, a greater degree of financial stability, an atmosphere of affirmation and respect, linkages to similar projects, assistance from regional and national resource centers, and ongoing cultivation and advancement of a powerful organizational vision.

Can't Get No Respect

Comedian Rodney Dangerfield never could get respect. Likewise, the media have been slow to grant youth-led organizing efforts the positive attention that they so richly deserve. Too often, young people are demonized or marginalized in the electronic and print media. Stereotypes abound, often of youth as unmotivated, poorly educated, lacking a strong work ethic, alienated from society, abusing various substances, running in violent gangs, and engaging in criminal activities. The negative images are particularly prevalent, offensive, and objectionable when applied to low-income youth of color. This media slant creates significant challenges for youth-led organizing efforts, especially those in multicultural urban areas with high poverty rates.

Positive media coverage can be a powerful weapon when community organizations pressure their targeted institutional decision makers to meet demands for social change. Third-party audiences—often the general public, made aware of the change initiative through media coverage—may help determine whether organizational goals are achieved. Likewise, positive or negative publicity impacts the ability of those decision makers to maintain or gain power and advance their careers. An organization's ability to bless or blast its targets, with media coverage, is an important source of power (Staples 2004a).

Positive publicity gives a group greater credibility, both internally "on the street" and externally with important people and institutions that have not been targeted. When community organizations are in the news, there's almost always a boost in recruitment. Beyond the community, good press coverage can win over potential allies, gain the respect of elected and appointed officials, attract volunteers from other groups, catch the attention of the general public, and enhance the organization's reputation as a serious player. Clippings of positive and prominent press coverage often go a long way toward establishing the group's legitimacy and viability in the eyes of possible funding sources.

When the media *fail* to cover an organization's protests, the group has lost important leverage, and unfortunately, this too often is the case for youth-led organizing initiatives. Mainstream media outlets tend to dismiss social-change campaigns led by young activists; therefore, securing more and better media coverage is a high priority for some youth-led organizations. Many groups put additional energy and time into cultivating good media relations; skills to work effectively with the media now are frequently incorporated into leadership development training programs for young activists. Old patterns of thinking and stereotypes often die hard, but when concerted efforts are made to develop and nurture relationships with the relevant media, there is reason for guarded optimism.

Adult Organizers in Waiting?

On the surface, it seems normal to view youth organizing positions as logical stepping stones toward an adult organizer role. However, this view can have inherent challenges and contradictions. HoSang notes:

A natural temptation exists to assess youth organizing efforts from this same vantage point—a "not quite" dry run in anticipation of a more bona fide effort to build "real" power as adults. Youth organizing projects are then either uncritically valorized and boosted without serious engagement, or all together dismissed as marginal and non-strategic. Adults may feel that youth members add "spirit" and "vitality" to actions and meetings, but do not expect them do to the heavy lifting of lobbying, advocacy, and turn-out crucial to sustaining social change projects. (Funders' Collaboration on Youth Organizing 2003, 17)

Evaluating Youth-Led Community Organizing: "Can't Live with it, and Can't Live without it"

The role of research and evaluation in the youth-led field is undeniable (Delgado 2006; Fernandez 2002; Fletcher 2004; Youth in Focus 2004). Funders increasingly have sought to demonstrate the effectiveness of these initiatives (Innovative Center for Community and Youth Development 2003); however, evaluation has also provided a venue for youth-involvement and leadership, regardless of the setting.

Schools are a prime example of the potential role students can play as evaluators (Fletcher 2004, 22):

By involving students as evaluators, schools can develop purposeful, impacting, and authentic assessments of classes, schools, teachers, and enact accountability and ownership for all participants in the learning process. Effective evaluations may include student evaluations of classes and schools; student evaluations of teachers; student evaluations of self; and student-led parent-teacher conferences, where students present their learning as partners with teachers and parents, instead of as passive recipients of teaching done "to" them.

Nevertheless, a word of caution is in order. For instance, the popularity of youth development no doubt will continue, influencing youth-led community organizing both in this country and internationally (Fernandez 2002). Research and evaluation in the youth development field can be expected to cross into youth-led organizing. Soon, these organizing initiatives will need to prepare for the arrival of social scientists and evaluators, who will be eager to document the processes and outcomes in their campaigns for social change. This phenomenon, in all likelihood, will not be well received by the youth-led organizing field.

New models of research and evaluation must be developed to take into account the unique aspects of this organizing approach (Delgado 2006). However, evaluation is a method heavily grounded in politics (Youth in Focus 2004, ii):

Everything is political and the drive towards evaluation is one of the most political movements in the current funding world. It is a two sided coin— when done for the right reasons, with the needed resources and support, evaluation becomes what it should be: a way for groups to take the time to reflect on their work to get feedback from participants, partners and the external environment and to find ways of becoming more effective. . . . At the same time, evaluation can serve as a dodge for the discomfort that some funders may have with supporting social justice and social change work.

Involving the young people doing the organizing in evaluating their own work will reduce some of this resistance. They can be instrumental in all facets of research and evaluation, thus generating support for more scientific investigations and ultimately strengthening the organizing at the same time as young activists develop new skill sets. The principles that govern youth-led community organizing are well served by similar guidelines for youth-led research. The integration of these two movements is a natural occurrence and in the long-run will benefit both fields.

It is imperative that the field avoid falling into long-established traps regarding what constitutes important questions in an evaluation effort. "In a society in which social policy is privatized and youth are mere commodities, the information all sides seek and relentlessly exploit is not the most important (no matter how accurate and topical), but the most salable (no matter how distorted, even ridiculous)" (Males 2004, 11). This caution should be heeded; evaluation is not value free and, as a result, is subject to sociopolitical forces and considerations.

No form of youth-led initiative or setting has escaped increased scrutiny (Delgado 2006). As a result, youth-led community organizing has had to contend with the challenges of evaluation. YouthAction (1998, 26) cautions: "Dispel the liberalism so often present when talking about youth, and youth organizing. Raise the level of expectations and seriousness about youth organizing efforts. Hold youth organizing to similar evaluation standards as other types of organizing." However, the fact that there should be rigorous criteria for evaluating youth-led community organizing does not mean that they are identical to the principles and methods applied to other youth-focused endeavors. Rather, the nature of the organizing process must be taken into account in determining the research questions, procedures, and conclusions. In short, a cookie-cutter approach is simply unacceptable (Delgado 2006).

As already noted, youth development and youth-led community organizing are not antithetical. Operating from a community context promotes the integration and achievement of both individual and social-change goals. Bridging the worlds of individual and community allows youth-led projects to set ambitious goals that can be tailored to complement community social-change goals. This flexibility, a hallmark of any good youth development project, facilitates the crafting of projects that take into account local circumstances. However, it also necessitates the creation of output objectives that stress both ends, making the project a challenge to evaluate.

Furthermore, documentation plays an important role in the evaluation process and helps maximize institutional memory. The evaluation process provides young people with an opportunity to share their stories with the outside world as well as promotes the organizational work and accomplishments. However, unless there are formal mechanisms in place to capture and document these experiences, much information will be lost. One youth organizer noted, "A lot of the best work happens off the radar screen. We are all so busy doing work . . . doing good work . . . we aren't doing the organizational promotion or being really effective in gathering new resources" (W.K. Kellogg Foundation 2000, 15).

Wheeler (2003) observes that documents such as manuals, guides, and curricula not only aid in the evaluation process but also help organizations achieve long-term sustainability. A grasp of history can ease the transition for new staff as they learn about the organization's philosophy and strategies; this process is particularly important in youth-led organizations because of the constant turnover of participants and leaders, owing to some participants' aging out and others' growing into these roles.

A number of scholars and organizations have addressed this challenge in highly responsive ways. For example, the Innovation Center for Community and Youth Development (2003) identified seven outcomes for individuals that should be a part of any youth-led community organizing effort:

1. Learning to navigate (moving in and out of various contexts with comfort and competence)
2. Learning to connect (communication and conflict resolution skills)
3. Learning to be productive (all aspects, from conceiving to completing projects)
4. Increasing political knowledge and skills
5. Increasing efficacy and agency (confidence and sense of voice)
6. Increasing democratic values (embracing equity and fairness-related values)
7. Developing strong personal and civic identity (sense of personal transformation and membership in community)

Each of these outcomes easily has a corresponding core element in a youth development paradigm, although different terms may be used.

There are important lessons to be learned from unsuccessful organizing campaigns, as noted by one youth organizer (LISTEN, Inc. 2004, 10):

> When you don't win, people don't say, you know that they don't want to be a part of things that lose. But I think the most important things are the development, because that's kind of the difference between advocacy and organizing. You can get a small group of lawyers or somebody to do something that might have the same impact, but in the long run that's not

really building power or not shifting the balance of that power, and its reliant on people who aren't experiencing the injustices.

Thus, emphasis on experience and lessons learned never should be lost in any campaign, regardless of the degree of success or failure! Furthermore, it would be irresponsible to imply that anything short of success constitutes absolute failure. Lessons with life-long application can be learned when young people draw positive outcomes from unsuccessful organizing efforts; this knowledge and perspective will aid them later in life, during times of great need. Indeed, this characteristic of youth-led organizing is one of many that must be present for young people to reap long-term benefits from their participation; a positive outlook also increases their likelihood of success in other efforts to bring about social change.

Not surprisingly, attributing community-centered change outcomes to youth-led organizing is much more difficult than evaluating efforts to bring knowledge and skills to participants (Innovation Center for Community and Youth Development 2003, 112):

> We were not able, within the scope of this evaluation, to assess community outcomes in any systematic way. Beyond not having the resources to measure community impacts, the field of community organizing and civic activism lacks clear established and tested benchmarks that we could use to assess community change. The complexity of political and social factors that influence shifts in community attitudes or policy makes community outcomes particularly difficult to measure.

However, this challenge must be met if the youth-led community organizing field hopes to find wider acceptance among funding and academic sources. Thus, evaluating social-change efforts embraces the following seven points (Korbin 2000; South 2000):

1. Lack of adequate funding
2. Importance of viewing outcomes longitudinally over a period of time
3. Emphasis on behavioral outcomes at the expense of attitudinal changes
4. A complex power construct, necessitating a broad perspective to capture both explicit and implicit changes in power relationships
5. Emphasis on significant social changes at the expense of more frequent incremental changes
6. Determination about whether social changes and neighborhood characteristics have affected all social and demographic groups in the same manner, and if not, in what ways they have differed
7. Validity of the historical tenet in the field of community organizing that the process of achieving change is of equal to or greater importance than the ultimate outcome

Any seasoned community-participatory evaluator will find the above points common considerations in carrying out an evaluation (Israel et al. 2005; Minkler and Wallerstein 2003). Community-focused interventions, by their very nature, are subject to a multitude of unanticipated forces and therefore have outcomes that are difficult to predict. Sometimes, these factors facilitate implementation; at other times, they hinder it. Nevertheless, the benefits of participation far outweigh the challenges and limitations of this form of social research.

On a final note, dissemination of the findings of any evaluation must go far beyond the conventional report and scholarly articles and books if the results are to reach young community activists and the adults instrumental in supporting them. The W.K. Kellogg Foundation (2000, 16) recommends a combination of methods for optimal dissemination:

- Print materials (program brochures, flyers, information sheets, how-to manuals
- Word of mouth
- Local radio, local television, public access cable
- Newspapers (local, city, and regional)
- Conferences (local, regional, and national)
- Speaking engagements, both to reach out to various audiences and in response to invitations
- Periodic and annual reports to funders and stakeholders
- Outreach to schools and community partners
- Youth-created/produced media (newspapers, "zines," radio/TV productions created by young people, video letters)
- Web sites and links
- E-mail and list serves
- Video (documentaries on issues, program information, training materials)
- Cultural and artistic performances (theater, spoken word, visual arts, photographic essays, video)
- Public service announcements on regional media, MTV spots, movie theater placements
- Gatherings for training and technical assistance
- Peer exchange programs

These are only a sampling of the ways to share evaluation results and promote youth-led organizing initiatives.

Youth Organizing: Stand Alone or in Unison with Others?

What is the best future for youth-led organizing? Is it preferable to go it alone, so to speak, because social-action agendas tend to make others feel uncomfortable about joining in? Or, should youth-led organizing reach across the conventional divides of human services (including the youth field)? James (2005) addresses this very point in describing how best to attend to the fragmentation of youth fields, particularly as the number of young people doing this work continues to increase.

James's call for a coordinated effort that serves young people speaks volumes about the growth of the field and its potential for benefiting all youth services. Although this exhortation is noble and its implications important, it will not be met with open arms. Competition between youth organizations for funding and participants often is fierce, and this will be a major impediment to cooperation across sectors. Nevertheless, an effort should be made, even though prospects for success are slim. Marginalized youth historically have suffered from insufficient resources, yet invariably there is a synergistic effect when one or more programs are merged to launch an initiative. This cooperation always is needed and can serve as a model for adult services to come together, as well.

Locating Resources for Training and Technical Assistance

We have stressed the importance of leadership development as a cross-cutting theme in the youth-led organizing model. However, lack of affiliation with large national or regional training networks and organizations is a common characteristic in the field. Intermediate support centers are few and far between. This situation poses a serious challenge for any approach that places a high priority on learning, consciousness raising, skills development, and personal growth. In essence, there is a significant shortfall of professional training resources available to most local youth-led programs around the United States.

Certainly, materials and information do exist, as evidenced in the scholarly work of Murphy and Cunningham (2003), Hardina (2002), and Homan (2004), not to mention the countless reports on youth organizing cited in this book; these all speak well for the field and its potential to increase in influence.

Intermediary organizations have been critical in moving the youth-led organizing field forward, as shown earlier in this chapter and in chapter 4. However, there is enormous need for expanded resources in this area. We believe that the major national foundations could accept this challenge and provide the requisite financial backing. Further, they could provide opportunities for youth organizers to learn and share their skills and information internationally.

Ultimately, regional and national support centers will be needed to transcend the training and technical assistance functions. If youth-led organizing holds true to its vision, it will continue to address major issues of oppression and social justice. If so, at some point the organizing campaigns will need to be made national, even international, in focus and scope. Such an ambitious organizing agenda cannot be initiated, nor sustained, from a purely local base. Larger structures will be necessary to drive and coordinate national and international campaigns, even as the issues are "localized" for neighborhood or school district arenas. This challenge to broaden the focus must be met if the youth-led organizing movement hopes to step up to the next level of power.

Strategic and Tactical Considerations: Outside or Inside Agents of Change?

Whether more can be accomplished from the inside or the outside is a classic question for any individual or group attempting to bring about social change. The inside strategy has the advantages of access to institutional decision makers, the potential for influencing opinions, the ability to obtain privileged information, opportunities to identify and cultivate allies in the power structure, a platform for legitimate criticism, and enhanced credibility with established powerful actors. But legitimacy can be a double-edged sword; it will cut back into the community if members perceive individuals having "sold out."

Furthermore, change from within can place a young person in a tenuous position regarding the organization. By joining the decision-making structure, to a large degree insider change agents forfeit their ability to criticize the process, since they have legitimized it through their participation. Once they are part of the official decision-making process, the members may be marginalized, viewed as tokens, compromised, or regularly outvoted as part of a relatively powerless minority, thereby becoming poster children for the concept of cooptation.

In contrast, outside strategies enable change agents to maintain a pure position, with total freedom to criticize targeted decision makers. When the campaign includes lively direct-action tactics, there also is potential, although no guarantee (see point number 8, above), that it will attract increased media coverage, since viewers, listeners, and readers often find the dynamics of contest and confrontation most engaging. Most important, an outside strategy has the greatest potential for using tactics that directly involve large numbers of the affected constituency—which is *the* fundamental source of power in community organizing—and it also increases "participatory competencies" (Kieffer 1984); the degree of organizational ownership (Staples 2004a); and the sense of collective self-efficacy (Pecukonis and Wenocur 1994).

However, those who use the outside approach always run the risk of being isolated and disregarded; the legitimacy of their claims may be questioned;

and they may fail to develop sufficient leverage to force decision makers to respond favorably. Outside strategies are labor-intensive, requiring aggressive and periodic recruitment, action research, strategic planning, and usually a series of direct-action tactics that mobilize large numbers of constituents to pressure institutional decision makers. Countertactics of the opposition must be anticipated and countered in turn; allies need to be enlisted; a media plan should be developed; and organizational leadership must be prepared for multiple roles and responsibilities.

Young activists, many of whom are marginalized in society, already are on the outside almost by definition; certainly, using customary social-action strategies to convince or coerce decision makers currently is the most prevalent approach in the field. Indeed, many of the examples in this book are instances when youth-led organizing has attempted to bring about change from the outside. Results have been mixed, but certainly they have been sufficient to justify this study. Indeed, a youth-led organizing social movement is beginning to emerge, and it has operated to bring about change essentially from the outside in.

However, youth-led organizing efforts at times may consider inside strategies. This approach can be problematic, especially if the group is vulnerable to countertactics by targeted adult decision makers with the intent of coopting the movement. The increased status and heady atmosphere of rubbing shoulders with adults in positions of power can be seductive. There can be the illusion of inclusion, and participation can seem like real power. The possibility that powerful adults will make benevolent decisions that provide much needed resources for youth-led organizations can be compelling.

Not all targeted adults will deal in bad faith, of course. Many will turn out to be legitimate allies who will engage youth leaders in authentic, genuine dialogue. Under such circumstances, an inside collaborative strategy may make sense and provide "organizational mileage" (Haggstrom 1971).

The strategic and tactical repertoire of youth-led organizations should include both inside, collaborative approaches and hard-hitting, outside adversarial methods. Choosing the appropriate strategy can be challenging, however. The key is to make decisions based on the following principle: Which approach is most likely to produce a positive result while simultaneously developing organizational capacity, or mileage, in the process?

Funding: Calling Youth-Led Organizing by Another Name?

The influence of funding on youth-led community organizing never should be overlooked or minimized. The funding process itself requires organizations to compete with one another; and this is problematic when youth-led organizations are forced to vie for monies with groups that sponsor popular, nonpolitical activities and services in addition to organizing.

When analyzing the sources of funding for Chicago youth-led organizing, Parham and Pinzino (2004) note that money can be funneled through "youth development" and "civic participation" projects. However, the majority of funding is received under the category of community organizing programming. This is important because this option provides the opportunity of including youth-led organizing under a familiar funding category. Indeed, ideally the funding for youth-led organizing should be its own category, because of the expectations for activities usually associated with this form of intervention.

Clash of Cultures

No, this section does not focus on conventional ways of looking at culture as it relates to ethnicity, race, socioeconomic class, or even youth culture. We refer to another meaning of *culture*, this one related to clashes between social-justice politics and the world of nonprofit organizations. At first glance it may seem strange to some readers that a culture of social-justice politics may not mesh with the culture of nonprofit work. However, upon further study, it should be clear that action for social justice is not necessarily synonymous with nonprofit work.

Sherwood and Dressner (2004, 57), in a rare reference to this potential tension, note:

> This clash is particularly evident around information sharing. Where funders, researchers and other interested outsiders assume that there is good will and mutual benefit in sharing information about organizations, programs, interests, and goals, some youth organizing groups do not. At a minimum, it can be time-consuming for a small organization to respond to requests for information. There might be questions about how the information will be used, including whether it will be accurately presented and whether it will ultimately support or undermine the cause of youth organizing. . . . Further, some youth organizing groups—not unlike previous generations of community-based organizations—analyze these interactions in the terms of power, dignity, and relationship that they use to develop their social justice campaigns.

Thus, Sherwood and Dressner (2004) do point out that social justice-related interventions may seem out of the mainstream for most nonprofit endeavors. This dislocation of social justice work is exacerbated by actions that are youth-led, because most nonprofit endeavors do not view young people as assets or potential decision makers. The tension between these two worlds will exist into the foreseeable future.

It would be irresponsible for us not to acknowledge this tension. Indeed, we think that a key factor here is the inherent *political* and *adversarial* nature of social justice work. It is about confronting the abuses of power, struggling for the redistribution of that power, and overcoming the inherent resistance to profound social change. In the true sense of the word, social justice work is radical, or root, change. On the other hand, the world of nonprofits is dominated by a service mentality that does little to alter existing power relations and patterns of oppression, which young people are so acutely aware of. The service provided by these institutions can be considered honest and valuable work, like most of social work, but it falls short of being reformist. Their targets of change invariably are the clients receiving services, rather than the unjust social systems that oppress people.

However, we believe that both forms of helping—as well as other forms— are necessary and worthy of respect. Because these two views have different basic operating assumptions and core values, there will be an inevitable and ongoing tension. It is no mistake that we end this chapter with this discussion. It would be simplistic to say that the entire nonprofit world is about service. Certainly, social action organizations are nonprofits themselves, as are CDCs, some prevention programs, public interest groups, think tanks, research centers, and training institutes. Consequently, all nonprofits can't be painted with the same brush. Nevertheless, we think that most readers will equate nonprofits with the *human service* sector.

Human services provide concrete benefits to individuals and groups who are in immediate need of assistance, and this worthy and beneficial activity should not be deprecated, dismissed, or devalued. Clearly, such services are important and necessary to reduce real pain and suffering, as they ameliorate the symptoms of many social problems. But frequently they are not sufficient to address the root causes of conditions that flow from inequality and oppression. Because services often help large numbers of people, they usually enjoy broad-based support among elected officials, the business community, and the general public—as long as they don't cost too much in tax dollars. Relations between service providers and institutional decision makers tend to be collaborative. Public- and private-sector leaders from the power structure frequently sit on the governing boards of service agencies, and may even provide some direct funding.

Service agencies typically are reluctant to upset these established leaders. However, organizing for social-action challenges the existing relations of power, and the same institutional leaders who support service programming may be targeted by organizations promoting social justice. At minimum, an ambitious agenda for social-action organizing almost can be guaranteed to make these power holders nervous. This situation has significant implications for available funding. Social service organizations take and receive monies from organizations where social action groups never would be welcomed. Indeed, many organizing projects would refuse to accept such funding, even if it were offered, because of the strings attached.

So, it should come as no surprise that funding sources for youth-led organizing are much more limited than those for youth services.

What can be done to close the gap between the culture of nonprofit services and the culture of community organizing? The initial, and we believe critical, step is to acknowledge that gap and to develop mechanisms for dialogue to occur. Only after a history of interactions whereby trust is developed will there be an effort to find the overlap between social justice and nonprofit work. However, while the disparities between the two certainly can be reduced, if not minimized, we do not believe that they can be eliminated. Thus, these two planets will continue in their separate orbits, and every once in awhile they may cross paths for a short time before continuing on their respective journeys.

Conclusion

No doubt other challenges will emerge as the field of youth-led organizing continues to develop and grow. But the fifteen dilemmas discussed in this chapter are hurdles enough as this book goes to press, with progress made in some areas more than in others. While a number of these topics are applicable to most, if not all, forms of community organizing, all have elements uniquely associated with the youth-led organizing examined here. And most of the solutions to these problems also will be youth specific. Given the creativity, energy, and commitment of the youth activists engaged in organizing, there is good reason for optimism, regardless of current challenges or future ones that inevitably lie ahead.

11

Epilogue

Understanding the everyday struggles and
creative interventions that youth deploy in
response to material and discursive processes of power, including those exercised by
the state, is key for theorizing the role of youth
in generating social change.
—Rios, *From Knucklehead to Revolutionary*
(2005)

Writing this book has been a fascinating and enlightening journey for us.
Youth-led community organizing must be solidly grounded in the context
of the youth-led movement. It is important to appreciate both the history of
this movement and the fact that its boundaries are ever changing. The be-
ginnings of the youth-led movement can be traced back several decades,
and there is no book that adequately captures its full breadth and depth
during the early part of the twenty-first century, both nationally and internationally. New developments continue to outpace our ability to study and
write about this dramatic growth (Cohen 2006). This dynamism has been
both exciting and frustrating for us; we believe that the reader may share
this sentiment.

Youth-led social change may be conceptualized as an expanding universe with all of the excitement and debate associated with such a phenomenon. There may be disagreement about where and when this worldwide youth-led movement started, just as there are differences of opinion
about the origins of the universe. There also are arguments about how far
this movement stretches and when it will contract—again, no different from
the universe analogy. And similar debates have transpired about the youth
development movement.

We believe that the reader must be prepared to tolerate this ambiguity about the youth-led movement's origins and destination. However, this does not mean that practitioners cannot enjoy the movement, both in the present and retrospectively. There is tremendous excitement for those of us involved with youth-led organizing. From the academic side, there is an understanding that this explosive growth is special, with prodigious implications for society and the education of future practitioners and academics. Academics and researchers alike will face all of the trials and tribulations associated with a field of practice that embraces the principles of social and economic justice and that is community centered. There will undoubtedly be debates in academic forums about youth-led community organizing and whether it is a subfield of adult organizing or a field of its own. Indeed, the presence of this debate signals a bright future for this field.

From the practitioner perspective, there also is excitement because of how youth-led organizing is transforming the lives of many young people whom this society essentially has written off. Yet, there also is the tension of trying to put boundaries around a phenomenon that simply defies being put into a box! If youth-led community organizing does eventually translate to a social movement, then its reach will be transnational or international, opening fertile fields for practitioners to teach and learn.

Community organizing, like any other form of social intervention that seeks to alter social circumstances, must never be conceptualized as a one-size-fits-all model. It requires modification, or tweaking, to maximize its potential for achieving noble goals of social and economic justice. Youth community organizing, whether youth-led or youth-involved, can take place in a wide range of settings and circumstances, as well as be based on different models. Practitioners must be prepared to view youth organizers from a broad perspective, modifying their strategies and constructs accordingly.

Clearly, there are distinct elements to youth-led community organizing that distinguish it from other approaches to working with young people, as well as other forms of organizing. Most fundamental is the central role of youth as decision makers and leaders in collective efforts to gain greater control over the conditions that impact their lives. Indeed, the term *youth-led* truly is both descriptive and instructive. The concept of leadership development takes on special significance with this model, even superceding its prominent position in all other forms of community organizing. We have devoted a full chapter to this topic, but in reality, leadership development is embedded in every aspect of youth-led organizing, as both an individual and collective manifestation of empowerment.

The emphasis on personal growth and development has led to an approach to youth organizing that is more holistic than most adult community organizing models. The focus is not limited to issue resolution and changes in policy, but also stresses the importance of promoting social relationships, educational attainment (often including pathways to college), community service, capacity enhancement, mentoring, individual support, increased self-esteem, and a very strong cultural component that is both a means to social change and an end in itself. Opportunities for training, role modeling, creativity, critical thinking, politicization, expression through multiple media forms, and skills development are built into every facet of the organizing. *And always there is the chance to socialize and have fun!*

This organizing process typically starts by raising consciousness about unequal power relationships, structural inequality, and oppression; then it is animated by a shared vision of both an end product and a process to achieve social and economic justice. The specific organizing goals and objectives tend to be multifaceted, depending on local circumstances, but almost always entail age-related issues. Therefore, target systems often include public and private schools, municipal government, police departments, criminal and juvenile justice systems, local housing authorities, private employers, nonprofits that provide youth services, recreation departments, public transportation carriers, and public youth employment programs. Nevertheless, youth organizing also may address issues related to racial discrimination, LGBT concerns, corporate pollution, or immigrant rights. Regardless of the particular focus of these youth-led organizing campaigns, they share a common ethos that is inclusive, participatory, and democratic as they pursue positive social change for individuals and the community.

Most youth-led organizing projects are locally based, and the change efforts usually are confined to the neighborhood or municipality. Organizational structures typically are streamlined; and only rarely are they formally affiliated with larger youth organizing networks at the state, regional, or national levels. This can cause youth-led projects to be isolated from age-peer efforts, with various initiatives sometimes reinventing the wheel. However, while there may be minimal connection among youth organizing programs, sponsorship by adult community organizations, coalitions, or community development corporations is quite common. Indeed, adults very seldom are completely out of the picture. Nevertheless, whether or not such linkages exist, the youth-led organizing model entails a high degree of autonomy.

As in all forms of community organizing, numbers count as a primary form of power, and ongoing recruitment is featured in all phases of this approach. This activity is tailored to engage young people in the context of their particular youth culture wherever they can be found, such as on streetcorners, in parking lots, at youth centers, on the Internet, in schools, on basketball courts, or wherever else they may hang. It may be done by formal outreach efforts or simply by word of mouth, recruiting along friendship lines or simply by loose networking, but it is done best by making personal connections, building relationships, appealing to self-interests, creating a sense of hope and possibility, and always stressing the importance of having a good time.

Once young people are engaged, there is strong emphasis on developing leadership capacities and learning new skills related to further recruitment, action research, facilitating meetings, strategic planning, communicating with their youth constituency and the broader community, reaching out to potential allies, building coalitions, developing action plans, implementing a wide range of tactics, public speaking, negotiating with decision makers, program development, media relations, fund-raising, and evaluation. Youth culture profoundly shapes an organizing process that integrates music, poetry, street theater, dance, film, creative writing, photography, newsletter production, fashion, graffiti, murals, and other art forms into all of its phases. And youth-led organizing increasingly uses information technology, such as cell phones, text messaging, e-mail, instant messaging, word processing, Web sites, Web pages, chat rooms, and other instruments and forms where young people often are more experienced and skilled than adults, especially as the digital divide continues to diminish.

Because the window of participation is relatively narrow, young activists and leaders age out after only several years. This chronological imperative demands that youth-led organizations not rely on the presence and skills of a small group of entrenched leaders. To do so is to commit the organization to an early demise, as the veteran cohort inevitably grows older and moves on, leaving a leadership vacuum in its wake. A leadership structure that is at once collective and constantly replenished is essential for organizational continuity and effectiveness over time.

In order to maintain a dynamic flow of new participants, recruiters usually must address challenges of competing time demands for potential activists, as well as the need for many young leaders to be paid. As discussed previously, support or opposition from a youth's family often will be an important determinant of participation. The need for immediate gratification, the ability to deal with the failure to achieve some organizing goals, and the threat of burnout caused by over involvement all serve to test a youth-led organizing project's ability to maintain its vitality and viability.

Currently, two of the greatest challenges facing youth-led organizing are the continued shortage of funds and the sometimes difficult relations with adults. The lack of funding has been discussed at a number of points in this book. Youth organizing projects frequently do not have adequate financial resources for staffing, work stipends for activists, rent, equipment, supplies, or payment to attend formal leadership training sessions. Questions may arise about whether accepting money from certain funding sources will compromise the organizing project's ability to conduct adversarial campaigns that may ruffle the feathers of adult decision makers. While adult organizations sometimes may provide space, technical assistance, administrative support, or even a degree of fiscal sponsorship, significant autonomy must be carved out and preserved in order for the initiative to meet the criteria for youth-led organizing. The phenomenon of adultism persists, and youth activists may have to contend with its consequences, regardless of whether they deal with intransigent targets or well meaning, but disrespectful allies.

These and other challenges aside, we are confident that youth-led organizing will continue to grow and increase its social impact in the years ahead. Youth activists bring idealism, high motivation, stamina, passion, and a sense of optimism to their organizing. They are able to draw on their own culture, as well as adult supports, to pursue their hopes and dreams. Young people bring fresh approaches, enthusiasm, and innovative tactics to their campaigns. The combination of campaigns on immediate concerns, the chance to make new friends, opportunities for personal growth, skills development, capacity enhancement, and the ability to have fun while working for progressive social change makes an attractive package. Indeed, this powerful blend contains the essence of the spirit and promise of youth-led organizing!

References

Age bias for young and old through the years. (2005, September 8). *Canberra Times*, p. A2.

Aglooba-Segurno, O. (1997). Impact of training on development: Lessons from a leadership training program. *Evaluation Review, 21*(6), 713–737.

Agnes, M. (ed.). (2000). *Webster's new world college dictionary* (4th ed.). Foster City, CA: IDG Books Worldwide, Inc.

Aitken, S. C. (2001). *Geographies of young people: The morally contested spaces of identity.* New York: Routledge.

Alexander, B. (2001, April 3). Youth organizing comes of age. *Youth Today*, p. 6.

Alinsky, S. (1971). *Rules for radicals.* New York: Random House.

American Youth Congress. (1936, July 4). The declaration of the rights of American youth. Accessed July 9, 2005, from http://newdeal.feri.org/students/ayc.htm

Anderson, M., Bernaldo, R., & David, J. (2004). *Youth speak out report.* Los Angeles, CA: National Conference for Community and Justice.

Ansari, W. E. (2005). Collaborative research partnerships with disadvantaged communities: Challenges and potential solutions. *Public Health, 119,* 758–770.

Arches, J. (1991). Social structure, burnout, and job satisfaction. *Social Work, 36*(3), 202–206.

Arendt, H. (1963). *On revolution.* New York: Viking Press.

Armour, S. (2003, October 7). Young workers say their age holds them back. *USA Today*, p. 1.

Arnstein, S. R. (1969). A ladder of citizen participation. *Journal of the American Institute of Planners, 35*, 216–224.

Austin, J., & Willard, M. N. (1989). Introduction: Angels of history, demons of culture. In J. Austin & M. N. Willard (eds.), *Generations of youth: Youth cultures and history in twentieth-century America* (pp. 1–20). New York: New York University Press.

Bales, R.F. (1970). *Personality and interpersonal behavior*. New York: Holt, Rinehart, and Winston.

Balsano, A. B. (2005). Youth civic engagement in the United States: Understanding and addressing the impact of social impediments on positive youth and community development. *Applied Developmental Science, 9*, 188–201.

Barich, C. (1998). Oh, the places we'll go! *New Designs for Youth Development, 14*, 6–9.

Bartik, T. J. (2001). *Jobs for the poor: Can labor demand policies help?* New York: Russell Sage Foundation.

Bass, M. (1997). Citizenship and young people's role in public life. *National Civic Review, 86*, 203–210.

Battles, S. (2002). African American males at a crossroad. *Journal of Health & Social Policy, 15*, 81–91.

Baxter, S., & Crockett, T. (2002, June 25). National organizing exchange brings young activists together. *WireTap Magazine*, pp. 1–2.

Bayer, A., & Bonilla, J. (2001). *Executive summary*. Washington, D.C.: Population Resource Center.

Beamish, A. (1999). Approaches to community computing: Bringing technology to low- income groups. In D. A. Schon, B. Sanyal, & W. J. Mitchell (eds.), *High technology and low-income communities: Prospects for the positive use of advanced information technology* (pp. 349–368). Cambridge, MA: Massachusetts Institute of Technology Press.

Bearse, J. (1998a, November 20). Kmart plan under fire. *Jamaica Plain Gazette*, pp. 1–2.

Bearse, J. (1998b, December 18). Urban Edge pushes for Kmart: Merchants oppose plan, friends of Kelly Rink may reconsider role in strategy process. *Jamaica Plain Gazette*, pp. 1–2.

Bearse, J. (1999a, January 8). Urban Edge backs off Kmart deal. *Jamaica Plain Gazette*, pp. 1–2.

Bearse, J. (1999b, February 5). JPNC opposes Kmart plan. *Jamaica Plain Gazette*, p. 1.

Bearse, J. (1999c, March 5). BRA steps in as planner. *Jamaica Plain Gazette*, p. 1.

Bell, J. (1995). *Understanding adultism: A key to developing positive youth-adult relationships*. Olympia, WA: The Freechild Project.

Benson, P. L. (2003). Developmental assets and asset-building community: Conceptual and empirical foundations. In R. M. Lerner & P. L. Benson (eds.), *Developmental assets and asset-building communities* (pp. 19–43). New York: Kluwer Associates.

Bergsma, L. A. (2004). Empowerment education: The link between media literacy and health promotion. *American Behavioral Scientist, 48*, 152–164.

Berson, Y., Shamir, B., Avolio, B., & Popper, M. (2001). The relationship between vision strength, leadership style and context. *Leadership Quarterly, 12*(1), 53–73.

Besharov, D. J. (ed.). (1999). *America's disconnected youth: Toward a preventive strategy*. Washington, D.C.: Child Welfare League of America.

Betten, N., & Austin, M. J. (eds.). (1990). *The roots of community organizing, 1917–1939*. Philadelphia: Temple University Press.

Beyond base: Insights about expansion and growth from YUCA and FCYO. (2004). *Pipeline*, (February), 5–7.

"Big-box" stores take the heat at meeting. (2000, May 21). *Boston Sunday Globe*, *Boston Notes*, p. 32.

Bjorhovde, P. O. (ed.). (2002). *Creating tomorrow's philanthropists: Curriculum development for youth*. San Francisco: Jossey-Bass.

Blum, R. (1988). Healthy youth development as a model for youth health promotion. *Journal of Adolescent Health, 22*, 368–375.

Bobo, K., Kendall, J., & Max, S. (2001). *Organizing for social change* (3rd ed.). Santa Ana, CA: Seven Locks Press.

Boehm, A., & Staples, L. (2004). Empowerment: The point of view of consumers. *Families in Society, 85*, 270– 280.

Boehm, A. & Staples, L. (2005). Grassroots leadership in task-oriented groups: Learning from successful leaders. *Social work with groups, 28*(2), 77–96.

Bombardieri, M. (2000, October 20). A plot of their own: Teens hope to see a youth center in Jackson Square. *Boston Globe*, p. B1.

Bonnichsen, S. (2005, December 2). Adult supremacism. Accessed January 12, 2006, from http://www.youthlib.com/generator/archieves/000147.php

Booth, A., & Crouter, A. C. (eds.). (2001). *Does it take a village? Community effects on children, adolescents, and families*. Mahwah, NJ: Lawrence Erlbaum Associates.

Boston Public Schools. (2004). School profile. Accessed February 10, 2005, from http://boston.k12.ma.us/schools/profiles.asp

Boyd, T. (2003, March 1). Hip hop: Today's civil rights movement? National Public Radio. Accessed January 3, 2005, from http://www.npr.org/templates/story.php?storyId=1178621

Boyte, H.C. (1980). *The backyard revolution*. Philadelphia: Temple University Press.

Brager, G., Specht, H. & Torczyner, J. (1987). *Community organizing* (2nd ed.). New York: Columbia University Press.

Breggin, P. R., & Breggin, G. R. (1998). *The war against children of color*. Monroe, ME: Common Courage Press.

Brown, M., Camino, L., Hobson, H., & Knox, C. (2000). Community youth development: A challenge to social injustice. *CYD Journal: Community Youth Development, 1*, 32–39.

Brueggemann, J. (2002). Racial considerations and public policy in the 1930s: Economic change and political opportunities. *Social Science History, 26*, 139–178.

Brueggemann, W.G. (2002). *The practice of macro social work* (2nd ed.). Belmont, CA: Brooks/Cole.

Building nations, changing nations: Youth action beyond communities. (2001). *Forum for Youth Investment, 2*, 55–57.

Burgess, J. (2002, Spring-Summer). Youth leadership for community change. *CYD Anthology*, pp. 25–30.

Burghardt, S. (1979). The tactical use of group structure and process in community organization. In F.M. Cox, J.L. Erlich, J. Rothman, and J.E. Tropman (eds.), *Strategies of community organization* (3rd ed., pp. 113–130). Itasca, IL: Peacock.

Burghardt, S. (1982). *The other side of organizing*. Cambridge, MA: Shenkman.

Burghardt, S., & Fabricant, M. (2004). Which side are you on? Social work, community organizing, and the labor movement. In M. Weil (ed.), *The handbook of community practice* (pp. 204–214). Thousand Oaks, CA: Sage Publications.

Burke, E. M. (1979). *A participatory approach to urban planning*. New York: Human Services Press.

Bynoe, Y. (2004). *Stand and deliver: Political actions, leadership, and hip hop culture*. New York: Soft Skull Press.

California Fund for Youth Organizing. (2004). Why youth organizing? Accessed March 3, 2005, from http://www.tidesfoundation.org/cfyo.cfm

Camino, L. (2000). Putting youth-adult partnerships to work for community change: Lessons from volunteers across the country. *CYD Journal: Community Youth Development, 1*, 27–31.

Camino, L. (2005). Youth-led community building: Promising practices from two communities using community-based service-learning. *Journal of Extension, 43*, 1–11.

Camino, L., & Shepard, Z. (2002). From periphery to center: Pathways to youth civic engagement in the day-to-day life of communities. *Applied Developmental Science, 6*, 213–220.

Camino, L. & Zeldin, S. (2002). Making the transition to community youth development: Emerging roles and competencies for youth-serving organizations and youth workers. *Community Youth Development Journal, 3*, 70–78.

Carlson, C. (2006). The Hampton experience as a new model for youth civic engagement. In B. N. Checkoway & L. Gutierrez (eds.), *Youth participation and community change* (pp. 89–105). New York: Haworth Press.

Carpini, M. X. D. (2003). Gen.Com: Youth, civic engagement, and the new information environment. *Political Communication, 17*, 341–349.

Carroll, G. B., Herbert, D. M., & Roy, J. M. (1999). Youth action strategies in violence prevention. *Journal of Adolescent Health, 25*, 7–13.

Center for Economic and Social Justice. (2005). Defining economic justice and social justice. Accessed January 9, 2006, from http://www.cesj.org/thirdway/economicjustice-defined.htm

Center for Economic and Social Justice. (2005). *Introduction to social justice*. Washington, D.C.: Author.

Cervone, B. (2002). *Taking democracy in hand: Youth action for educational change in the San Francisco Bay area. An occasional paper prepared by What Kids Can Do with The Forum for Youth Investment*. Takoma Park, MD: Forum for Youth Investment.

Cervone, B., & Cushman, K. (2002). Moving youth participation into the classroom: Students as allies. In B. Kirshner, J. L. O'Donoghue, & M. McLaughlin (eds.), *Youth participation: Improving institutions and communities* (pp. 83–99). San Francisco: Jossey-Bass.

Chan, B., Carlson, M., Trickett, B., & Earls, F. (2003). Youth participation: A critical element of research on child well-being. In R. M. Lerner & P. L. Benson (eds.), *Developmental assets and asset-building communities* (pp. 65–96). New York: Kluwer Associates.

Chang, J. (2003). *Constant elevation: The rise of Bay Area hip-hop activism.* San Francisco: Author. Accessed May 12, 2006, from http://www.cantstopwonstop.com/power.cfm

Charles, M. M. (2005). *Giving back to the community: African American inner city teens and civic engagement.* Circle Working Paper 38. College Park, MD: Circle, University of Maryland School of Public Policy.

Checkoway, B. (1996). *Adults as allies.* Ann Arbor, MI: University of Michigan School of Social Work.

Checkoway, B. (1998). Involving young people in neighborhood development. *Children and Youth Services Review, 20,* 765–795.

Checkoway, B. (2005). Foreword: Youth participation as social justice. *Community Youth Development Journal, 6* (Fall), 15–17.

Checkoway, B., Dobbie, D., & Richards-Schuster, K. (2003). Involving young people in community evaluation research. *CYD Journal: Community Youth Development, 4,* 7–11.

Checkoway, B., Figueroa, L., & Richards-Schuster, K. (2003). Democracy multiplied in an urban neighborhood: Youth Force in the South Bronx. *Children, Youth and Environment, 13.* Accessed October 23, 2006, from http://www.colorado.edu/journals/cye/13_2/Checkoway/DemocracyMultiplied.htm

Checkoway, B. & Gutierrez, L.M. (2006). Youth participation and community change: An introduction. In B. N. Checkoway & L. Gutierrez (eds.), *Youth participation and community change* (pp. 1–9). New York: Haworth Press.

Checkoway, B., & Norsman, A. (1986). Empowering citizens with disabilities. *Community Development Journal, 21,* 270–277.

Checkoway, B., & Richards-Schuster, K. (2002). *Youth participation in community evaluation research.* Ann Arbor, MI: Center for Community Change, School of Social Work, University of Michigan.

Checkoway, B., & Richards-Schuster, K. (2004). Youth participation in evaluation and research as a way of lifting new voices. *Children, Youth and Environments,14.* Accessed October 30, 2006, from http://www.colorado.edu/journals/eye

Checkoway, B., Richards-Schuster, K., Abdullah, S., Aragon, M., Facio, E., Figueroa, L., Reddy, E., Welsh, M., & White, A. (2003). Young people as competent citizens. *Community Development Journal, 38,* 298–309.

Cherniss, C. (1980). *Staff burnout: Job stress in the human services.* Beverly Hills, CA: Sage Publications.

Child across the borders. (2003). Social justice framework. Accessed January 12, 2006, from http://www.sws.soton.ac.uk/cwab/Session3/ICWs34.htm

ChildStats.gov. (2001). Accessed January 3, 2005, from http://www.childstats.gov/ac2001/detail.asp

City of Boston. (1998). *Jackson Square Profile Report: National decision systems.* Boston: Author.

Cohen, S. (2006). African American youth: Broadening our understanding of politics, civic engagement and activism. Youth Activism: A web forum organized by the Social Science Research Council. Accessed October 23, 2006, from http://ya.ssrc.org/african/Cohen

Community Unity Matters. (2000). Youth-led community meetings, forums, and summits. Accessed April 10, 2005, from http://www.commatters.org/youth/summit.htm

Community Youth Development Program. (2005). Best practices. Accessed November 15, 2005, from http://www.tnoys.org/T&TA Programs/CYD/BestPractices.html

Conover, P. J., & Seering, D. D. (2000). A political socialization perspective. In L. M. McDonnell, P. M. Timpane, & R. Benhamine (eds.), *Rediscovering the democratic purposes of education* (pp. 91–124). Lawrence, KS: University of Kansas Press.

Cook, T. E., & Morgan, P. M. (1971). An introduction to participatory democracy. In T. E. Cook & P. M. Morgan (eds.), *Participatory democracy* (pp. 1–40). San Francisco: Canfield Press.

Coombe, C. M. (2005). Participatory evaluation: Building community while assessing change. In M. Minkler (ed.), *Community organizing and community building for health* (2nd ed., pp. 368–385). New Brunswick, NJ: Rutgers University Press.

Costello, J., Totes, M., Spielberger, J., & Wynn, J. (2000). History, ideology and structure shape the organizations that shape youth. In *Youth development: Issues, challenges and directions* (pp. 185–231). Philadelphia: Public/Private Ventures.

Cowan, J. J. (1997). The war against apathy: Four lessons from the front lines of youth advocacy. *National Civic Review, 83*, 193–202.

Cowger, C. D. (1994). Assessing client strengths: Clinical assessment for client empowerment. *Social Work, 39*, 262–268.

Cox, E. O. (1991). The critical role of social action in empowerment oriented groups. *Social Work with Groups, 14*(3/4), 77–90.

Cutler, D. (2002). *Taking the initiative—Promoting young people's involvement in public decision making in the USA.* London: Carnegie Young People Initiative.

Dahl, R. A. (1982). *Dilemmas of pluralist democracy.* New Haven: Yale University Press.

Damon, W., & Gregory, A. (2003). Bringing in a new era in the field of youth development. In R. M. Lerner & P. L. Benson (eds.), *Developmental assets and asset-building communities* (pp. 47–64). New York: Kluwer Associates.

Daniel, S. (2000, March 31). Survey supports Kmart-style store: Many neighborhood groups dispute results. *Jamaica Plain Gazette*, pp. 1–2.

Davis, D. (2004). When youth protest: Student actions, civil disobedience and the Mississippi civil rights movement, 1955–1970. *Mississippi History Now.* Accessed November 19, 2004, from http://mshistory.k12ms.us/index.html

Delgado, G. (1997). *Beyond the politics of place.* Oakland, CA: Applied Research Center.

Delgado, L. (2005, 12 August). Tragedy brought a plan to woo teen-agers from gangs. *Boston Globe*, p. 25.

Delgado, M. (1996). Puerto Rican food establishments as social service organizations: Results of an asset assessment. *Journal of Community Practice, 3*(2), 57–77.

Delgado, M. (1999). *Social work practice in nontraditional urban settings.* New York: Oxford University Press.

Delgado, M. (2000). *New arenas for community social work practice with urban youth: Use of the arts, humanities, and sports.* New York: Columbia University Press.

Delgado, M. (2002). *New frontiers for youth development in the twenty-first century: Revitalizing and broadening youth development.* New York: Columbia University Press.

Delgado, M. (2004). *Social youth entrepreneurship: The potential for youth and community transformation.* Westport, CT: Praeger Publishers.

Delgado, M. (2006). *Designs and methods for youth-led social research.* Thousand Oaks, CA: Sage Publications.

Delgado, M. (2007). *Social work practice with Latinos using a cultural assets paradigm.* New York: Oxford University Press.

Delgado, M., Jones, K., & Rohani, M. (2005). *Social work practice with immigrant and refugee youth in the United States.* Boston: Allyn & Bacon.

Delgado, M. & Zhou, M. (in press). *Youth-led health promotion in urban communities.* New York: Aronson Publishers.

van Dijk, J., & Hacker, K. L. (2000). Summary (chap. 12). In K. L. Hacker, & J. van Dijk (eds.), *Digital democracy: Issues of theory and practice.* London: Sage Publications.

Dodd, P., & Gutierrez, L. (1990). Preparing students for the future: A power perspective for community practice. *Administration in Social Work, 14*(2), 63–78.

Dowdy, Z., & McGrory, B. (1993, January 17). Gang shooting brings calls for action. *Boston Sunday Globe,* p. 34.

Downing, J., Frasano, R., Friedland, P. A., McCullough, M. F., Mizarahi, T., & Shapiro, J. J. (eds.). (1991). *Computers for social change and community organizing.* New York: Haworth Press.

Downton, J. V., Downton, J., Jr., & Wehr, P. E. (1997). *The persistent activist: How peace commitment develops and survives.* Boulder, CO: Westview Press.

DuBois, D. L., Neville, H. A., Parra, G. R., & Pugh-Lilly, A. O. (2003). In J. E. Rhodes (ed.). *A critical view of youth mentoring* (pp. 21–57). San Francisco, CA: Jossey-Bass.

Dworkin, R. (1977). *Taking rights seriously.* London: Duckworth.

Earls, F., & Carlson, M. (2002). Adolescents as collaborators in search of well-being. In M. Tienda & W. J. Wilson (eds.), *Youth in cities: A cross-national perspective* (pp.58–83). Cambridge, MA: Harvard University Press.

Eccles, J., & Gootman, J. A. (eds.). (2002). *Community programs to promote youth development.* Washington, D.C.: National Research Council.

Edelman, A., Gill, P., Comerfort, K., Larson, M., & Hare, R. (2004). *A background paper: Youth development and youth leadership.* National Collaborative for Workforce & Disability for Youth.

Edelman, P. (1977). The children's rights movement. In B. Gross & R. Gross (eds.), *The children's rights movement: Overcoming the oppression of young people* (pp. 203–213). Garden City, NY: Anchor Press/Doubleday.

Elikann, P. (1999). *Superpredators: The demonization of our children by the law.* New York: Insight Books.

Ephross, P. H. & Vassil, T. V. (2005). *Groups that work: Structure and process* (2nd ed.). New York: Columbia University Press.

Etzioni, A. (1969, August 25). The fallacy of decentralization. *The Nation*, pp. 145–147.

Evans, W. D., Ulasevich, A., & Blahut, S. (2004). Adult and group influences on participation in youth empowerment programs. *Health Education & Behavior, 31*, 564–576.

Eyler, J., & Giles, D. E. (1999). *Where's the learning in service-learning?* San Francisco: Jossey-Bass.

Faircloth, P. (1998, September 25). Kmart looks at JP location. *Jamaica Plain Gazette*, p. 7.

Fanon, F. (1965). *The wretched of the earth.* New York: Grove Press.

Farson, R. (1974). *Birthrights.* New York: MacMillan.

Felix, A. (2003). Making youth voice a community principle. *Youth Service Journal, 10*, 1–8.

Ferber, T., Pittman, K., & Marshall, T. (2002). *State youth policy: Helping all youth to grow up fully prepared and fully engaged.* Takoma Park, MD: The Force for Youth Involvement.

Fernandez, M. A. (2002). *Creating community change: Challenges and tensions in community youth research.* Stanford, CA: John W, Gardner Center for Youth and Their Communities.

Fine, J. (2001). Community unionism in Baltimore and Stamford. *Working USA, 4*(3), 59– 85.

Finks, D.P. (1984). *The radical vision of Saul Alinsky.* New York: Paulist Press.

Finn, J. L. (1994). The promise of participatory research. *Journal of Progressive Human Services, 5*(2), 25–42.

Finn, J. L., & Checkoway, B. (1998). Young people as competent community builders: A challenge to social work. *Social Work, 43*, 335–345.

Fisher, R. (1984). *Let the people decide: Neighborhood organizing in America.* Boston: Twayne.

Fisher, R. (1994). *Let the people decide: Neighborhood organizing in America (Social movements past and present)* (2nd ed.). Boston: Twayne.

Fisher, R. (2005) History, context, and emerging issues for community practice. In M. Weil (ed.), *The handbook of community practice* (pp. 34–58). Thousand Oaks, CA: Sage Publications.

Fisher, R. & Shragge, E. (2000). Challenging community organizing: Facing the 21st century. *Journal of Community Practice, 8*(3), 1–19.

Fisher, R., Weedman, A, Alex, G., & Stout, K. D. (2001). Graduate education for social change: A study of political social workers. *Journal of Community Practice, 9*, 43–64.

Flanagan, C. A., & Galley, L. S. (2001). *Nurturing democratic character in teens: The potential of information technology.* Washington, D.C.: Benton Foundation.

Flanagan, C. A., & Van Horn, B. (2003). Youth civic engagement: A logical next step in community youth development. In F. A. Villarruel, D. F. Perkins, L. M. Borden, & J. G. Keith (eds.), *Community youth development: Programs, policies, and practices* (pp. 273–296). Thousand Oaks, CA: Sage Publications.

Flasher, J. (1978). Adultism. *Adolescence, 13*, 517–523.

Flay, B. R. (2002). Positive youth development requires comprehensive health promotion programs. *American Journal of Health Behavior, 26*, 407–424.

Fletcher, A. (2004). *Stories of meaningful student involvement.* Olympia, WA: The Freechild Project.

Flores, J. (1994). Puerto Rican and proud, boyee!: Rap roots and amensia. In A. Ross & T. Rose (eds.), *Microphone fiends: Youth music & youth culture* (pp. 89–98). New York: Routledge.

The Forum for Youth Investment. (2006). *Engaging young people in community change: The Youth Impact Approach*. Washington, D.C.: Author.

Foster, J. (1998). *Youth empowerment and civil society*. Paper presented at the Commonwealth Youth Ministers' Meeting (May 28–30, 1998), Kuala Lumpur, Malaysia.

Frank, K. I. (2006). The potential of youth participation in planning. *Journal of Planning Literature, 20,* 351–371.

Freire, P. (1970). *Pedagogy of the oppressed*. New York: Seabury Press.

Freire, P. (1973). *Education for critical consciousness*. New York: Seabury Press.

Freire, P. (1990). M. Moch (trans.). A critical understanding of social work. *Journal of Progressive Human Services, 1*(1), 3–10.

Friar, M. (2000). Personal communication via e-mail, March 12, 2000.

Funders' Collaborative on Youth Organizing. (2003). *An annotated bibliography on youth organizing*. New York: Author.

Furstenberg, F. F., Cook, T. D., Eccles, J., Elder, G. H., & Sameroff, A. (1999). *Managing to make it: Urban families and adolescent success*. Chicago: University of Chicago Press.

Gail Sullivan Associates, Inc. (2001). Putting the pieces together: A report on Jackson Square Planning Initiatives. Boston: City of Boston and Boston Redevelopment Authority.

Gainwright, S. & James, T, (2002). From assets to agents of change: Social justice, organizing, and youth development. In B. Kirshner, J.L. O'Donoghue & M. McLaughlin (eds.). *Youth participation: Improving institutions and communities* (pp. 27–46). San Francisco: Jossey-Bass.

Gambone, M.A., Yu, H. C., Lewis-Charp, H., Sipe, C. L., & Lacoe, J. (2004). *A comparative analysis of community youth development strategies*. Circle Working Paper 23. College Park: University of Maryland School of Public Policy.

Gambone, M.A., Yu, H. C., Lewis-Charp, H., Sipe, C. L., & Lacoe, J. (2006). Youth organizing, identity-support, and youth development agencies as avenues for involvement. In B. N. Checkoway & L. Gutierrez (eds.), *Youth participation and community change* (pp. 235–253). New York: Haworth Press.

Garbarino, J., Dubrow, N., Kostelny, K., & Pardo, C. (1992). *Children in danger: Coping with consequences of community violence*. San Francisco: Jossey-Bass.

Garrett, J. (2005). Rawls' mature theory of social justice: An introduction for students. Accessed January 5, 2006, from http://www.wku.edu/-jan.garrett/ethics/matrawls.htm

Garrett, L. (2006, June). Greetings! *Pipeline: Funders' Collaborative on Youth Organizing*, pp. 1–4.

Garvin, C.D. & Cox, F.M. (2001). A history of community organizing since the Civil War with special reference to oppressed communities. In J. Rothman, J.L. Erlich & J.E.Tropman, (eds.), *Strategies of community intervention* (6th ed., pp. 65–100). Itasca, IL: Peacock.

Gauthier, M. (2003). The inadequacy of concepts: The rise of youth interest in civic participation in Quebec. *Journal of Youth Studies, 6,* 265–276.

Gaventa, J., & Cornwall, A. (2001). Power and knowledge. In P. Reason & H. Bradbury (eds.), *Handbook of action research: Participative inquiry and practice* (pp. 70–80). London: Sage Publications.

Generator. (2005, September 15). Exploration: Criteria for YL organizations. Accessed July 7, 2006, from http://www.youthlib.com/generator/archives/2005/09/exploration_cri.html

Gibb, C.A. (1969). *Leadership*. Baltimore: Penguin.

Gibson, C. (2001). *From inspiration to participation: A review of perspectives on youth civic engagement*. New York: Grantmaker Forum on Community and National Service.

Gil, D. G. (1998). *Confronting injustice and oppression: Concepts and strategies for social workers*. New York: Columbia University Press.

Gillis, J. R. (1981). *Youth and history: Tradition and change in European age relations, 1770–present*. New York: Academic Press.

Ginwright, S. (2003). *Youth organizing: Expanding possibilities for youth development*. Occasional Paper Series on Youth Organizing, no. 3. New York: Funders' Collaborative on Youth Organizing.

Ginwright, S. (2006). Toward a politics of relevance: Race, resistance and African American youth activism. Youth activism: A web forum organized by the Social Science Research Council. Accessed October 23, 2006, from http://ya.ssrc.org/african/Ginright

Ginwright, S., & Cammarota, J. (2002). Toward a social justice model of youth development. *Social Justice, 29*, 82–94.

Ginwright, S., & James, T. (2002). From assets to agents of change: Social justice, organizing, and youth development. In B. Kirshner, J. L. O'Donoghue, & M. McLaughlin (eds.), *Youth participation: Improving institutions and communities* (pp. 27–46). San Francisco: Jossey-Bass.

Ginwright, S., Norguera, P., & Cammarota, J. (eds.). (2006). *Beyond resistance: Youth activism and community change: New democratic possibilities for policy and practice for America's youth*. Oxford, UK: Routledge.

Giroux, H. A. (1996). *Fugitive culture: Race, violence & youth*. New York: Routledge.

Giroux, H. A. (1998). *Channel surfacing: Racism, the media, and the destruction of today's youth*. New York: St. Martin's Griffin.

Gitlin, T. (1989). *The sixties: Years of hope, days of rage*. New York: Bantam Books.

Golombek, S. B. (ed.). (2002). *What works in youth participation: Case studies from around the world*. Baltimore, MD: International Youth Foundation.

Golombek, S. B. (2006). Children as citizens. In B. N. Checkoway & L. Gutierrez (eds.), *Youth participation and community change* (pp. 11–30). New York: Haworth Press.

Granger, R. C. (2002). Creating the conditions linked to positive youth development. In R. M. Lerner, C. S. Taylor, & A. von Eye (eds.), *Pathways to positive development among diverse youth* (pp. 149–164). San Francisco: Jossey-Bass.

Green, R. (2004). *Taking the initiative: Promoting young people's involvement in public decision making for NI*. Belfast, NI: Youth Council for Northern Ireland.

Gross, B., & Gross, R. (eds.). (1977). *The children's rights movement: Overcoming the oppression of young people*. Garden City, NY: Anchor Press/Doubleday.

Gruber, M. S. Q., Frommeyer, J., Weisenbach, A., & Sazama, J. (2003). Giving youth a voice in their own community and personal development. In F. A. Villarruel, D. F. Perkins, L. M. Borden, & J. G. Keith (eds.), *Community youth development: Programs, policies, and practices* (pp. 297–323). Thousand Oaks, CA: Sage Publications.

Gutierrez, L. M. (1990). Working with women of color: An empowerment perspective. *Social Work*, *35*(2), 149–153.

Gutierrez, L. M., & Lewis, E. A. (1994). Community organizing with women of color: A feminist approach. *Journal of Community Practice*, *1*, 23–44.

Hagen, M. B. (2005, April 14). Students use silence to protest discrimination against gays, lesbians. *Herald-Sun* (Durham, NC), p. B1.

Haggstrom, W.C. (1971). The theory of social work method. (Unpublished paper.)

Halfon, N. (2003). Afterword: Toward an asset-based policy agenda for children, families, and communities. In R. M. Lerner & P. L. Benson (eds.), *Developmental assets and asset-building communities: Implications for research, policy, and practice* (pp. 223–229). New York: Kluwer Academic Publisher.

Halpern, R. (2005). Instrumental relationships: A potential relationship model for inner-city youth programs. *Journal of Community Psychology*, *33*, 11–20.

Hanson, P.G. (1972). What to look for in groups. In J.W. Pfeiffer and J.J. Jones (eds.), *The 1972 annual handbook for group facilitators* (pp. 21–24). La Jolla, CA: University Associates.

Hardcastle, D.A., Wenocur, S. and Powers, P.R. (1997). *Community practice: Theories and skills for social workers*. New York: Oxford University Press.

Hardina, D. (2002). *Analytical skills for community organization practice*. New York: Columbia University Press.

Hardley, R. (2004). *Young people and mentoring: Towards a national strategy*. Sydney, Australia: Big Brothers Big Sisters Australia, Ltd.

Hargittai, E. (2002). *Second-level digital divide: Differences in people's online skills*. Accessed September 2, 2005, from http://www.firstmonday.dk/isssues/issues7_4/hargittai/

Harper, G. W., & Carver, L. J. (1999). Out-of-the-mainstream youth as partners in collaborative research: Exploring the benefits and challenges. *Health Education & Behavior*, *26*, 250–265.

Harrison, W. (1980). The role of strain and burnout in child protective service workers. *Social Service Review*, *54*, 31–44.

Hart, D. & Atkins, R. (2002). Civic competence in urban youth. *Applied Developmental Science*, *6*, 227–236.

Hart, R. (1992). *Ladder of participation, children's participation: From tokenism to citizenship*. New York: UNICEF.

Haslam, S.A. & Platow, M.J. (2001). The link between leadership and followership: How affirming social identity translates vision into action. *Personality and Social Psychology Bulletin*, *27*(11), 1469–1479.

Hayden, T. (1970, July). On trial. *Ramparts*, pp. 53–58.

Haynes, K. S. (1998). The one-hundred-year debate: Social reform versus individual treatment. *Social Work*, *43*, 501–509.

Hefner, K. (1998). The movement for youth rights, 1945–2000. *Social Policy*, *30*, xx.

Heifetz, R.A. (1994). *Leadership without easy answers*. Cambridge, MA: Harvard University Press.

Heifetz, R.A. & Linsky, M. (2002). *Leadership on the line: Staying alive through the dangers of leadership*. Cambridge, MA: Harvard Business School Press.

Hine, T. (2000). *The rise and fall of the American teenager*. New York: Perennial.

Hohenemser, L. K., & Marshall, B. D. (2002). Utilizing a youth development framework to establish and maintain a youth advisory committee. *Health Promotion Practice*, *3*, 155–165.

Hollander, E.F. (1978). *Leadership dynamics*. New York: The Free Press.

Hollister, C.D. & Mehrotra, C.M.N. (1999). Utilizing and evaluating ITV workshops for rural community leadership training. *Journal of Technology in Human Services, 16*(2/3), 35–45.

Holt, J. (1974). *Escape from childhood*. New York: Dutton.

Holt, J. (1977). Why not a bill of rights for children? In B. Gross & R. Gross (eds.), *The children's rights movement: Overcoming the oppression of young people* (pp.319–325). Garden City, NY: Anchor Press/Doubleday.

Homan, M. S. (2004). *Promoting community change: Making it happen in the real world* (3rd ed.). Belmont, CA: Brooks/Cole.

Hoose, P. (1993). *It's our world, too! Stories of young people who are making a difference*. Boston: Little, Brown.

HoSang, D. (2003). Youth and community today. Occasional Papers Series on Youth Organizing (no. 2). New York: Funders' Collaborative on Youth Organizing.

HoSang, D. (2004). Youth and community organizing today. *Social Policy, 34*, 1–6.

HoSang, D. (2005). *Traditions and innovations: Youth organizing in the Southwest*. New York: Funders' Collaborative on Youth Organizing.

Huber, M.S.Q., Frommeyer, J., Weisenbach, A. & Sazama, J. (2003). Giving youth a voice in their own community and personal development. In F.A. Villarruel, D.F. Perkins, L.M. Borden & J.G. Keith (eds.), *Community youth development* (pp. 297–323). Thousand Oaks, CA: Sage Publications.

Hyde, C. (1986). Experiences of women activists: Implications for community organizing theory and practice. *Journal of Sociology and Social Welfare, 13*, 545–562.

Hyde, C. (1994). Commitment to social change: Voices from the feminist movement. *Journal of Community Practice, 1*, 45–64.

Hyde, C. (1996). A feminist response to Rothman's Interweaving of community intervention approaches. *Journal of Community Practice, 3*, 127–145.

Hyde, C. (2004). Feminist community organizing. In M. Weil (ed.), *Handbook of community practice* (pp.360–371). Thousand Oaks, CA: Sage Publications.

Hyde-Jackson Square Youth Community Organizing Project. (1999). Internal flyer. Boston: Hyde Square Task Force, Inc.

Hyde Square Task Force, et al. (1999). An open letter to the community. Internal flyer.

Immigration Update. (2002). Executive summary. Accessed January 19, 2005, from www.predc.org/summaries/immigration/changingnation.html

Innovation Center for Community and Youth Development. (2001) Rejecting the isolation of youth adult and organizations dramatically benefit. *The Nonprofit Quarterly, 8*, 2–9.

Innovations Center for Community & Youth Development. (2003). *Extending the reach of youth development through civic activism: Research results from the Youth Leadership for Development Initiative*. New York: Author.

Innovation Center for Community & Youth Development. (2004). *Creating change: How organizations connect youth, build communities, and strengthen themselves*: Takoma Park, MD: Author.

Institute for Education and Social Policy. (2004). *Lessons from the field of school reform organizing: A review of strategies for organizers and leaders*. New York: Steinhardt School of Education, New York University.

Irby, M., Ferber, T., & Pittman, K. (2001). *Youth action: Youth contributing to Communities, communities supporting youth.* Community & Youth Development Series (vol. 6). Takoma Park, MD: Forum for Youth Investment.

Israel, B. A., Eng, E., Schulz, A. J., & Parker, E. A. (eds.). (2005). *Methods in community-based participatory research for health.* San Francisco, CA: Jossey-Bass.

Itzhaky, H., & York, A. S. (2002). Showing results in community organization. *Social Work, 47,* 125–131.

Jackson Square Development Priorities. (2003, September). Boston: Jackson Square Coordinating Group.

James, T. (2005). *Bringing it together: Uniting youth organizing, development and services for long-term sustainability.* Oakland, CA: Movement Strategy Center.

Jarrett, R. L., Sullivan, P. J., & Watkins, N. C. (2004). Developing social capital through participation in organized youth programs: Qualitative insights from three programs. *Journal of Community Psychology, 33,* 41–55.

Jason, W. (2005, June 2). Long-awaited Jackson Square plan now reality. *Jamaica Plain Bulletin,* p. 1.

Jayaratne, S. & Chess, W. (1984). Job satisfaction, burnout, and turnover: A national study. *Social Work, 29,* 448–453.

Jefferson, T. (1824). Letter to John Cartwright, June 5. In M.D. Peterson (ed.). (1984). *Thomas Jefferson: Writings.* New York: Library of America.

Jenkins, R. R. (2001). The health of minority children in the year 2000: The role of government programs in improving the health status of America's children. In N. J. Smelser, W. J. Wilson, & F. Mitchell (eds.), *America becoming: Racial trends and their consequences* (vol. 2, pp. 351–370). Washington, D.C.: National Academy Press.

Jennings, L. B., Parra-Median, D. M., Messias, D. K. H., & McLoughlin, K. (2006). Toward a critical social theory of youth empowerment. In B. N. Checkoway & L. Gutierrez (eds.), *Youth participation and community change* (pp. 31–55). New York: Haworth Press.

Johnson, D.W. & Johnson, F. P. (2003). *Joining together: Group theory and group skills* (7th ed.). Englewood Cliffs, NJ: Prentice Hall.

JP council lowers voting age to 16. (2000, December 24). *Boston Sunday Globe, City Weekly,* p. 1.

Kahn, R. (2000, April 9). Survey upsets Kmart foes in Jackson Square. *Boston Sunday Globe, City Weekly,* p. 24.

Kahn, S. (1994). *How people get power.* Washington, D.C.: National Association of Social Workers.

Kant, I. & J. Ladd. (trans.). (1797/1965). *The metaphysical elements of justice.* Indianapolis: Bobbs-Merrill Co.

Karger, H. (1981). Burnout as alienation. *Social Service Review, 55,* 271–283.

Katz, J. (2004). *The rights of kids in the digital age.* Accessed February 20, 2005, from http://www.wired.com/wired/archieve/4.07/kids.html

Kids First. (2003). *Student voices count: A student-led evaluation of high schools in Oakland.* Oakland, CA: Author.

Kieffer, C. H. (1984). Citizen empowerment: A developmental perspective. In J. Rappaport & R. Hess (eds.), *Studies in empowerment: Steps toward understanding and action* (pp. 9–36). New York: Haworth Press.

Kim, J., de Dios, M., Caraballo, P., Arciniegas, M., Abdul-Matin, I., & Taha, K. (2002). *Future 500: Youth organizing and activism in the United States*. New Orleans: New Mouth from the Dirty South.

Kim, J., & Sherman, R. F. (2006). Youth as important civic actors: From the margins to the center. *National Civic Review, 95* (Spring), 3–6.

Kipke, M. D. (1999). *Risks and opportunities: Synthesis of studies on adolescence.* Washington, D.C.: National Academy Press.

Kirshner, B., O'Donoghue, J. L., & McLaughlin, M. (eds.). (2003). *Youth participation: Improving institutions and communities.* San Francisco: Jossey-Bass.

Kiselica, M. S., & Robinson, M. (2001). Bringing advocacy counseling to life: The history, issues, and human dramas of social justice work in counseling. *Journal of Counseling & Development, 79,* 387–397.

Kitlan, M. (2004). *The digital divide: Economical class.* University Park, PA: Pennsylvania State University Press.

Kitwana, B. (2002). *The hip-hop generation: Young blacks and the crisis in African-American culture.* New York: Basic Books.

Klau, M. (2006). Exploring youth leadership in theory and practice: An empirical study. In M. Klau, S. Boyd, & L. Luckow (eds.), *Youth leadership: New directions for youth development* (pp. 57–87). San Francisco: Jossey-Bass.

Klau, M., Boyd, S., & Luckow, L. (eds.). (2006a). *Youth leadership: New directions for youth development.* San Francisco: Jossey-Bass.

Klau, M., Boyd, S. & Luckow, L. (eds.). (2006b). Editors' notes. In M. Klau, S. Boyd, & L. Luckow (eds.), *Youth leadership: New directions for youth development* (pp. 3–7). San Francisco: Jossey-Bass.

Knox, L., Bracho, A., Sanchez, J., Vasques, M., Hahn, G., Sanderas, M., & Kaupfner, C. J. (2005). Youth as change agents in distressed immigrant communities. *Community Youth Development Journal, 6* (Fall), 19–28.

Korbin, J. E. (2000). Context and meaning in neighborhood studies of children and families. In A. Booth & A. C. Crouter, *Does it take a village? Community effects on children, adolescents, and families* (pp. 79–86). Mahwah, NJ: Lawrence Erlbaum Associates.

Kreider, A. (2002). *Student power.* Accessed February 7, 2005, from http://www.campusactivism.org

Kress, C. A. (2006). Youth leadership and youth development: Connections and questions. In M. Klau, S. Boyd, & L. Luckow (eds.), *Youth leadership: New directions for youth development* (pp. 43–56). San Francisco: Jossey-Bass.

Kumpher, K. L. (1999). Factors and processes contributing to resilience: The resilience framework. In M. D. Glantz & J. L. Johnson (eds.), *Resilience and development: Positive life adaptations* (pp. 179–224). New York: Kluwer Academic/Plenum.

Kurland, N.G. (2004). The just third way: Basic principles of economic and social justice. Paper presented at the Fifth Annual Conference of the Center for the Study of Islam and Democracy (CSID), Washington, D.C., May 28–29.

Lafferty, C. K., Mahoney, C. A., & Thombs, D. L. (2003). Diffusion of a developmental asset-building initiative in public schools. *American Journal of Health Behavior, 27,* S35–S44.

Lane, R. P. (1939). The field of community organization: Report of discussions. Proceedings of the National Conference of Social Work: Selected papers from

Sixty-sixth Annual Conference, Buffalo, New York, June 18–24 (vol. 66, pp. 95–124). New York: Columbia University Press.

Larson, R. W., & Hansen, D. (2005). The development of strategic thinking: Learning to impact human systems in a youth activism program. *Human Development, 48,* 327–349.

Larson, R. W., Walker, K., & Pearce, N. (2004). A comparison of youth-driven and adult-driven youth programs: Balancing inputs from youth and adults. *Journal of Community Psychology, 33,* 57–74.

Lawrence, K., Sutton, S., Kubisch, A., Susi, G. & Fullbright-Anderson, K. (2004). Structural racism and community building. Washington, D.C.: The Aspen Institute.

Leadbeater, B. J. R., & Way, N. (eds.). (1996). *Urban girls: Resisting stereotypes, creating identities.* New York: New York University Press.

Leadership? (2003, October). *Pipeline,* pp. 2–3.

Lee, J. (1997). The empowerment group: The heart of the empowerment approach and an antidote to injustice. In J. Parry (ed.), *From prevention to wellness through group work* (pp. 25–32). New York: Haworth Press.

Lerner, R. M. & Benson, P. L. (2003). (eds.). *Developmental assets and asset-building communities: Implications for research, policy, and practice.* New York: Kluwer Academic/Plenum Publishers.

Lerner, R. M., Bretano, C., Dowling, E. M., & Anderson, P. M. (2002). Positive youth development: Thriving as the basis of personhood and civil society. In R. M. Lerner, C. S. Taylor, & A. von Eye (eds.), *Pathways to positive development among diverse youth* (pp. 11–33). San Francisco: Jossey-Bass.

Lerner, R. M., Taylor, C. S., & von Eye, A. (eds.). (2003). *Pathways to positive development among diverse youth.* San Francisco: Jossey-Bass.

Levitt, P. (2001). *The transnational villagers.* Berkeley, CA: University of California Press.

Libby, M., Sedonaen, M., & Bliss, S. (2006). The mystery of youth leadership development: The path to just communities. In M. Klau, S. Boyd, & L. Luckow (eds.), *Youth leadership: New directions for youth development* (pp. 13–26). San Francisco: Jossey-Bass.

Lindberg, L. D., Boggess, S., Porter, L., & Williams, S. (2000). *Teen risk-taking: A statistical portrait.* Washington, D.C.: Urban Institute.

Linden, J. A., & Fertman, C. I. (1998). *Youth leadership: A guide to understanding leadership development in adolescents.* San Francisco: Jossey-Bass.

Lipsitz, G. (1998). The hip hop hearings: Censorship, social memory, and inter-generational tensions among African Americans. In J. Austin & M. N. Willard (eds.), *Generations of youth: Youth cultures and history in twentieth-century America* (pp. 395–411). New York: New York University Press.

LISTEN, Inc. (2003). *An emerging model for working with youth: Community organizing + youth development = youth organizing.* Occasional Paper Series on Youth Organizing. New York: Funders' Collaborative on Youth Organizing.

LISTEN, Inc. (2004). *From the frontlines: Youth organizers speak.* Washington, D.C.: Author.

Lombardi, K. (2000, December 29). JP lowers the voting age. *Boston Phoenix,* p. 12.

Lombardo, C., Zakus, D., & Skinner, H. (2002). Youth social action: Building a global latticework through information and communication technologies. *Health Promotion International, 17,* 363–371.

London, J., & Young, A. (2003). *Youth empowerment and community action in the Central Valley: Mapping the opportunities and challenges.* Davis, CA: Youth in Focus.

Lopez, M. H. (2002). *Youth demographic fact sheet.* Washington, D.C.: Center for Information and Research on Civic Learning & Engagement.

Lorion, R. P., & Sokoloff, H. (2003). Building assets in real world communities. In F. A. Villarruel, D. F. Perkins, L. M. Borden, & J. G. Keith (eds.), *Community youth development: Programs, policies, and practices* (pp. 121–156). Thousand Oaks, CA: Sage Publications.

Lupo, A. (1989, April 1). Staying on guard in the war on drugs. *Boston Globe,* p. 23.

Lupo, A. (1999, February 7). Competing visions for Jackson Square. *Boston Sunday Globe, City Weekly,* p. 1.

Lupo, A. (1999, March 7). BRA steps in on dispute over future of Jackson Square. *Boston Sunday Globe,* p. 29.

Lurie, H. L. (1959). *The community organization method of social work education. Vol. IV, A project report of the curriculum study.* New York: Council on Social Work Education.

Lurie, H. L. (1965). *Encyclopedia of social work* (issue 15). New York: National Association of Social Workers Press.

Lynd, S. (1967, July). Bicameralism from below. *Liberation,* pp. 15–19.

MacDonald, C. (2003, October 12). At Jackson Square, a new day is coming: Broad outlines of plan get local OK. *Boston Globe,* p. A16.

MacGregor, M.G. (2005). *Designing student leadership programs: Transforming the leadership potential of youth.* Morrison, CO: Youthleadership.com.

MacIntyre, A. (1981). *After virtue* (2nd ed.). Notre Dame, IN: University of Notre Dame Press.

MacNeil, C. A. (2006). Bridging generations: Applying adult leadership theories to youth leadership development. In M. Klau, S. Boyd, & L. Luckow (eds.), *Youth leadership: New directions for youth development* (pp. 27–42). San Francisco: Jossey-Bass.

MacNeil, C. A., & McClean, J. (2006). Moving from youth leadership development to youth in governance: Learning leadership by doing leadership. In M. Klau, S. Boyd, & L. Luckow (eds.),*Youth leadership: New directions for youth development* (pp. 99–106). San Francisco: Jossey-Bass.

Macnicol, J. (2006). *Age discrimination: An historical and contemporary analysis.* Cambridge, UK: Cambridge University Press.

Males, M. (2004). *Youth and social justice.* Accessed January 13, 2006, from home .earthlink.net/-mmales/socjust.doc

Malick, B., & Ahmad, S. (2001). A conversation with organizers from South Asian Youth Action (SAYA), Desis Rising Up & Moving (DRUM), and Youth Solidarity Summer (YSS). *Samar (South Asian Magazine for Action and Reflection), 14,* 1–6.

Mangum, S., & Waldeck, N. (1997). Investments in people matter. In *A generation of challenge: Pathways to success for urban youth* (pp. 45–55). Baltimore, MD: Sar Levitan Center for Policy Studies.

Martineau, P. (2005, May 5). Focused on equality: Davis group helps teens promote racial tolerance among peers. *Sacramento Bee*, pp. B1, B4.

Martinez, C., & Tangvik, K. (1998, December 4). Op-ed: Needs of youth must be priority for Jackson Square development. *Jamaica Plain Gazette*, p. 16.

Martinez, E. (1996, September). Back in the Early 1990s: Latino/a youth activism and its promise for us all. *Z Magazine*, pp. 29–34.

Martsudaira, J., & Jefferson, A. (2006). Anytown: NCCJ's youth leadership experience in Social justice. In M. Klau, S. Boyd, & L. Luckow (eds.), *Youth leadership: New directions for youth development* (pp. 107–116). San Francisco: Jossey-Bass.

Marx, K. (1975). *Early writings*. R. Livingstone & G. Benton (trans.). London: Harmondsworth.

Mary, N. L. (2001). Political activism of social work educators. *Journal of Community Practice, 9*, 1–20.

Maslach, C. (1982). *Burnout: The cost of caring*. Englewood Cliffs, NJ: Prentice Hall.

Mason, D. (1999). *Official memorandum: Shopper survey*. Boston: Urban Edge.

Massey, D. (2001). The prodigal paradigm returns: Ecology comes back to Sociology. In A. Booth, & A. C. Crouter, *Does it take a village? Community effects on children, adolescents, and families* (pp. 41–47). Mahwah, NJ: Lawrence Erlbaum Associates.

Masten, A. S., Best, K. M., & Garmezy, N. (1990). Resilience and development: Contributions from the study of children who overcome adversity. *Development and Psychopathology, 2*, 425–444.

May, J. P., & Pitts, K. R. (eds.). (2000). *Building violence: How America's rush to incarcerate creates more violence*. Thousand Oaks, CA: Sage Publications.

McCall, D. S., & Shannon, M. M. (1999). *Youth led health promotion, youth engagement and youth participation*. Ottawa, Canada: Health Canada.

McDermott, C. J. (1989). Empowering the elderly nursing home resident: The resident rights campaign. *Social Work, 34*, 155–157.

McElroy, A. (2001, June 4). Former McDonogh 35 Senior High School student honors black leadership. *Louisiana Weekly*, p. 1.

McGillicuddy, K. (2003, May). *A veteran activist talks about the power of youth organizing*. Providence, RI: What Kids Can Do.

McGillicuddy, K., & James, T. (2001). Building youth movements for community change. *Nonprofit Quarterly, 8*, 1–3.

McKnight, J. (1995). *The careless society*. New York: Basic Books.

McLaughlin, M. W. (1993). Embedded identities: Enabling balance in urban contexts. In S. B. Heath & M. W. McLaughlin (eds.), *Identity & inner-city youth: Beyond ethnicity and gender* (pp. 36–68). New York: Teachers College Press.

McNamara, R. P. (1999). *Beating the odds: Crime, poverty, and life in the inner city*. Washington, D.C.: Child Welfare of America Press.

McNutt, J. (2000). Organizing by cyberspace: Strategies for teaching about community practice and technology. *Journal of Community Practice, 7*, 95–109.

McNutt, J., & Hick, S. (2002). Organizing for social change: Online and traditional community practice. In S. Hick & J. McNutt (eds.), *Advocacy, activism, and the Internet* (pp. 73–79). Chicago: Lyceum Books.

Mediratta, K., & Fruchter, N. (2001). *Mapping the field of organizing for school improvement: A report on education organizing in Baltimore, Chicago, Los Angeles, the Mississippi Delta, New York City, Philadelphia, San Francisco and Washington D.C.* Accessed August 6, 2005, from http://www.ci.chi.il.us/Human Services/sub/youthnet.html

Mendel, D. (2004, March). Is civic action the answer? *Youth Today,* p. 31.

Miao, V. (2003). *Youth organizing: Expanding possibilities for youth development.* Occasional Papers Series on Youth Organizing. New York: Funders' Collaborative on Youth Organizing.

Michels, R. (1949). *Political parties: A sociological study of the oligarchical tendencies of modern democracy.* New York: Free Press.

Michelsen, E., Zaff, J. F., & Hair, E. C. (2002). *Civic engagement programs and youth development: A synthesis.* Washington, D.C.: Child Trends.

Miley, K., & Dubois, B. (1999). Empowering processes for social work practice. In W. Shera & L. M. Wells (eds.), *Empowerment practice in social work: Developing richer conceptual foundations* (pp. 2–13). Toronto: Canadian Scholars Press.

Mill, J. S. (1849/1973). On liberty. In J. Bentham (ed.), *The utilitarians: An introduction to the principles of morals and legislation* (pp. 473–600). Garden City, NY: Doubleday Books.

Mill, J. S. (1861). *Considerations on representative government.* Reprinted in J. Gray (ed.), *John Stuart Mill: On liberty and other essays.* Oxford, UK: Oxford University Press.

Miller, D. (1999). *Principles of social justice.* Cambridge, MA: Harvard University Press.

Miller, M. (2004). Editor's introduction: Organizing youth. *Social Policy, 34*(3), 65.

Miller, Y. (1998, November 20). Guess who's coming to Roxbury: Kmart? *The Bay State Banner,* pp. 1–2.

Miller, Y. (1999, November 18). Youth activists seek input in Jackson Square. *The Bay State Banner,* pp. 9–10.

Miller, Y. (1999, November 25). Kmart, *The Bay State Banner,* pp. 1–2.

Miller, Y. (2000, October 26). Jackson Square teens push for youth center. *The Bay State Banner,* pp. 1–2.

Minkler, M. (1997). Community organizing among the elderly poor in San Francisco's Tenderloin District. In M. Minkler (ed.), *Community organizing & community building for health* (pp. 272–87). New Brunswick, NJ: Rutgers University Press.

Minkler, M., & Pies, C. (2005). Ethical issues and practical dilemmas in community organization and community participation. In M. Minkler (ed.), *Community organizing and community building for health* (2nd ed., pp. 116–133). New Brunswick, NJ: Rutgers University Press.

Minkler, M., & Wallerstein, N. (eds.). (2003). *Community-based participatory research for health.* San Francisco, CA: Jossey-Bass.

Mizrahi, T. (1993). *Community organizers: For a change.* Accessed November 9, 2005, from http://www.hunter.cuny.edu/socwork/ecco/cocareer.htm

Mohamed, I. A., & Wheeler, W. (2001). *Youth leadership for development initiative: Broadening parameters of youth development and strengthening civic activism.* Chevy Chase, MD: Innovation Center for Community and Youth Development.

Mokwena, S. (2000). Young people taking responsibility for change in Latin America. *CYD Journal: Community Youth Development, 1,* 26–31.

Mokwena, S., et al. (1999). *Youth participation, development, and social change: A synthesis of core concepts and issues.* Baltimore, MD: International Youth Foundation.

Morales, J., & Reyes, M. (1998). Cultural and political realities for community social work practice with Puerto Ricans in the United States. In F. G. Rivera & J. L. Erlich (eds.), *Community organizing in a diverse society* (3rd ed., pp. 49–66). Boston: Allyn & Bacon.

Moreau, M. (1990). Empowerment through advocacy and consciousness raising. *Journal of Sociology and Social Welfare, 17*, 53–67.

Morrell, E. (2004). *Becoming critical researchers: Literacy and empowerment for urban youth.* New York: Peter Lang Publishers.

Morsillo, J., & Prilleltensky, I. (2005). *Social action with youth: Interventions, evaluation, and psychopolitical validity.* Victoria, Australia: St. Albans Campus, Victoria University.

Mortimer, J. T., & Larson, R. W. (2002). *The changing adolescent experience: Societal trends and the transition to adulthood.* New York: Cambridge University Press.

Moss, P., & Tilly, C. (2001). *Stories employers tell: Race, skill, and hiring in America.* New York: Russell Sage Foundation.

Movement Strategy Center. (2005). *Bringing it together: Uniting youth organizing, development and services for long-term sustainability.* Oakland, CA: Author.

Moynihan, D. (1969). *Maximum feasible misunderstanding.* New York: Free Press.

Mullahey, R., Susskind, Y., & Checkoway, B. (1999). *Youth participation in community planning.* Washington, D.C.: American Planning Association.

Murase, K. (1992). Organizing in the Japanese American community. In F. G. Rivera & J. L. Erlich (eds.), *Community organizing in a diverse society* (pp. 91–112). Boston: Allyn & Bacon.

Murashige, M. (2001). *The future of change: Youth perspectives on social justice and cross- cultural collaborative action in Los Angeles.* Los Angeles: A Multicultural Collaborative Report.

Murphy, P. W., & Cunningham, J. V. (2003). *Organizing for community controlled development: Renewing civil society.* Thousand Oaks, CA: Sage Publications.

Murphy, R. (1995). *Training for youth workers: An assessment guide for community-based youth-serving organizations to promote youth development.* Washington, D.C.: Center for Youth Development and Policy Research, Academy for Educational Development.

Nagle, A., Nignaraja, Wignaraja, M., Fullwood, P. C., & Hempel, M. (2003). *Power & possibilities.* New York: Ms. Foundation for Women.

Nasaw, D. (1985). *Children of the city at work and at play.* New York: Oxford University Press.

National Youth Rights Association. (2003). *Three types of youth liberation: Youth equality, youth power, youth culture.* Accessed January 10, 2005, from http://www.youthrights.org/articles/threetypes.html

Networks for Youth Development. (1998a). *The handbook for positive youth outcomes* (2nd ed.). New York: Author.

Networks for Youth Development. (1998b). *Core competencies for youth work.* New York: Author.

Newman, K. S. (1999). *No shame in my game: The working poor in the inner city.* New York: Russell Sage Foundation.

Nisbet, R. (1953). *The quest for community.* New York: Oxford University Press.

Noack, P., & Kracke, B. (1997). Social change and adolescent well-being: Healthy country, healthy teens. In J. Schulenberg, J. L. Maggs, & K. Hurrelmann (eds.), *Health risks and developmental transitions during adolescence* (pp. 54–84). New York: Cambridge University Press.

Norris, P., & Curtice, J. (2004). *If you build a political website, will they come?* National Centre for Social Research. Cambridge, MA: Harvard University, John F. Kennedy School of Government.

Notepad. (2003). Objections to calling adultism an oppression. Accessed January 12, 2006, from http://www.youth;ib.com/notepad/archieves/2003/12/objections_to_c.html

Nozick, R. (1974). *Anarchy, state, and utopia.* New York: Basic Books.

Nussbaum, E., with Mazer, R. (2006). Arts-based leadership: Theatrical tributes. In M. Klau, S. Boyd, & L. Luckow (eds.), *Youth leadership: New directions for youth development* (pp. 117–124). San Francisco: Jossey-Bass.

Nygreen, K., Kwon, S. A., & Sanchez, P. (2006). Urban youth building community social change and participatory research in schools, homes, and community-based organizations. In B. N. Checkoway & L. Gutierrez (eds.), *Youth participation and community change* (pp. 107–123). New York: Haworth Press.

O'Donoghue, J. L. (2003). *Youth civic engagement: Annotated bibliography.* Palo Alto, CA: John W. Gardner Center for Youth and their Communities.

O'Donoghue, J. L., Kirshner, B., & McLaughlin, M. (2002). Introduction: Moving youth participation forward. In B. Kirshner, J. L. O'Donoghue, & M. McLaughlin (eds.), *Youth participation: Improving institutions and communities* (pp. 15–26). San Francisco: Jossey-Bass.

Ogbu, O., & Mihyo, P. (eds.). (2000). *African youth on the information highway: Participation and leadership in community development.* Ottawa, Canada: International Development Research Centre.

O'Hare, W., & Mather, M. (2003). *Kids count/PRB report on census 2000. The growing number of kids in severely distressed neighborhoods: Evidence from the 2000 Census.* Baltimore, MD: Annie E. Casey Foundation.

O'Kane, C. (2002). Marginalized children as social actors for social justice in South Asia. *British Journal of Social Work, 32,* 697–710.

One and Four. (2005, October 13). Ageism vs. adultism. Accessed January 12, 2006, from http://www.oneandfour.org/archieves/2005/10/ageism_vs_adult.htm

Open Society Forum Institute. (2002). *Move the crowd: The emergence of hip-hop activism.* New York: Author.

Open Society Institute. (1997). Funding youth organizing: Strategies for building power and youth leadership. Paper presented at the Open Society Institute, New York.

Otis, M.D. (2006). Youth as engaged citizens and community change advocates through the Lexington Youth Leadership Academy. In B. N. Checkoway & L. Gutierrez (eds.), *Youth participation and community change* (pp. 71–89). New York: Haworth Press.

Pancer, M. (2001). *Does research tell the whole story?* Literature Review Report no. 1. Toronto: Centre of Excellence for Youth Engagement.

Pantoja, A. and Perry, W. (1998). Community development and restoration: A perspective and case study. In F. G. Rivera & J. L. Erlich (eds.), *Community organizing in a diverse society* (3rd ed.). Boston: Allyn Bacon.

Parenti, M. (2002). *Democracy for the few* (7th ed.). Boston: Bedford/St. Martin's.

Parham, A., & Pinzino, J. (2004). The Chicago School of youth organizing: A case study. *Social Policy, 34*, pp. 7–15.

Parson, R. (1977). A child's bill of rights. In B. Gross & R. Gross (eds.), *The children's rights movement: Overcoming the oppression of young people* (pp. 325–328). Garden City, NY: Anchor Press/Doubleday.

Pecukonis, E. V., & Wenocur, S. (1994). Perceptions of self and collective efficacy in community organization theory and practice. *Journal of Community Practice, 1*(1/2), 5–21.

Perry, J. L., & Imperial, M. T. (2001). A decade of service-related research: A map of the field. *Nonprofit and Voluntary Sector Quarterly, 30*, 462–479.

Petterman, D.M. (2002). Empowerment evaluation: Building communities of practice and culture building. *American Journal of Community Psychology, 30*(1), 89–102.

Pinderhughes, E.B. (1983). Empowerment for our clients and ourselves. *Social Casework, 64*, 331–338.

Pines, A. & Maslach, C. (1978). Characteristics of staff burnout in mental health settings. *Hospital and Community Psychiatry, 29*(4), 233–237.

Pintado-Vertner, R. (2004). *The West Coast study: The emergence of youth organizing in California*. Occasional paper series on youth organizing (no. 5). New York: Funders' Collaborative on Youth Organizing.

Pitkin, H. F., & Shumer, S. M. (1982). On participation. *Democracy, 2*(4, Fall), 43–54.

Pittman, K. (1991). *Bridging the gap: A rationale for enhancing the role of community organizations promoting youth development*. Report for the Task Force on Youth Development and Community Programs at the Carnegie Council on Adolescent Development. Washington, D.C.: Academy for Educational Development.

Pittman, K. (2000). Balancing the equation: Communities supporting youth, youth supporting communities. *CYD Journal, 1*, 8–10.

Pittman, K., & Zeldin, S. (1995). *Premises, principles and practice: Defining the why, what, and how of promoting youth development through organizational practice*. Washington, D.C.: Center for Youth Development and Policy Research, Academy for Educational Development.

Piven, F. F. & Cloward, R. A. (1977). *Poor people's movements: Why they succeed, how they fail*. New York: Vintage Books.

Polk, E., & Clayborne, J. (2004). Voices from the field: Forum interviews with youth mobilizers. *Youth Focus, 2*, 5–9.

Powell, G. Jr., & Bingham, G. (1989). Constitutional design and electoral control. *Journal of Theoretical Politics, 1/2*, 107–130.

Price, C., & Diehl, K. (2004). *A new generation of southerners: Youth organizing in the south*. Occasional Paper Series on Youth Organizing (no. 6). New York: Funders' Collaborative on Youth Organizing.

Prilletensky, I. (2003). Understanding, resisting, and overcoming oppression: Toward psychopolitical validity. *American Journal of Community Psychology, 31*, 195–201.

Prilletensky, I., Nelson, G., & Peirson, L. (2001). The role of power and control in children's lives: An ecological analysis of pathways toward wellness, resilience, and problems. *Journal of Community and Applied Social Psychology, 11*, 143–158.

Putnam, R. D. (2000). *Bowling alone*. New York: Simon & Schuster.

Putnam, R. D. (2003). *Better together*. New York: Simon & Schuster.

Quioroz-Martinez, J., HoSang, D., & Villarosa, L. (2004). *Changing the rules of the game: Youth development & structural racism*. Findings from the Youth and Racial Equity Project. Washington, D.C.: Philanthropic Initiative for Racial Equity.

Quiroz-Martinez, J., Wu, D. P., & Zimmerman, K. (2005). *ReGeneration: Young people shaping environmental justice*. Oakland, CA: Movement Strategy Center.

Rajani, R. (2001). *The participation rights of adolescents: A strategic approach*. Working Paper of the United Nations Children's Fund. New York: UNICEF Programme Division.

Ramphele, M. (2002). Steering by the stars: Youth in cities. In M. Tienda & W. J. Wilson (eds.), *Youth in cities: A cross-national perspective* (pp. 21–30). Cambridge, MA: Harvard University Press.

Rappaport, J. (1981). In praise of paradox: A social policy of empowerment over prevention. *American Journal of Community Psychology, 9*, 1–25.

Rauner, D. M. (2000). *They still pick me up when I fall: The role of caring in youth development and community life*. New York: Columbia University Press.

Rawls, J. (1999). *A theory of justice*. Cambridge, MA: Harvard University Press.

Rhodes, J. E. (2002). *A critical view of youth mentoring*. San Francisco: Jossey-Bass.

Rhodes, J. E., Grossman, J. B. & Roffman, J. (2002). The rhetoric and reality of youth mentoring. In J. E. Rhodes (ed.). *A critical view of youth mentoring* (pp. 9–20). San Francisco, CA: Jossey-Bass Publisher.

Rhodes, J. E., & Roffman, J. G. (2003). Nonparental adults as asset builders in the lives of youth. In R. M. Lerner & P. L. Benson (eds.), *Developmental assets and asset-building communities* (pp.195–209). New York: Kluwer Associates.

Riessman, F. & Gartner, A. (1984). *The self-help revolution*. New York: Human Science.

Riessman, F. & Carroll, D. (1995). *Redefining self-help: Policy and practice*. San Francisco: Jossey-Bass.

Rios, V. M. (2005, January). From knucklehead to revolutionary: Urban youth culture and social transformation. *Online Journal of Urban Youth Culture*. Accessed October 18, 2006, from http://www.juyc.org/current/0501/hiphop.html

Rivera, F. G., & Erlich, J. L. (eds.). (1998). *Community organizing in a diverse society* (3rd ed.). Boston: Allyn & Bacon.

Rizzini, I., Barker, G., & Cassaniga, N. (2002). From street children to all children: Improving the opportunities of low-income urban children and youth in Brazil. In M. Tienda & W. J. Wilson (eds.), *Youth in cities: A cross-national perspective* (pp.113–137). Cambridge, MA: Harvard University Press.

Roach, C. L., Sullivan, L., & Wheeler, W. (1999). *Youth leadership for development initiative: Broadening the parameters of youth development and strengthening civic activism*. New York: Innovation Center for Community & Youth Development.

Roach, C., Yu, H. C., & Lewis-Charp, H. (2001). Race, poverty and youth development. *Poverty & Race, 10*, 3–6.

Roberts, D. (2002). *Shattered bonds: The color of child welfare*. New York: Basic Civitas Books.

Roberts-DeGennaro, M. (2004). Using technology for grassroots organizing. In L. Staples (ed.), *Roots to power: A manual for grassroots organizing* (2nd ed., pp. 270–281). Westport, CT: Praeger.

Roche, J. (1999). Children: Rights, participation, and citizenship. *Childhood, 6,* 475–493.

Roessler, C. (2003). *From exclusion to inclusion: Strengthening community-led organizations with effective technology.* St. Paul, MN: Progressive Technology Project.

Roffman, J. G., Suarez-Orozco, C., & Rhodes, J. E. (2003). Facilitating positive development in immigrant youth: The role of mentors and community organizations. In F. A. Villarruel, D. F. Perkins, L. M. Borden, & J. G. Keith (eds.), *Community youth development: Programs, policies, and practices* (pp. 90–117). Thousand Oaks, CA: Sage Publications.

Roosevelt, E. (1940). Why I still believe in the Youth Congress. *Liberty, 17* (April), 30–32.

Rose, T. (1994). A style nobody can deal with: Politics, style and the postindustrial city in hip hop. In A. Ross and T. Rose (eds.), *Microphone fiends: Youth music & youth culture* (pp. 71–88). New York: Routledge.

Ross, A., & Rose, T. (eds.). (1994). *Microphone fiends: Youth music & youth culture.* New York: Routledge.

Ross, M. G. (1955). *Community organization: Theory and principles.* New York: Harper & Brothers.

Rosseau, J. J. (1762). *The social contract.* G. D. H. Cole (trans.). London: J.M. Dent & Sons.

Rost, J.C. (1991). *Leadership for the twenty-first century.* Westport, CT: Praeger.

Roth, J., Murray, L. F., Brooks-Gunn, J., & Foster, W. H. (1999). Youth development programs. In D. J. Besharov (ed.), *America's disconnected youth: Toward a preventive strategy* (pp. 267–294). Washington, D.C.: Child Welfare League of America.

Rothman, J. (1964). An analysis of goals and roles in community organization practice. *Social Work, 9,* 24–31.

Rothman, J. (1968). Three models of community organization practice. From National Conference on Social Welfare, *Social Work Practice.* New York: Columbia University Press.

Rothman, J. (1995). Approaches to community intervention. In J. Rothman, J. L. Erlich, & J. E. Tropman (eds.), *Strategies of community intervention,* (5th ed., pp. 26–93). Itasca, IL: Peacock.

Rubin, H. J. and Rubin, I.S. (2001). *Community organizing and development* (3rd ed.) Boston: Allyn & Bacon.

Rubin, H. J., & Rubin. I. S. (2004). The practice of community organizing. In M. Weil (ed.), *The handbook of community practice* (pp. 189–203). Thousand Oaks, CA: Sage Publications.

Ruch, J. (2003, September 12). Development rules completed. *Jamaica Plain Gazette,* pp. 1–2.

Ruch, J. (2005, February 4). Two developers submit proposals. *Jamaica Plain Gazette,* pp. 1–2.

Rudavsky, S. (2002, November 17). Youths looking for a place to go, and they won't settle for no. *Boston Sunday Globe, City Weekly,* p. 8.

Russell, S. T. (2002). Queer in America: Citizenship for sexual minority youth. *Applied Developmental Science, 6,* 258–263.

Sabo, K. (ed.), (2003). *Youth participatory evaluation: A field in the making.* San Francisco: Jossey-Bass.

Saito, R. N., & Blyth, D. A. (1995). *Understanding mentoring relationships.* Minneapolis: Search Institute.

Saleeby, D. (ed.). (1992). *The strengths perspective in social work practice: Power in the people.* White Plains, NY: Longman.

Sanchez-Jankowski, M. (2002). Minority youth and civic engagement: The impact of group relations. *Applied Developmental Science, 6,* 237–245.

Sandel, M. J. (1982). *Liberalism and the limits of justice.* Cambridge, UK: Cambridge University Press.

Sanyal, B., & Schon, D. A. (1999). Information technology and urban poverty: The role of public policy. In D. A. Schon, B. Sanyal, & W. J. Mitchell (eds.), *High technology and low-income communities: Prospects for the positive use of advanced information technology* (pp.371–393). Cambridge, MA: Massachusetts Institute of Technology Press.

Sashkin, M. (1988). The visionary leader. In J. A. Conger & R.N.K. Kanungo (eds.), *Charismatic leadership* (pp. 120–160). San Francisco: Jossey Bass.

Scales, P. C., & Leffert, N. (1999). *Developmental assets: A synthesis of the scientific research on adolescent development.* Minneapolis, MN: Search Institute.

Scheie, D. (2003). *Organizing for Youth Development and School Improvements: Final Report from a Strategic Assessment.* Prepared for the Edward W. Hazen Foundation. Minneapolis, MN: Rainbow Research, Inc.

Scheve, J., Perkins, D. F., & Mincemoyer, C. (2006). Collaborative teams for youth engagement. In B. N. Checkoway & L. Gutierrez (eds.), *Youth participation and community change* (pp. 219–234). New York: Haworth Press.

Schoberg, D. (2001, June 12). A conversation with a Jamaica Plain police officer. *Emerson College Newspaper* (Boston, MA), p. 1.

Schon, D. A., Sanyal, B. & Mitchell, M. J. (1999). *High technology and low-income communities: Prospects for the future use of advanced information technology.* Cambridge, MA: Massachusetts Institute of Technology Press.

Seamans, J. (1991, December 19). Hundreds turn out for Baez Dinner: JP unites in face of tragedy. *Jamaica Plain Citizens,* p. 3.

Sears, A. (2005). *A good book, in theory: A guide to theoretical thinking.* Peterborough, Ontario: Broadview Press.

Selznick, P. (1948). Foundations of the theory of organization. *American Sociological Review, 13,* 25–35.

Sen, I. (2003, June 8). Teens get lesson in activism, civility in Jackson Square. Forum. *Bay State Banner,* p. 8.

Sen, R. (2003). *Stir it up.* San Francisco: Jossey-Bass.

Sheffield, R. (1998, December 18). Day events focus on neighborhood issues: Marchers call for Peace/Paz in Hyde Sq. *Jamaica Plain Citizens,* p. 5.

Sherman, R. F. (2002). Building young people's public lives: One foundation's strategy. In B. Kirshner, J. L. O'Donoghue, & M. McLaughlin (eds.), *Youth participation: Improving institutions and communities* (pp. 65–82). San Francisco: Jossey-Bass.

Sherrod, L. R., Flanagan, C., & Youniss, J. (2002). The development of citizenship: Multiple pathways and diverse influences. *Applied Developmental Science, 6,* 221–226.

Sherwood, K. E., & Dressner, J. (2004). *Youth organizing: A new generation of social activism*. Philadelphia, PA: Public/Private Ventures.

Shragge, E. (ed.). (1997). *Community economic development: In search of empowerment* (2nd ed.). Montreal: Black Rose Books.

Simmons, L. (2004). Community labor coalitions. In L. Staples, *Roots to power: A manual for grassroots organizing* (2nd ed., pp. 302–308).Westport, CT: Praeger.

Simon, B. L. (1994). *The empowerment tradition in American social work history*. New York: Columbia University Press.

Simpson, A. R., & Roehlkepartain, J. L. (2003). Asset building practices and family life. In R. M. Lerner & P. L. Benson (eds.), *Developmental assets and asset-building communities* (pp.157–193). New York: Kluwer Associates.

Sistas and Brothas United. (2005). Focus on education. Bronx, NY. Accessed April 7, 2005, from http://www.whatkidscando.org/featurestories/yobronx.html

Skelton, N., Boyte, H. C., & Leonard, L. S. (2002). *Youth civic engagement: Reflections on an emerging public idea*. Minneapolis, MN: Center for Democracy and Citizenship.

Smith, G. W. (2004). *The politics of deceit*. Hoboken, NJ: John Wiley.

Smith, T. A., Genry, L. S. & Ketring, S. A. (2005). Evaluating a youth leadership life skills development program. *Journal of Extension, 41*, 1–8.

Solomon, B. B. (1976). *Black empowerment: Social work in oppressed communities*. New York: Columbia University Press.

Sonenshein, R. (1998). Making the rules: Youth participation and Los Angeles charter reform. *New Designs for Youth Development, 14*, 39–40.

South, S. J. (2000). Issues in the analysis of neighborhoods, families, and children. In A. Booth & A. C. Crouter (eds.), *Does it take a village? Community effects on children, adolescents, and families* (pp. 87–93). Mahwah, NJ: Lawrence Erlbaum Associates.

Spann, E. K. (2003). *Democracy's children: The young rebels of the 1960s and the power of ideals*. Wilmington, DE: Scholarly Resources, Inc.

Spatz, M. (2005). *At a crossroads: Youth organizing in the Midwest*. New York: Funders' Collaborative on Youth Organizing.

Specht, H., & Courtney, M. (1995). *Unfaithful angels: How social work has abandoned its mission*. New York: Free Press.

Spector, J. M. (1994). Computers for social change and community organizing: A review. *Computers in Human Behavior, 10*, 411–413.

Stahlhut, D. (2004). The people closest to the problem. *Social Policy, 34*(3), 71–74.

Staples, L. (1984). *Roots to power: A manual for grassroots organizing*. Westport, CT: Praeger.

Staples, L. (1990). Powerful ideas about empowerment. *Administration in Social Work, 14*, 29–42.

Staples, L. (1999). Consumer empowerment in a mental health system: Stakeholder roles and responsibilities. In W. Shera & L. M. Wells (eds.), *Empowerment practice in social work* (pp. 119–141). Toronto, Ontario: Canadian Scholars' Press.

Staples, L. (2004a). *Roots to power: A manual for grassroots organizing* (2nd ed.). Westport, CT: Praeger.

Staples, L. (2004b). Social action groups. In C. D. Garvin, L. M. Gutierrez, & M. J. Galinsky (eds.), *Handbook of social work with groups* (pp. 344–359). New York: Guilford.

Steiner, J. (1930). *Community organization: A study of its theory and current practice* (rev. ed.). New York: Century.

Stepick, A., & Stepick, D. (2002). Becoming American, constructing ethnicity: Immigrant youth and civic engagement. *Applied Developmental Science, 4,* 246–257.

Stoddard, L. (2000, November 3). Op-ed. *Jamaica Plain Gazette,* p. 4.

Stoecker, R. (2002). Cyberspace vs. face-to-face: Community organizing in the new millennium. *Perspectives on Global Development and Technology, 1,* 143–164.

Stogdill, R.M. (1974). *Handbook of leadership research: A survey of theory and research.* New York: Free Press.

Stokes, C. F., & Gant, L. M. (2002). Turning the tables on the HIV/AIDS epidemic: Hip hop as a tool for reaching African-American adolescent girls. *African-American Perspectives, 8,* 70–81.

Stoneman, D. (2002). The role of youth programming in the development of civic engagement. *Applied Developmental Science, 6,* 221–226.

Strand, K., Marullo, S., Cutforth, N., Stoecker, R., & Donohue, P. (2003). *Community-based research and higher education: Principles and practices.* San Francisco: Jossey-Bass.

Suleiman, A.B., Soleimanpour, S., & London, J. (2006). Youth action for health through youth-led research. In B. N. Checkoway & L. Gutierrez (eds.), *Youth participation and community change* (pp. 1025–1045). New York: Haworth Press.

Sullivan, L. (1997) Hip-hop nation: The undeveloped social capital of black urban America. *National Civic Review, 86,* 3–5.

Sullivan, L. (2001). Emerging Model for Working with Youth, 2000. In J. Tolman, & K. Pittman (eds.), *Youth acts, community impacts: Stories of youth engagement with real results* (vol. 7). Washington, D.C.: Forum for Youth Investment.

Sullivan, L.Y. (2003). The state of youth organizing 1990–2000. In *The state of philanthropy 2002* (pp. 25–30). Washington, D.C.: National Committee for Responsive Philanthropy.

Susskind, Y. (2003). A framework for youth empowerment. *Children, Youth and Environments, 13,* 1–3.

Swan, J. (1999, December 3). Teens organize to work for youth center. *Jamaica Plain Gazette,* p. 24.

Swart-Kruger, J., & Chawla, L. (2002). Children show the way: Participatory programs for children of South African streets and squatter camps. In M. Tienda & W. J. Wilson (eds.), *Youth in cities: A cross-national perspective* (pp. 31–57). Cambridge, MA: Harvard University Press.

Tacchi, J. (2004). Researching creative applications of new information and communication technologies. *International Journal of Cultural Studies, 7,* pp. 91–103.

Tangvik, K. (2004). Personal interview, December 16.

Tardieu, B. (1999). Computer as community memory: How people in very poor neighborhoods made use of a computer of their own. In D. A. Schon, B. Sanyal, & W. J. Mitchell (eds.), *High technology and low-income communities:*

Prospects for the positive use of advanced information technology (pp. 287–313). Cambridge, MA: Massachusetts Institute of Technology Press.

Tasker, T. (1999). You like Tupac, Mary? *Families in Society: The Journal of Contemporary Human Services, 80,* 216–218.

Tate, T. F., & Copos, B. L. (2003). Insist or enlist? Adultism versus climates of excellence. *Reclaiming Children and Youth, 12,* 40–47.

Taylor, C. S. (2004, January). Hip-hop and youth culture: Contemplations on an emerging cultural phenomenon. *Online Journal of Urban Youth Culture.* Accessed August 28, 2006, from http://www.juyc.org/current/0401/hiphop.html

Taylor, G. (2000). Community organizing for youth development: A strategy for network building. *Community Youth Development Journal, 1,* 10–11.

Tayo, O. (2002). An adult's dilemma on youth participation. In S. Golombek (ed.), *What works in youth participation: Case studies from around the world* (p. 14). Baltimore, MD: International Youth Foundation.

Terrin, N. (2000). Personal communication via e-mail, February 2, 2000.

Terry, J., & Woonteiler, D. (2000). An interview with Craig Kielburger, founder of Free the Children. *CYD Journal Community Youth Development, 1,* 14–19.

Thornton, S. (1996). *Club cultures: Music, media and subcultural capital.* Hanover, NH: Wesleyan University Press.

Tienda, M., & Wilson, W. J. (2002a). Comparative perspectives of urban youth: Challenges for normative development. In M. Tienda & W. J. Wilson (eds.), *Youth in cities: A cross-national perspective* (pp. 3–18). Cambridge, MA: Harvard University Press.

Tienda, M., & Wilson, W. J. (2002b). Prospect and retrospect: Options for health youth developing in changing urban worlds. In M. Tienda & W. J. Wilson (eds.), *Youth in cities: A cross-national perspective* (pp. 269–277). Cambridge, MA: Harvard University Press.

Tocqueville, A. de (1840/1945). *Political effects of decentralized administration in the United States* (vol. I). H. Reeve (ed.), P. Bradley (trans.). New York: Vintage.

Tolman, J., & Pittman, K. (2001). Youth acts, community impacts: Stories of youth engagement with real results. Community and Youth Development Series (vol.7). Washington, D.C.: Forum for Youth Investment.

Tomlinson, F., & Egan, S. (2002). From marginalization to (dis)empowerment: Organizing training and employment services for refugees. *Human Relations, 55,* 1019–1043.

Transformative leadership in youth organizing. (2004, June). *Pipeline,* pp. 2–4.

Traynor, B. (1993, March/April). Community development and community organizing. *Shelterforce,* pp. 4–7.

Tropman, J.E. (1997). *Successful community leadership: A skills guide for volunteers and professionals.* Washington, D.C.: National Association of Social Workers.

Tully, C. T., Craig, T., & Nugent, G. (1994). Should only gay and lesbian community organizers work in gay and lesbian communities? In M. A. Austin & J. I. Lowe, (eds.), *Controversial issues in communities and organizations* (pp. 86–96). Boston: Allyn & Bacon.

Turning the leadership corner. (2004). *Insight, 5,* 1–7.

Two decades of youth action ideas. (2002). *Forum for Youth Investment, 2,* 11–12.

Two teens win spots on JP council. (2001, June 10). *Boston Sunday Globe, City Weekly,* p. 23.

United Nations. (2005). *Final report of the Ad Hoc Working Group for Youth and the Millennium Development Goals*. New York: Author.

Urban Edge (1998). *Egleston-Jackson strategy: A comprehensive development approach proposed by Urban Edge*. Boston: Author.

U.S. Census Bureau. (2000). Child population statistics. Accessed April 4, 2004, from www.census.gov/population/estimates/nation/intfile2-1.txt

U.S. Department of Health and Human Services. (2002). *Profile of America's youth*. Washington, D.C.: Author.

Valaitis, R. K. (2005). Computers and the Internet: Tools for youth empowerment. *Journal of Medical Internet Research, 7*(5), pp. 1–18.

Velazquez Jr., J., & Garin-Jones, M. (2003, January/February). Adultism and cultural competence. *Children's Voice*, pp. 1–4.

Vibrations. (2003, Spring). Newsletter of LISTEN, Inc. Intermediary Movement Strategy Center. Accessed March 23, 2005, from http://www.movementstrategy.org/index.html://www.ejcc.org/CJCorps2004/CJCorps2004.html

Villarruel, F. A., Perkins, D. F., Borden, L. M., & Keith, J. G. (2003a). *Community youth development: Programs, policies, and practices*. Thousand Oaks, CA: Sage Publications.

Villarruel, F.A., Perkins, D. F., Borden, L. M., & Keith, J. G. (2003b). Community youth development: Youth voice and activism. In F. A. Villarruel, D. F. Perkins, L. M. Borden, & J. G. Keith (eds.), *Community youth development: Programs, policies, and practices* (pp. 394–403). Thousand Oaks, CA: Sage Publications.

Walker, J.A. (2003). The essential youth worker: Supports and opportunities for professional success. In F. A. Villarruel, D. F. Perkins, L. M. Borden, & J. G. Keith (eds.), *Community youth development: Programs, policies, and practices* (pp. 373–393). Thousand Oaks, CA: Sage Publications.

Walzer, M. (1983). *Spheres of justice*. New York: Basic Books.

Wang, C. C. (2006). Youth participation in photovoice as a strategy for community change. In B. N. Checkoway & L. Gutierrez (eds.), *Youth participation and community change* (pp. 147–181). New York: Haworth Press.

Warren, R. (1975). Types of purposive change at the community level. In R.M. Kramer & H. Specht (eds.), *Readings in community organization practice* (2nd ed.). Englewood Cliffs, NJ: Prentice Hall, Inc.

Wasler, R. (1998). Clamor and community in the music of Public Enemy. In J. Austin & M. N. Willard (eds.), *Generations of youth: Youth cultures and history in twentieth-century America* (pp. 293–310). New York: New York University Press.

Watts, R. J., & Serrano Garcia, I. (2003). The quest for a liberating community psychology: An overview. *American Journal of Community Psychology, 31,* 73–78.

Watts, R. J., Williams, N. C., & Jagers, R. J. (2003). Sociopolitical development. *American Journal of Community Psychology, 31,* 195–201.

Weale, A. (1999). *Democracy*. New York: St. Martin's Press.

Weil, M. (1986). Women, community and organizing. In N. Van DenBergh & L. Cooper (eds.), *Feminist visions for social work* (pp.187–210). Silver Springs, MD: National Association of Social Workers.

Weil, M. (1996). Model development in community practice: An historical perspective. *Journal of Community Practice, 3,* 5–67.

Weil, M. (2004). Introduction: Contexts and challenges for 21st century communities. In M. Weil (ed.), *Handbook of community practice* (pp. 30–33). Thousand Oaks, CA: Sage Publications.

Weil, M. & Gamble, D.N. (1995). Community practice models. In R.L. Edwards (ed.), *Encyclopedia of social work* (19th ed., pp. 577–593). Washington, D.C.: National Association of Social Workers Press.

Weisbrod, B. A. (1997). What policy makers need from the research community. In B. A. Weisbrod & J. Worthy (eds.), *The urban crisis: Linking research to action* (pp. 205–221). Evanston, IL: Northwestern University Press.

Weiss, M. (2003). *Youth rising*. Oakland, CA: Applied Research Center.

Welton, N., & Wolf, L. (2001). *Global uprising: Confronting the tyrannies of the 21st century: Stories from a new generation of activists*. Gabriola Island, BC, Canada: New Society Publications.

Werner, E. E., & Smith, R. S. (1977). *Kauai's children come of age*. Honolulu: University of Hawaii Press.

Werner, E. E., & Smith, R. S. (1982). *Vulnerable but invincible: A longitudinal study of resilient children and youth*. New York: McGraw-Hill.

Werner, E.E., & Smith, R. S. (1992). *Overcoming the odds*. Ithaca, NY: Cornell University Press.

Westheimer, J., & Kahne, J. (2002). What kind of citizen? The politics of educating for democracy. *American Educational Journal, 41*, 237–269.

What Kids Can Do. (2001). *Making youth known: Philadelphia students join a union to improve their schools*. Providence, RI: Author.

What is the impact of meaningful youth action? On youth? On Communities? (2002). *Forum for Youth Investment, 2*, 7–8.

Wheeler, W. (2003). Youth leadership for development: Civic activism as a component of youth development programming and a strategy for strengthening civil society. In F. Jacobs, D. Wertlieb, & R. Lerner (eds.), *Enhancing the life chances of youth and families: Contributions of programs, policies, and service systems* (pp. 491–505). Thousand Oaks, CA: Sage Publications.

Wheeler, W. (2005). Maximizing opportunities for young people to participate in and lead community change. *The Kellogg Leadership for Community Change Newsletter, III*, 9.

Wheeler, W., & Edlebeck, C. (2006). Leading, learning, and unleashing potential: Youth leadership and civic engagement. In M. Klau, S. Boyd, & L. Luckow (eds.), *Youth leadership: New directions for youth development* (pp. 89–98). San Francisco: Jossey-Bass.

Why youth development is our business. (2001). Op-ed. *The Nonprofit Quarterly, 8*, 1.

Wikipedia. (2006). Youth rights. Accessed January 8, 2006, from http://en.wikipedia.org/wiki/Youth_rights

Wilhelm, A. G. (2000). *Democracy in the digital age: Challenges to political life in cyberspace*. New York: Routledge.

Williams, R. J. (2003). *The hell with status quo! A practical guidebook on youth organizing*. Washington, D.C.: Urban Education, Inc.

Wilson, N., Minkler, M., Dasho, S., Carrillo, R., Wallerstein, N., & Garcia, D. (2006). Training students as facilitators in the Youth Empowerment Strategies (YES) Project. In B. N. Checkoway & L. Gutierrez (eds.), *Youth participation and community change* (pp. 201–217). New York: Haworth Press.

Wilson-Ahlstrom, A., Tolman, J., & Jones, K. (2004). *Youth action for educational change: A resource guide.* Washington, D.C.: Forum for Youth Investment.

Withorn, A. (1984). *Serving the people: Social services and social change.* New York: Columbia University Press.

W.K. Kellogg Foundation. (2000). *Youth in community, youth in citizenship: Weaving in a future tense.* Battlecreek, MI: Author.

Wohlfeiler, D. (1997). Community organizing and community building among gay and bisexual men: The STOP AIDS Project. In M. Minkler (ed.), *Community organizing & community building for health* (pp. 230–243). New Brunswick, NJ: Rutgers University Press.

W.T. Grant Commission on Women, Families and Citizenship. (1988). *The forgotten half-non-college graduates in America.* Washington, D.C.: Author.

Wulfert, E., Block, J. A., Santa Ana, E., Rodriguez, M. L., & Colsman, M. (2002). Delay of gratification: impulse choices and problem behaviors in early and late adolescence. *Journal of Personality, 70,* 533–552.

Yohalem, N. (2003). Adults who make a difference: Identifying the skills and characteristics of successful youth workers. In F. A. Villarruel, D. F. Perkins, L. M. Borden, & J. G. Keith (eds.), *Community youth development: Programs, policies, and practices* (pp. 358–372). Thousand Oaks, CA: Sage Publications.

Young Wisdom Project. (2004). *Making space, making change: Profiles of youth-led and youth-driven organizations.* Oakland, CA: Movement Strategy Center.

Youniss, J., Bales, S., Christmas-Best, V., Diversi, M., McLaughlin, M., & Silberecisen, R. (2002). Youth civic engagement in the twenty-first century. *Journal of Research on Adolescence, 12,* 121–148.

Youniss, J., McLellan, J., & Yates, M. (1997). What we know about engendering civic identity. *American Behavioral Scientists, 40,* 620–631.

YouthAction. (1998). *Why youth organizing?* Albuquerque, NM: Author.

Youth in Focus. (2004). *Measuring up and throwing down! Evaluation and self-assessment tools for youth organizing groups.* Oakland, CA: Movement Strategy Center.

Youth Liberation Program. (1977). Youth liberation of Ann Arbor. In B. Gross & R. Gross (eds.), *The children's rights movement: Overcoming the oppression of young people* (pp. 329–333). Garden City, NY: Anchor Press/Doubleday.

Youth Organizing (1998). Notes from the Field. A report from a youth organizer/funder. Retreat, Pocantico Center, New York, December 11–12.

Youth United for Change. (2005). *Mobilizing students.* Philadelphia, PA: Author.

Zachary, E. (2000). What makes up community leadership competence? *Journal of Community Practice, 7*(1), 71–93.

Zeldin, S., McDaniel, A. K., Topitzes, D., & Calvert, M. (2001). *Youth in decision-making: A study on the impacts of youth on adults and organizations.* Washington, D.C.: Innovation Center for Community and Youth Development.

Zelizer, V. A. (1985). *Pricing the priceless child: The changing social value of children.* New York: Basic Books.

Zimmerman, K. (2004). *Making space, making change: Profiles of youth and youth-driven organizations.* Oakland, CA: Young Wisdom Project.

Zimmerman, M. A., & Warshausky, S. (1998). Empowerment theory for rehabilitation research: Conceptual and methodological issues. *Rehabilitation Psychology, 43,* 3–16.

Index

DATE DUE
